PEDESTAL

PEDESTAL

The convoy that saved Malta
70th Anniversary Edition

by
PETER C SMITH

Foreword by
Admiral of the Fleet
the Lord Lewin
KG GCB LVO DSC

Crécy Naval
from
Crécy Publishing Limited

First published in 1970 by William Kimber, London
Italian edition published in 1972 by Longanesi, Milan
Second edition published in 1987 by William Kimber, London
Audio Cassette editions by Calibre, Aylesbury, 1987-2002
Third edition published in 1994 by Crécy Books, Bristol
Fourth edition published in 1999
by Crécy Publishing, Manchester
Fifth (Maltese) edition published in 2002
by Crécy Publishing, Manchester
Reprinted 2007, 2012, 2017 and 2018
by Crécy Publishing, Manchester

See other Peter C Smith books at www.dive-bombers.co.uk

Jacket photographs courtesy of Imperial War Museum
A CIP record of this book is available from the British Library

Printed in Malta by Melita Press

ISBN 9 780907 579199

A Crécy Naval paperback published by

Crécy Publishing Limited
1a Ringway Trading Estate, Shadowmoss Road, Manchester M22 5LH
www.crecy.co.uk

Contents

List of Photographs

Admiral of the Fleet the Lord Lewin *(Crown Copyright)*

Rear-Admiral Sir Harold Burrough *(Imperial War Museum)*

Vice-Admiral Sir Neville Syfret *(Imperial War Museum)*

Operation '*Berserk*': the carriers *Indomitable* and *Argus* *(Imperial War Museum)*

The convoy passes into the Mediterranean *(Imperial War Museum)*

The *Eagle* after being hit by four torpedoes *(Cdr C. C. Crill)*

The sinking *Eagle* *(Cdr C. C. Crill)*

Short-range guns crew aboard the *Manchester* *(L. McDonald)*

Captain Drew of the *Manchester* *(L. McDonald)*

Pom-pom crews aboard the destroyer *Pathfinder* *(J. G. Buchan)*

The Junkers Ju 88 dive-bombers of LG 1 *(Nicola Malizia)*

Rodney in action against dive-bombers *(Ufficio Storico, Roma)*

Bombs fall alongside the *Clan Ferguson* *(Cdr C. C. Crill)*

Bombs in the convoy lanes *(Cdr C. C. Crill)*

Manchester turns to meet an attack from an Italian torpedo-bomber.
   An Italian torpedo-bomber attacking at close range *(Admiral Burrough)*

Bombs explode in the wake of a merchantman *(G. F. Jones)*

One of the Italian Ju.87 Stuka's is hit by the warships anti-aircraft fire
   and plunges into the Mediterranean *(Imperial War Museum, London)*

Ithuriel closing the Italian submarine *Cobalto* *(Crown Copyright)*

Ithuriel rams *Cobalto* *(Crown Copyright)*

Cobalto seconds before she sank *(Crown Copyright)*

Italian ground crew load torpedoes in Sicily *(Ufficio Storico, Roma)*

Savoia Marchetti SM79 torpedo-bombers approach the convoy
   (Ufficio Storico, Roma)

An Italian aerial reconnaissance photograph of the convoy, August 12
   (Imperial War Museum)

Torpedo aircraft SM.79 of 132 Squadron, starting to attack, August 12
   (Imperial War Museum)

An Italian SM.79 torpedo-bomber attacking the convoy, August 12
   (Imperial War Museum)

The destroyer H.M.S. *Foresight* under torpedo-bomber attack
   (Ufficio Storico, Roma)

A Junkers Ju 87D dive-bomber over the Mediterranean coastline
   (National Archives, Washington)

A Ju 88 escorting an Italian cruiser *(Hanfried Schliephake)*

Heinkel 111T on a Sicilian airstrip *(Franz Selinger)*

Sea Hurricanes aboard *Indomitable* during the battle *(Arthur Lawson)*

The ordeal of *Indomitable* *(Arthur Lawson)*

Indomitable's forward starboard guns receive a direct hit *(Arthur Lawson)*

Indomitable sailing through a hail of bombs *(Imperial War Museum)*

Indomitable lies enshrouded in a pall of her own smoke *(Arthur Lawson)*
Ohio receives what should have been her death blow *(Cdr C. C. Crill)*
The Italian submarine *Axum (Ufficio Storico, Roma)*
The Italian E-boat *MASS 563 (Ufficio Storico, Roma)*
Nigeria after the torpedo attack in the Narrows *(Admiral Burrough)*
The Merchantmen under attack *(Ufficio Storico, Roma)*
The final blows *(Ufficio Storico, Roma)*
SM79's circle the funeral pyre of several proud ships *(Ufficio Storico, Roma)*
The damaged *Kenya* under heavy air attack *(Cdr C. C. Crill)*
Kenya in dry-dock *(Cdr C. C. Crill)*
Port Chalmers arrives at Malta *(Imperial War Museum)*
Brisbane Star limps in *(Imperial War Museum)*
The *Melbourne Star* safely in *(Imperial War Museum)*
MM Rochester Castle enters the Grand Harbour *(Lieut. H.E.Cook)*
The *Rochester Castle* unloads her precious cargo *(Imperial War Museum)*
Unloading supplies at Malta 21st August 1942 *(Imperial War Museum)*
All the stops were pulled out to unload valuable cargo *(Imperial War Museum)*
Barely, afloat, the *Ohio* enters Grand Harbour Malta *(Imperial War Museum)*
The damaged tanker *OHIO* being 'nursed' into harbour *(Sgt. Deakin)*
Ohio surrounded by auxiliary craft in the Grand Harbour Malta
    (Imperial War Museum)

Maps and Diagrams

Foreword

By the late Admiral of the Fleet the Lord Lewin,
KG, GCB, LVO, DSC

THE late Admiral Sir Richard Onslow who, as Acting Captain, was in command of HMS *Ashanti* during the *Pedestal* operation wrote the foreword to the first edition of this book. It was my good fortune to serve under him in this Tribal Class destroyer; he was a truly great destroyer captain and I and many others owe much to him and the example he set. I therefore feel especially honoured to have been asked to offer some of my own memories before the reader embarks on this revised edition, particularly as I have always considered Peter Smith's narrative to be the most accurate and comprehensive account there is of the battle.

In 1942 I was a junior lieutenant, *Ashanti*'s Gunnery Control Officer. My knowledge of the strategic background to great events was limited, my view merely that from the Gunnery Control Tower above the bridge of one destroyer. We all realised that this was an important convoy from the strength of the escort and the fast, modern merchant ships which formed it; but few of us were aware of the vital importance of its cargo for Malta's survival, or just how close the island was to surrender.

Some memories remain vivid. Perhaps surprisingly, first, the warm sunshine as we entered the Mediterranean – with the comforting prospect of a warm sea if ill fortune forced us to swim for it. Those of us from the Home Fleet were used to going north from Scapa towards Iceland and the Arctic. *Ashanti* had returned only a few weeks before from escorting convoy PQ16 to Murmansk. To sit in the AA director in shirtsleeves seemed like a summer holiday. The sinking of *Eagle* was a blow but we tried to console ourselves that we had escorted the convoy for over a week through the Atlantic U-boat packs and that this was our first loss.

At the end of the next day – a day of heavy air attacks – our tails were high. Despite some damage to one or two warships the convoy was almost unscathed, one merchant vessel had been hit by a bomb but despite reduced speed was still on course for Malta. The battleships and carriers were to turn back and we had 'only' to get through the Narrows during the night and on to Malta. Then almost at dusk came that devastating salvo of torpedoes that scored hits on three important ships, *Nigeria* (the Flagship), *Cairo* and the vital British-manned tanker *Ohio*, and suddenly the scales tipped against us.

The next twenty-four hours from that moment were a blur of almost continuous incident. We caught up with the convoy after transferring Admiral Burrough from *Nigeria*, too late to help much with the air attacks that came at dusk. The frustration of trying to find something to shoot at as the E-boats weaved in among our ranks in the blackness. I saw the explosion as their torpedoes hit *Manchester*. We heard men talking and shouting on her upper decks as she lost way and we slid close past her. Air attacks the next morning were unending. Not surprisingly by then the merchant ships and escorts had become somewhat spread out in small groups and up in the director we had no idea how many were left afloat. Our spirits lifted when *Ohio* reappeared from astern, going well. *Ashanti* took station close alongside to give her protection. I remember engaging a Stuka which grew larger and larger in my sights as it seemed to be diving straight at us until, at the last moment, it passed overhead and crashed into *Ohio*. With relief we saw the cliffs of Malta on the horizon and we handed over our few remaining charges to be led in by the minesweepers, turning then to the west at twenty-five knots.

The remaining air attacks on the following day had a different feel to them. We no longer had the responsibility of the convoy, we had only ourselves to defend. Each mile took us further from the enemy air bases and soon we would be beyond their reach. There was no need to conserve ammunition and we used it freely at any possible target. The news that four ships had entered Grand Harbour and that *Ohio* was almost there added to our euphoria. As the book describes, *Ashanti* was always short of fresh water. As we climbed down from the director after some sixty hours of action stations, I remember the incident described in these pages – a naked Admiral elbowing his way under a crowded salt-water shower rigged on the upper deck – indeed we all needed a bath!

Pedestal was far from being my first convoy but it set the seal for all time on my already strong admiration and respect for the men of the Merchant Navy. It was so much easier for us in our well-armed ships, with high speed and manoeuvrability, to feel that we had a reasonable chance, in the face of such concentrated and determined attacks. They on the other hand must have felt like sitting ducks. It would have been easy and understandable for a ship already damaged and reduced in speed to turn back, yet their determination to press on to Malta to deliver their cargoes was an inspiration to us all. Their crews were the heroes of Pedestal as of so many other hard-fought convoys.

With hindsight, illuminated by Peter Smith's meticulous and wide-ranging research, it is possible to see that Operation Pedestal was the first ripple of the turning tide, and, despite the losses, an important if not vital strategic victory. Without the 55,000 tons of stores and fuel that the five remaining ships were able to deliver, Malta would have been forced to surrender within a month. If Pedestal had failed, there would have been no time, let alone ships, to mount another attempt. The consequences of failure can only be a matter of conjecture. But with Malta's stranglehold on Rommel's supply lines released, increased war material and oil would have flowed to North Africa and the Axis forces might then well have succeeded in their thrust to Alexandria, Cairo and the Suez Canal. Instead they were forced to halt so temptingly close to their ultimate goal, short of both fuel and ammunition, on the Alam Halfa ridge. Certainly, Rommel would have been in much better shape at El Alamein if he had received the hundreds of thousands of tons of urgently needed supplies that were sent to the bottom in the September and October after Pedestal by Malta-based submarines and aircraft.

1982 brought the fortieth anniversary of Operation Pedestal. It brought also Operation Corporate, the campaign in the South Atlantic to recover the Falklands and South Georgia. Both operations, although involving all three services and the Merchant Navy, were predominantly maritime in nature. Broadly, the same number of servicemen took part in both campaigns. Corporate cost the Royal Navy two destroyers, two frigates, a landing ship and a large merchantman. Pedestal's cost was an aircraft carrier, two cruisers, a destroyer and nine merchant ships. With Corporate the action was spread over some fifty days while with Pedestal the fighting lasted five. Both operations were successful in achieving their objectives but at a price. Corporate cost 250 lives, Pedestal 350. The first British loss in the latter campaign, HMS *Sheffield*, shocked the nation. Realisation that war involved sacrifice grows dim in time of peace.

In September 1982, with the South Atlantic campaign behind us, some sixty of those who took part in Pedestal, with Peter as our guest, met to commemorate the fortieth anniversary. We held a service of remembrance and thanksgiving at the seafarers' church, All Hallows by the Tower. We laid a wreath at the Merchant Navy War memorial on Tower Hill and we exchanged memories with old shipmates over luncheon in Trinity House. Three years later, in 1985, I was in Malta at Pedestal time. The subject of this convoy came up in conversation with the Prime Minister and without premeditation he decided that as the next day, 15th August, was the anniversary of *Ohio*'s arrival, it should be marked by a Remembrance Ceremony at the National War Memorial, the first such ceremony to be held since the final withdrawal of the British services in 1979. A year later, in 1986, this precedent was repeated in greater style. HMS *Brazen*, flying the flag of the Commander-in-Chief, Fleet, was in Grand Harbour, the first of Her Majesty's ships to return in seven years. She was given a welcome that recalled that given to Pedestal's surviving merchantmen. Admiral Sir Nicholas Hunt and the *Brazen*'s ships company took part in the Remembrance Ceremony. Hopefully, a tradition has now been established and each year on 15th August the Feast of Santa Marija and a Maltese National Holiday will see a fitting tribute paid to all those who gave their lives to save Malta. They justly deserve to be remembered. Peter Smith's fine history is in itself a lasting tribute to all those brave men.

Woodbridge, Suffolk

Introduction
to the Sixtieth Anniversary Edition

I am especially proud and gratified that my history of the *Santa Marija* convoy (as Operation *Pedestal* is more usually known to the Maltese themselves) should see a fifth edition to celebrate the 60th Anniversary of the battle. That it is being produced largely at the behest of the Maltese themselves makes is particularly poignant for the author. The gallantry of the islanders themselves matched exactly the gallantry of the Royal and Merchant Navies who sacrificed themselves to bring succour to the hardy defenders. The unique distinction of the award of the George Cross to the whole of Malta by King George VI was a fitting tribute to their steadfastness and loyalty.

In these days of 24-hour media exposure there is, in Britain, a constant clamour for instant results by television and radio presenters. In their impatient and intolerant ignorance, they frequently undermine rather than support those who fight evil for all our sakes. It would be good if some of these gentleman and ladies, with their colossal ego's, might be reminded of some constant truths. The might remind themselves that the losses sustained in this single convoy operation came in the midst of a war that had already lasted more than three years, and whose end was still another three weary years in the future. A quick fix in order to produce a good news story was not the way of the world in 1942 any more than it is in 2002.

In the Introduction to the First edition of this book, written in 1970, Admiral Sir Richard Onslow, KCB, that very gallant destroyer skipper, reminded us of the words of Sir Francis Drake. "It is not the beginning but the continuing of the same until it be thoroughly finished that yielded the true glory" How *very* apt these words ring today, and what pity that they are not more frequently applied.

PETER C. SMITH
Riseley, Bedford.

Acknowledgements

I should like to take this opportunity to thank the following people who have very kindly assisted me in my research into Operation 'Pedestal', both for the time and help they unselfishly gave me and for the patience with which they answered my many questions: Mr W. G. Allen, US Department of Commerce; Captain Jack Broome, DSC, RN; Rear-Admiral P. N. Buckley, CB, DSO; Admiral Sir Harold Burrough, GCB, KBE, DSO; Mr N. P. Collei, Shaw, Saville & Albion; Miss J. Collett, Central Office of Information; Mr Jim David; Admiral Sir Michael Denny, CB, DSO; Mrs I. English, Imperial War Museum Film Library; Freggattenkapitan F. Forstmeier, Federal German Navy; Capitano di Vascello Franco Gnifetti, Italian Navy; Mr M. L. Gordon, New Zealand Shipping Company; Vice-Admiral Sir Peter Gretton, KCB, DSO, OBE, DSC; Mr Hine, Imperial War Museum Photographic Library; Mr Jackets, Air Historical Branch, MOD; Commander C. B. Lamb, DSO, DSC, RN; Captain F. Kent Loomis, United States Navy; General Lionello Leone; Mr Alan Linder; Herr Doktor Mauergifer, Federal German Archives; Capitano de Vascello G. Martucci, Italian Navy; Mr W. T. Mills, Air Historical Branch, MOD; Signor C. De Grossi Mazzorin, Director of the Associazione Nazionale Marinai d'Italia; Mr A. H. Murphy; Colonel V. Marotta, Italian Air Attache; Mr J. G. Norton, Cayzer, Irvine and Company; Admiral Sir Richard Onslow, KCB, DSO, RN; Mr Hugh Popham; Mr Alfred Price; Rear-Admiral C. K. Roberts, DSO, RN; Herr Franz Selinger; Mr Squires, Imperial War Museum Photographic Library; General Giuseppe Santoro, Ufficio Storico, Italy; Mr. J. Richard Smith; Commissario Attilio Silvestri, Ufficio Administrativo, Italy; Mr Peter Vikery; Mr Edwin Walker; and finally a special thank-you to my old friend John Dominy for drawing the diagrams.

For this edition I would like to add my sincere thanks and gratitude to the following:

The late Admiral of the Fleet Lord Lewin (*Ashanti*), Les Wright (*Ashanti*), J. G. Buchan (*Pathfinder*), Robert W. Gant, Captain D. A. G. Dickens (*Dorset)*, John C. Waine (*Brisbane Star*), Gerd Stamp (Pilot, LG 1), Generale Antonio Cumbat (Stuka Commander, Italian Air Force), E. Kenward (*Eagle*), Henry Rathbone (*Eagle*), J. F. Bleasdale (*Nigeria*), Mrs Charlotte Bailey, window of Frank Bailey (*Sirius*), Rolando Perasso (*MAS* 552-Italian Navy), L. McDonald (*Manchester* Survivors Association), Alf Lawson (*Indomitable*), Captain J. A. Pearson (*Rye*), G. F. Jones (*Manchester*), W. Stroud (*Manchester*), G. V. Towell (*Manchester*), W. Butler (*Manchester*), E. Hodgson (*Manchester*), David Royale (*Charybdis* Association), Commander, C. G. Crill (*Kenya*), Charles W. McCoombe *(Sirius)*, Les Owen (*Eagle*), Mrs Doreen Pilling, Alan Smith (*Indomitable*), Charles Corder (Beaufighter navigator, RAF), Douglas Clare (1st DF Association), Mrs Barbara Broadwater (Fleet Air Arm Museum, Yeovilton), A. J. H. King (*Cairo*), Rowland Charles Marshall (*Waimarama*), J. W. Izard, son of DEMS gunner W. T. Izard (*Santa Elisa*), J. Carvana (Malta).

When originally researching this book the official Admiralty papers, records and data on Operation *Pedestal* were still 'classified information'. Nonetheless the author received special dispensation to examine almost all the documents concerned then held at the Admiralty in Whitehall. The only condition, made at the time, was that *no* acknowledgement of this fact should be made in the book. The author duly complied with this proviso and continued to do so for the second edition, published several years later, even though there was no longer any secrecy attached to them and all the papers were available to view at the Public Record Office, Kew. This led to some ill-founded and unsustainable criticism by people who should have known much better.

For the record, and to help students and others who wish to consult the originals, a list of those Admiralty files are given in the 'Source Notes' section.

For

PAUL DAVID

In the years since the first edition of
this book you have grown from a
small boy of whom I was immensely
proud, to a grown man in whom my
pride is even greater.
Thank you, Son.

Chapter One

Malta in Subjection

I

IN 1940 there were two schools of thought with regard to the importance of Malta in modern war. The RAF and the Army contended that, lying as it did within half an hour's flying time from the network of Italian airfields in Sicily, it could be rendered untenable within a very short time and would therefore be a useless drain on our resources. The Navy took the opposite viewpoint, pointing out its great importance astride the enemy supply routes to North Africa. It was fortunate indeed that Winston Churchill took a similar attitude for very early on in the conflict, upon Italy's entry in the war, the strangulation of these arteries of supply was found to be the most telling single factor in curbing the Duce's designs on Egypt, the Suez Canal and the Middle East.

Although the island's defences were in a deplorable state, in fact almost non-existent, submarines and torpedo-bombers operating from Malta were quickly to demonstrate how easy it was for them to restrict even the most powerful moves of the enemy. The island soon became, for the Italians, a threat to their supplies. The effect of continued strikes from this base reduced them to the expedient of carrying the bulk of their supplies in warships, for each time a large convoy put to sea, they felt sure that they would lose every ship. Count Ciano, the Italian Foreign Minister, recorded one typical example, which took place in 1941 when the island's strike forces had been built up to include surface forces of cruisers and destroyers:

November 9: Since September we have given up trying to get convoys through to Libya; every attempt has been costly, and the losses suffered by our merchant marine have reached such proportions as to discourage any further experiments. Tonight we tried again; Libya needs materials, arms, fuel, more and more every day. A convoy of seven ships left accompanied by two ten-thousand-ton cruisers and ten destroyers, because it was known that at Malta the British had two battleships intended to act as wolves among the sheep.[1] An engagement occurred, the results of which are inexplicable. All, I mean *all*, our ships were sunk and one or maybe two or three destroyers. The British returned to base having slaughtered us. Naturally, today our various headquarters are pushing out their usual inevitable and imaginary sinking of British cruiser by a torpedo plane; nobody believes it. This morning Mussolini was depressed and indignant. This will undoubtedly have profound repercussions in Italy, Germany and above all in Libya. Under the circumstances we have no right to complain if Hitler sends Kesselring as commander in chief in the South.

November 10: The photographs taken by our reconnaissance planes show four British ships moored in the port of Malta. Notwithstanding, it is reported in the bulletin that one of the cruisers has been hit. Pricolo[2] insists on it and argues that this ship has been moored near the dry-dock. This is the equivalent to declaring that a man is probably slightly dead because he has gone to live near a cemetery!

The increasing destruction of their seaborne supplies led to a frantic reappraisal by the Italians of their position and plans with regard to Malta. Hitler, too, was jolted into a belated realisation of the importance of seaborne communications.

Only two forces had proved up to that time that they could effectively curtail either operations from Malta or the activities of the Royal Navy in general and these were the Luftwaffe and the German U-boats stationed in the Mediterranean. Fliegerkorps X and the handful of German submarines available could claim credit for almost all the major casualties suffered by

[1] Actually two 6-inch cruisers, *Aurora* and *Penelope*, which, together with the destroyers *Lance* and *Lively*, formed Force K. In the course of this action which took place on the night of 8th/9th November, they sank seven merchant ships (39,000 tons), and one of the escorting destroyers, while another destroyer was finished off by one of our submarines. The two Italian heavy cruisers failed to stop them and Force K suffered no damage whatsoever.

[2] General Francesco Pricolo: Chief of Staff for Air 1940.

the British fleets during 1941; the Italian effort, although larger, had in comparison achieved little. It was clear that the re-introduction of these forces was necessary to restore the balance of operations in the Mediterranean back in the favour of the Axis. Swallowing their pride, the Italians were now forced to accept Hitler's ideas for their salvation.

Grand-Admiral Raeder had long been pleading the case for an offensive in the Mediterranean. He envisaged a linking up in the Middle East during 1942, of the two German offensives through the Ukraine and Egypt respectively. To achieve this end he stressed that Malta must be taken. The Fuehrer, engrossed as he was with the crushing of the Soviet hordes, had not been very enthusiastic before, but now, with his armies held up by appalling weather just short of their main objectives on the Eastern Front, he was able to focus his attention on to this alternative strategy. He soon came to a decision. Directive Number 38, dated 17th November 1941, laid down his conclusions in no uncertain manner.

Briefly, he intended to withdraw a complete Air Corps from the Russian wastes and re-deploy it in Sicily, to relieve the by now exhausted Fliegerkorps X, which was transferred to Greece.

This force was to dominate the Central Mediterranean sea routes and to crush Malta's strike capacity and defensive capability as a prelude to the planned occupation of the island.[1] Fliegerkorps II, commanded by Bruno Loerzer, was accordingly withdrawn from the threshold of the Soviet capital and shifted south to the Mediterranean sunshine. To supervise this transfer, and also to assume command of all the German forces in the area, Hitler appointed Field Marshal Kesselring Commander-in-Chief South. To him he allocated the following tasks:

1. To secure the mastery of the air and sea in the Central Mediterranean area in order to secure sea communications with Cyrenaica and Libya and in particular to keep Malta in subjection.
2. To help the Axis land forces in their final drive on Egypt.

[1] Operation Hercules.

19

3. To operate with Axis Naval forces in closing the Mediterranean to British sea traffic.

As a sop to the Italians, Kesselring was placed under the nominal control of the Duce; a proviso – which is of some importance with regard to our story – was that requests by Kesselring for combined operations by Axis Naval forces would be referred to the German Navy-Admiral Weichold – and the Italian High Command.

When the new dispositions were completed during the early part of 1942 Kesselring had available to carry out these duties some 2,000 frontline aircraft and these he now organised in Sicily, Greece and Crete. However, everything was not to his liking:

'Every day [he recorded in his memoirs] showed more plainly the naval and air supremacy of the British in those waters.' He therefore came to the conclusion that Malta was of 'decisive importance' as a strategic keypoint and his primary object at the beginning was to safeguard the Axis supply lines by 'smoking out that hornet's nest'.

He still required time to build up his newly arrived forces and contented himself with familiarising himself with the area arid his allies. It was early April before he felt ready to fulfil his instructions and unleash his aircraft against the stubborn island. Final detailed plans had been drawn up by the German Chief of Staff, Air Marshal Deichmunn, at Messina. The main objectives were laid down as airfields, harbour installations and shipping; Valletta itself was to be spared as much as possible. Daylight attacks were to be concentrated and incessant and given such powerful fighter protection that the British fighters would be kept away from the bombers until they were totally eliminated. In addition heavy minelaying of the waters around the island was to be undertaken as a further measure of blockade – and this soon reaped a rich harvest.

In its general outlines the plan resembles the one under which the Battle of Britain had been fought. On that occasion the British had been able to husband their fighter strength in the untouched north until they were needed, but in Malta there was no such area and it soon became apparent that Kesselring's assault would probably attain its objectives.

The main assault [Kesselring later recorded] was begun at the beginning of April. On the 10th of May I could regard the task as accomplished.

In those six grim weeks, the people of Malta and the British defenders endured the greatest scale of air attack yet released against the island up to that time and by the end of them the survival of the island, had the scale of attacks been maintained, was doubtful.

Although the Germans intended to spare Valletta it was inevitable that, with the bombers concentrating on the harbour, the surrounding cities themselves would suffer heavily, and so they did. Already badly battered from two years of bombing by Italian and German aircraft alike, Valletta was to undergo what the Official Naval Historian described as her 'supreme ordeal'. Conditions on the island became critical. The two thousandth air raid occurred on the 8th April and the result of the subsequent overwhelming weight of bombs which followed was terrifying. No less than 6,700 tons of bombs rained down in a single month and this mass of explosive was concentrated on an area around the dockyards. The fighter air strips were also devastated until they resembled the aerial photographs of the Somme, in 1916, but somehow the few surviving fighters continued to rock and scrape off from these shattered areas to offer combat with the German and Italian hordes. Despite their bravery, and the losses they inflicted on the Axis bombers, there were too few of them to protect the island – an area smaller than Greater London.

Over ten thousand houses were demolished; the island's reservoirs were destroyed; stores of food were gutted and gun emplacements blasted. Worse still was the havoc caused in Valletta harbour. The cranes and installations were pulverised, wharfs gutted and warehouses knocked flat. As for the ships themselves, many of them were damaged and unable to escape. One eyewitness aboard the cruiser *Penelope*, which was in dock repairing damage, gives this account of one typical raid during April:

At 1650 we got our biggest dose. Observers on the bridge agreed that this raid looked the worst of the lot from our point of view. It was certainly brilliantly executed. Ju88s and 87s seemed to be coming in, in ones and twos, from every direction at the same time. There was a nasty collection of bombs to be seen in the air at any given moment, and they all appeared to be right on the mark and to get larger as you watched them. One particular stick arrived and we ducked and felt the ship jump violently up and down several times. People who were watching from other ships said afterwards that it was a most remarkable sight. Luckily our guns' crews didn't duck but went on firing coolly, giving the enemy everything they'd got, and shifting from one target to another without anything like wild firing. There can be little doubt that it was only the intensity and accuracy of their firing that made even this dangerous effort a near miss instead of a direct hit.

It was a very near thing indeed; between the ship and the jetty, and the bomb burst in the water and made a sizeable hole in the ship's bottom. Damage control parties were on the job immediately – a good many of the lower compartments were flooded, but the ship was still there. We found afterwards that cordite in the magazine had begun to char, but that the water had entered before anything could explode.

While we were clearing up the mess another very heavy raid began, and again the bombs seemed to fall everywhere but on the ship. We had a near miss aft this time, and one of the close-range guns disappeared from the top of Y Turret and was never seen again. We had our first casualties of the commission, but none of them were very serious.

Penelope was to undergo worse trials before the dockyard, working whenever there was a brief lull in the raids, got her fit enough to make a break for Gibraltar. It was plain that every ship in the harbour would be sunk if they remained and desperate efforts were made to sail them to safety. The *Carlisle* and four 'Hunts' were got safely away to Alexandria on 25th March and the *Aurora* and *Avonvale* followed them there four days later. Other ships, more damaged and unable to get clear, were not so lucky. Under the hail of bombs, casualties were as heavy as those suffered in the battle for Crete the year before.

On 1st April the submarines *Pandora* and *P.36* were sunk and several more of the 10th Flotilla were damaged. On the 9th the destroyer *Lance* was destroyed in dry-dock and in the same raid the destroyer *Gallant*, still under repair from the damage received the year before, was hit and beached. Meantime the *Havock* completed her repairs and started out for Gibraltar, but she never made it; running aground off the Tunisian coast, she became a total loss. Her crew were interned but her broken hull became a new feature of the coastline south of Cape Bon; as such she was destined to play another part in this story.

There was no respite and casualties continued to mount. On the 7th the tug *Emily* was destroyed and the following day another destroyer, the *Kingston*, which had been damaged a few days earlier, was hit again in dock and wrecked. On the 1st minesweeper *Sunset*, went down and next day a third, the *Jade*, was bombed. *Abingdon* followed on the 4th. It now became impossible safely to clear the channels in and out of Valletta harbour and it was obvious that unless the remaining vessels got away at once they would be bottled up and demolished.

On the 8th the *Penelope* had sailed for Gibraltar, so full of holes from bomb splinters was she that she had been dubbed 'HMS Pepperpot'. The Luftwaffe made determined attempts to hit her on her journey to safety, but although she fired off all her anti-aircraft shells fighting her way through, she reached the Rock on the 10th. She was one of the more fortunate ones; on 28th April the 10th Submarine Flotilla lost another boat, the *Urge*, which was caught by Italian destroyers as she ran for Alexandria. In Valletta harbour another two minesweepers, *Hellespont* and *Coral*, were sunk by bombing. The virtual elimination of the minesweeping force was to lead to even greater tragedy when the submarine *Olympus*, packed with survivors from the two submarines sunk earlier, was mined and sunk off the island on 8th May with severe loss of life.

By 12th May the dockyard was out of action save for a few underground workshops. Only the limestone rock formations of the island, which the authorities rapidly chiselled out to make deep secure air-raid shelters and hospitals, prevented a mass slaughter. Even so loss of life was heavy, over eight hundred people being killed in the first quarter of the year and almost another thousand seriously injured. Debris from the thirty thousand smashed or damaged houses choked the streets of the larger towns and hindered rescue operations. The island was rapidly grinding to a halt. Worse yet, starvation was almost upon them. Already food and all other commodities were rationed more strictly than anything known in Britain. Even milk and water were rationed. Witness the report made by Malta's Governor, General Dobbie, on 1st April:

Our supply position has been reassessed and may be summarised as follows:

a. *Wheat and flour*: No material cuts seem possible, as these are staple foods. Present stocks will, with care, last until early June.

b. *Fodder*: Issues already inadequate were recently cut; stocks will now last until the end of June.

c. *Minor foodstuffs*: Meat stocks are entirely exhausted. Most other stocks will last until June.

d. *White oils*: Aviation fuel till mid-August; benzene till mid-June; kerosene till early June.

e. *Black oils*: We have only 920 tons of diesel oil – five weeks' supply – and 2,000 tons of furnace fuel, all of which will be needed for fuelling HM Ships now in dock. The black oil position is thus becoming precarious and very urgent action appears necessary to restore it.

f. *Coal*: Welsh coal will last only until the end of May, other grades until mid June.

g. *Ammunition*: Consumption of ack-ack ammunition has greatly increased and we have only one and a half months' stock left.

Due to insufficient escorts to carry out two convoy operations, no supplies were possible during the month of May; Russia took priority and preparations to run the biggest convoy of freighters yet assembled to Murmansk were in train in the Arctic. The emphasis was not finally shifted away from the Arctic and back to Malta until the Russia-bound convoy PQ16 had got through. Meantime, the island, blasted, bombed and on the brink of starvation, had to hold on while Marshal Stalin's capacious appetite was assuaged.

'Malta's need is for Spitfires, Spitfires and more Spitfires', wrote Air Vice-Marshal Sir Hugh Lloyd, The Air Officer Commanding Malta's air defences.

This urgent request was promptly complied with and the United States Navy aircraft-carrier *Wasp* and the British carriers *Eagle* and *Argus* all made sorties into the western basin and flew off substantial numbers of fighters to reinforce the island's wilting garrison. These additions coincided with a diversion of the main Luftwaffe strength to other theatres of war and by the end of May the aerial defences of Malta had recovered. The Axis had overtaxed themselves and had suffered severe losses.

Although the island now was in a better position to defend herself, she still could not sustain her population for longer than another two months at the outside. Also, now that the bulk of her air and sea striking forces had been eliminated, she could not operate offensively and interfere with the enemy's communications. The Axis soon noticed the effect of a neutralised Malta: fast convoys laden with fuel and supplies poured into Libya and Rommel was able to renew his offensive against the Eighth Army. He surrounded Tobruk and forced the main front line back to within sixty miles of Alexandria.

It was essential that fuel and food should reach the island and the Admiralty decided that the best way was to use both the Home Fleet from the west and the reinforced Mediterranean Fleet from the east in an attempt to split the Axis defences by running two small fast convoys, one from each end of the Mediterranean, at the same time. The idea was sound and plans were laid accordingly. Unfortunately the enemy was to prove that he had adequate forces at his disposal to ensure the destruction of both convoys.

Time was short; on 16th April the King had awarded the island the George Cross as a tribute from the rest of the Empire to her people's bravery and stubborn resistance, but wars cannot be fought on medals; with a lack of proper diet comes a decline in morale and efficiency. Malta was nearing the crisis point beyond which she would be lost.

It is impossible to carry on without food and ammunition [the Commander-in-Chief wrote]. It is obvious that the worst must happen if we cannot replenish our vital needs, especially flour and ammunition....

II

The planning for the double convoy – Operation 'Harpoon' from the west and 'Vigorous' from the east – was soon set in motion, but at a time of the greatest adversity for the Royal Navy finding sufficient ships to provide anything like the escort required to fight these convoys through to Malta was an extremely difficult problem. Never before had our Navy suffered such heavy losses as between December 1941 and May 1942. There were just not enough ships to cover the Atlantic, the Arctic, the Indian Ocean and the Mediterranean.

Of capital ships and carriers we had very few; cruisers were needed everywhere and the bulk of our destroyer strength was also severely stretched; the same handful of ships had to be shuffled continually from one war zone to another without time for the refits that most of them urgently required. It was not therefore a very impressive escort which assembled at Gibraltar to sail with the 'Harpoon' convoy on 12th June.

The convoy itself comprised five freighters fully loaded, the British *Burdwan*, *Orari* and *Troilus*, the Dutch *Tanimbar*, and the American *Chant*; also included was one of the very few fast tankers made available to us from the United States, the *Kentucky*. Force H had been reinforced from vessels scraped together mainly from the Home Fleet and consisted of the ancient battleship *Malaya* and the equally antiquated carriers *Eagle* and *Argus*. These were supported by the modern cruisers *Kenya* and *Liverpool*, with the anti-aircraft cruiser *Charybdis* and eight destroyers. But Force H would only escort the convoy as far as the Narrows – the channel between Sicily and the coast of North Africa.

The usual 'through escort' which was to sail to Malta itself after Force H had turned back, was also very small numerically for the task required of it. Commanding this group was Captain C. C. Hardy in the old light cruiser *Cairo*; she had been converted before the war into an anti-aircraft ship and carried eight 4-inch HA guns plus smaller weapons. In such a function she was useful but against surface forces would be able to play no part whatsoever. Accompanying her were nine destroyers, five of them big 'Fleet' types, *Bedouin*, *Marne*, *Matchless*, *Ithuriel* and *Partridge*. Also forming part of the close escort were four 'Hunt' class destroyers, boats with good anti-aircraft armaments but no torpedo tubes, the *Blankney*, *Middleton*, *Badsworth* and the Polish *Kujawiak*. Also to go right through to Malta – in fact they were to be stationed there – were the four minesweepers' of the 17th Flotilla, to replace those vessels recently lost there. Six motor launches of the 6th Flotilla, some of them fitted with minesweeps to perform a similar function, were also to accompany the convoy.

The whole force, convoy and escort, under the command of Vice-Admiral A. T. B. Curteis, sailed into the western basin on 12th June. It was perhaps the immunity that the recent Gibraltar-mounted convoys had enjoyed from intervention by the enemy surface fleet which resulted in the decision not to include one or two of the 6-inch cruisers in the through escort. Certainly not since the balmy days of 1940 had the Italians sent their surface vessels out to hinder the convoys from this end of the Mediterranean. The Battle of Spartivento during which Force H had pursued a larger enemy fleet back into its own ports had set the seal on subsequent convoys. Nevertheless it was always known that the Italians had the capacity to confront the close escort with superior strength whenever they so wished.

With the benefit of hindsight it can now be seen that more heavy metal than one old AA cruiser was needed, but it must be remembered that the protection of the two carriers, which, although obsolete, were all that were available, loomed large in the minds of the planners. Perhaps *Malaya* and two cruisers would have been sufficient, but in any case losses soon made it clear that not more than one cruiser could be spared.

On the 13th they were sighted by the enemy who made arrangements to attack them with a heavy bombing raid from Sardinia and another from Sicily, and further, to sail a cruiser squadron to intercept them at first light on the 15th, south of Sicily. The convoy itself was not attacked this day but the 14th brought submarine alarms and the air raids.

It was now that the age of the two carriers began to tell against them. Both were old and slow, and the maximum number of aircraft they were able to put up against the waves of Axis aircraft was only ten at a time. Although valiantly flown they could not stop many of the bombers getting through to the convoy. The *Argus* also experienced extreme difficulty in regaining her station at her slow speed after turning into the wind to operate her planes.

The first attacks started at 10.30 am and comprised high-level and torpedo-bombers, the usual Italian formations, and in addition the appearance of the Ju87 dive-bomber with Italian crews. These had recently been trained in the dive-bombing technique by the Luftwaffe in return for torpedo-bomber facilities for the newly formed Heinkel 111 squadrons being formed by Germany. The Italians had evidently not gained the same proficiency in their use, as had the Luftwaffe.

All the same, the torpedo-bombers scored successes and the *Tanimbar* was sunk, while the *Liverpool* was hit in the engine-room, disabling her – so one of the modern cruisers had to be sent back to Gibraltar where she arrived safely after a tow by the destroyer *Antelope*. This one damaged ship seemed to act as irresistible bait to the subsequent waves of Italian airmen and they concentrated on her for the rest of the day, which afforded the convoy some respite.

The Germans had different priorities and the attack they mounted in the evening was directed exclusively upon the main force. All types of bombing took place and penetrations by the powerful

Junkers Ju88s proved most difficult to counter for the slow Fleet Air Arm fighters. Despite this and the fact that dive-bombing attacks were pressed well home, no further vessel suffered damage. By 9 pm the big ships of Force H had hauled round to the west.

The night passed without incident as the convoy steamed past Cape Bon and by morning they had struck out east towards Malta, taking a course south of Pantelleria. It was here that the Italians sprang their surprise.

A force comprising the 6-inch cruisers *Raimondo Montecuccoli* and *Eugenio di Savoia*, with the destroyers *Vivaldi*, *Malocello*, *Premuda*, *Oriani* and *Ascari*, under the command of Admiral da Zara, had sortied out from Palermo on the 14th and now fell upon the convoy.[1]

Warning of their approach had just been received from the patrolling aircraft from Malta, but the Italian commander, as usual, was not so well served by his scouting planes and, according to his report, had no idea of the actual strength of the British escort. Be this as it may, his subsequent tactics were hardly aggressive enough to reveal this information to him.

The first Italian salvo from the cruisers arrived at 6.40 am and was followed by a second which straddled the *Cairo*. Such a high standard of shooting was an unpleasant surprise for Captain Hardy, all his ships being outranged and unable to reply. The third and fourth enemy salvoes landed in among the merchantmen from about 20,000 yards' range, before the covering smoke screen shielded them mercifully from the Italian gunlayers.

While *Cairo* and the 'Hunts' continued laying smoke, the five big British destroyers, led by Commander Scurfield in the *Bedouin*, unhesitatingly steamed out to engage the enemy cruisers and their destroyer escorts. Da Zara was forced to divert his main armament towards these fast-oncoming aggressors and the convoy ran clear to the south.

Subjected to heavy and accurate fire from both Italian cruisers as they approached, two of the British ships were hit and disabled before coming into range with their own guns. The *Bedouin* took a

---

[1] Two other destroyers of this force had turned back on the 14th.

6-inch shell amidships while the *Partridge* was struck in the stern. Both destroyers slid to a halt. As they did so the remaining three burst past them dividing formation as they did so.

Ithuriel very gallantly took on the nearest enemy cruiser and was rewarded by scoring two hits at 8,000 yards' range. After receiving these, the Italian cruisers turned quickly away, three of their destroyers trailing behind them. The other two were made of sterner stuff and attempted to reach the convoy, but the two 'Ms' headed them off and at close range the *Vivaldi* was hit forward in the boiler room by a 4.7-inch shell, which perforated steam and oil pipes and started a fire in an adjacent magazine. Her companion, the *Malocello*, circled her laying a protective smoke screen, while *Vivaldi* fired two torpedoes at her tormentors.[1] She was saved from certain destruction by the recall of the three active British boats.

The recall signal was made necessary when a shift of the wind had rolled back *Cairo*'s smokescreen revealing her once more to the two Italian cruisers. Splitting their armaments they concentrated two turrets on her and two on *Ithuriel* and at 7.10 scored hits on Captain Hardy's ship. Almost simultaneously a force of German bombers arrived over the convoy, now protected solely by the 'Hunts'. Despite a good barrage put up by these little vessels the enemy planes pushed in to score a devastating three-bomb stick on the *Chant*, which blew up and sank in seconds. The only tanker, *Kentucky*, was luckier, but a near miss disabled her and she was taken under tow by the minesweeper *Hebe*. An ugly situation was developing and Captain Hardy re-concentrated his remaining warships. Fortunately da Zara was not too keen to re-close his adversaries. Convinced he was up against a cruiser of the 'Colony' class he kept a respectful distance while circling around to the southwest.

All the British escorts were now making smoke and clouds of this were obscuring da Zara's rangefinders. He declined to plunge straight through this with his cruisers for fear of torpedo attack and

[1] The Italian Admiral Cocchia, describing this incident in his book *Submarines Attacking* (William Kimber, 1956), states that she thus forced the British destroyer *H.68* to withdraw. H.68 was the pennant number of HMS *Foresight*, which was not present. Cocchia makes no mention of the two Italian cruisers, which *were* present.

his remaining three destroyers showed no inclination to do so either. Soon after 8.30 he withdrew to the north to weigh up the situation. *Cairo* and the destroyers shadowed him for a while then returned to their charges.

At 11.20 another heavy air attack developed over the convoy and Captain Hardy reluctantly decided that he ought to concentrate all his resources on getting his two undamaged merchantmen into Valletta and he therefore instructed the escorts that *Kentucky* and the *Burdwan*, disabled by bombs in this second raid, should both be sunk. This was done, and the *Cairo* and the 'Fleets' rejoined the convoy, now under the protection of the Malta Spitfires, for the final dash.

Meantime, aboard the two stationary British destroyers they were working feverishly to get under way again. *Partridge* eventually managed to move but *Bedouin* could not. Lieutenant-Commander Hawkins passed a tow to her sister ship and started the long haul towards Malta. Alas, their efforts were doomed to failure. Isolated enemy torpedo-bombers made individual attacks and at 1.30 the Italian cruisers lamely reappeared hoping to gain something from the battle by finishing off any damaged stragglers.

As soon as they were sighted *Partridge* slipped her tow and laid smoke to protect *Bedouin*. She held off the Italian naval squadron for almost an hour on her own but the odds were too great. A torpedo-bomber slipped past her and hit *Bedouin* amidships. She sank very quickly and *Partridge* was forced to use avoiding action. Commander Scurfield and the other survivors were finally rescued by the Italians. *Partridge* herself, after many adventures, got into Gibraltar.

The much-reduced convoy was undergoing even further trials. Despite their fighter cover the two surviving merchantmen were attacked again and again as they struggled eastwards. There was a final savage assault by twelve dive-bombers at 7 pm and the enemy had shot his bolt; both ships survived.

The convoy was almost safely in when final tragedy struck. Owing to a misunderstanding the *Cairo* and the destroyers pushed on into the channel approach to Valletta ahead of the minesweepers. The Germans had been industriously sowing mines here for months and the area was thick with them. First one, then another ship, was mined and brought to a halt.

Within a short while two of the 'Hunts', *Badsworth* and *Kujawiak*, the *Matchless*, the minesweeper *Hebe* and the *Orari* were likewise damaged. The Polish vessel finally sank, but the others were brought into Malta. Within a short time the two freighters had been unloaded and 20,000 tons of vital cargo was ashore. It was not a moment too soon for the Luftwaffe returned with a vengeance, blasting the harbour and dockside once more. *Cairo* and her four remaining destroyers refuelled and with the minelayer *Welshman*, which had slipped in ahead of the main convoy, fought their way back to the west again where they were met by Admiral Curteis's cruisers. For *Matchless* and *Badsworth* it meant a long period of repair in the battered dockyard, but with the arrival of only two ships, 'Harpoon', although not the unqualified defeat claimed by the Italians, had turned out to be a much-blunted instrument. Unfortunately the companion convoy from Alexandria was even less successful.

III

The Commander-in-Chief of the Mediterranean Fleet, Admiral Sir Henry Harwood, needed a great deal of persuasion that the convoy from the east – Operation 'Vigorous' – was necessary, or, more pertinent, possible. The fleet had been reduced during the preceding six months to a pale shadow of its former self, with a handful of 'Dido' class cruisers, the redoubtable 15th Cruiser Squadron of Rear-Admiral Vian, and less than a score of battleworthy destroyers. They were in an even less favourable position than Force H to fight through such a convoy.

Plans had been made to include at least one modern carrier before the attempt was made, but in fact not one could be found. To act as a substitute for a battle line, every attempt was made to co-ordinate early aerial reconnaissance and bomber strikes from Middle East Air Command with heavy submarine concentrations south of Taranto. There were certainly no illusions about the capacity of the enemy to interpose a battleship force between the convoy and Malta, for he had already twice done so and, although they had on both occasions been out-manoeuvred by Vian, there was no certain guarantee in the long hours of midsummer daylight that the Italians would allow this to occur again.

It was known that the enemy had reinforced his bomber squadrons in Crete and with the German airfields so close at hand, within bombing range of the main British Naval base, no measure of secrecy could conceal the assembly and sailing of a big convoy from them. The ships could expect to be under continuous air attack for the whole journey to Malta and back, and as a further hazard the German 6th E-boat Flotilla at Derna had also been brought up to full strength.

In addition to air and submarine deterrents the covering force for 'Vigorous' was reinforced by the addition of the cruisers *Birmingham*, *Newcastle* and *Arethusa* and the destroyers *Pakenham*, *Paladin*, *Norman*, *Nizam*, *Napier*, *Nestor*, *Fortune*, *Griffin*, *Hotspur*, *Hasty* and *Javelin* which sailed up through the Suez Canal from the Indian Ocean in May.

A long-shot deception was the sailing of a dummy convoy, escorted by seven 'Hunts' and the AA cruiser *Coventry* on 11th June. This force was to sail west in order to draw the Italian fleet out prematurely and thus subject it to attack – with the hope that such a sortie with their big ships would use up valuable fuel and force them to withdraw before the 'Vigorous' convoy reached the danger area. This diversionary group sailed as planned and was duly reported. On the meridian of Tobruk the following morning it reversed course to join up with the main body which had sailed in two groups from Haifa and Port Suez. Before they could do so the first waves of bombers found them, and fifteen Ju88s, although scoring no hits, planted near misses alongside one freighter, the *City of Calcutta*, forcing her to fall back and she was sent into Tobruk.

The main convoy also started ingloriously and one MT ship, the *Elizabeth Bakke*, was found to be too slow to maintain her position and she too limped back to harbour. She was joined in this sorry procession shortly afterwards by two of the escorts, the corvettes *Erica* and *Primula*, both with engine defects. No one could deny that 'Vigorous' seemed to be a shambles from the start; soon yet another cargo ship, the Dutch *Aegterkirk*, was sent back as she started to drop behind. Her unhappy crew were to pay dearly for their vessel's faults, slow and without air cover she was still some twelve miles from port when a jubilant group of Ju87s found her. Ideal Stuka bait, she soon went down under a hail of bombs. Her destroyer escort, the *Tetcott*, shot down three bombers but could do little to stop such a concentrated assault.

As if this were not enough. Admiral Harwood and Air Marshal Tedder found themselves bedevilled by lack of information filtering back to their headquarters. Like blindfolded chess players they moved their pieces to the best of their knowledge, but their opponents were kept better informed.

All through the night of the 13th/14th enemy planes circled the convoy, dropping flares and sending back a constant stream of movement reports. Fighters from the Western Desert managed to keep some of the heaviest enemy bombing raids away from the ships and broke up others, but all too soon the convoy was out of range of the short endurance Hurricanes and Kittyhawks of Middle East Command. The escorts stood to throughout the long hot day as wave after wave of Axis planes came in.

During the afternoon the enemy formations grew heavier and the *Bhutan* was stuck by three bombs and sank, while another merchant ship was damaged. Many ships were near-missed but their barrage had so far protected the convoy well. An alarmingly high rate of anti-aircraft fire was found necessary to beat off so many determined attacks and soon Admiral Vian began to be troubled with thoughts of shortages in all the escorts. Some of these vessels had already fired off about 50 per cent of their HA shells in just one day, and Vian knew that there was much worse to come.

Indeed reports of the sailing of the Italian fleet: two battleships, *Vittorio Veneto* and *Littorio*; two 8-inch and two 6-inch cruisers; and twelve destroyers. Our air and underwater substitutes for battleships did their best, but they were too few in number to affect the issue to our satisfaction. One heavy cruiser, the *Trento*, was hit by an aerial torpedo and finished off by the submarine *Umbra*. One battleship was claimed hit by bomb and torpedo but these failed to slow her down or impede her in any way. It was plain that this large force would cross Vian's path by dawn and he therefore signalled back to Harwood for instructions.

Admiral Harwood told him to hold his course until 2 am and then reverse it. He was probably hoping that a further day of air attacks would cause the Italians to return to port. Thus it was that around two in the morning of the 15th forty ships started the complicated manoeuvring to turn round in formation. With perfect timing the German E-boat flotilla chose this moment to attack and was quickly rewarded with successes among the warship escorts.

The 4th Cruiser Squadron had dropped astern during the turn and was hurrying to overtake the formation again when the enemy drove in out of the night, engines snarling, and delivered their torpedo assault. Swinging to avoid one torpedo the *Newcastle* took another for'ard which stopped her for a time, although she was able to catch up at 24 knots later. The destroyer *Hasty* was hit by another torpedo, from the *S.55* and had to be sunk by her sister ship the *Hotspur*. This attack was taken to have been made by a submarine and a fruitless hunt followed.

The sorry tale continued the next day. Throughout the 15th air attacks on the Italian fleet already described led to a succession of conflicting signals from the pilots of hits and damage inflicted, coupled with sighting reports which proved that the enemy was still astride the British convoy's intended route. While the convoy itself sailed up and down in 'Bomb Alley' the Axis airmen were presented with the opportunity of continuous bombing practice against the massed formation of ships whose ability to defend themselves was rapidly fading away.

In the morning the *Birmingham* was subjected to a Stuka attack with the usual result that when she emerged from it she was badly damaged. A neat- miss had shaken her very badly and dislocated some of her gun turrets. This afternoon the destroyer *Airedale* went down and another merchant ship dropped out with defects. While the old battleship *Centurion* – one of the original 'Super-Dreadnought' types dating back to *before* the First World War and armed with multiple Oerlikons – drew much fire, it was clear that the convoy was rapidly being decimated.

A last attempt to race the convoy through was called off when it was learnt just how low the escorts had now become anti-aircraft ammunition. It was at this point that the Italian warships finally turned back, leaving the route open, but it was plainly suicide to attempt to run the gauntlet now. Even as this news came through a further air raid got under way. The *Centurion* and *Arethusa* were both hit and the destroyer *Nestor* damaged and later scuttled. With a heavy heart Vian turned his ships for the last time back to Alexandria. Even then the enemy harried them and during the following night the unhappy convoy suffered the loss of yet another fine vessel when the *U-205* sank the cruiser *Hermione* with two torpedoes.

'Vigorous' was undoubtedly a major victory for the Axis, at trifling damage to himself – a cruiser and about a dozen aircraft; he had not only denied the sea lane to Malta from the east but had inflicted severe losses on the already exhausted and depleted Mediterranean Fleet.

If this operation can be claimed to have achieved anything, it can only be that it drew much of the weight of the German air force from our retreating armies in Egypt and at a critical time gave them some respite from the pounding their fleeing columns had received during the rout. The German War Diary admits that the main air strength was employed against the convoy, but this was of little consolation to the tired men of the fleet as they brought their battered vessels back to the now doubtful haven of Alexandria.

Admiral Vian, who had fought so brilliantly and hard to relieve Malta in January and March, had this to say:

> So ended, in distressing failure, the last attempt made under my command to relieve the necessities of Malta.
>
> [Typical of the man, he also added] … a more resolute commander than I was on this occasion might have held on regardless. Something might have got through.

A study of the operation reveals that Vian was being less than fair to himself. Whether anything would have got through at all is open to speculation, but it is certain that the price would have proved prohibitive had it been attempted.

The dismal end of the June convoy operations left a gloomy outlook for the officers and men most concerned with the continued resistance of Malta. The Germans were soon found to be at the gates of Cairo; Malta's days were clearly numbered. On the 20th Rommel captured Tobruk in his usual lightning manner and proceeded with hammer blows against the Army of the Nile, driving them rapidly back to Mersa Matruh. Evacuation of the naval base at Alexandria was seriously considered, and there was widespread panic in the rear echelons at Cairo itself. Many ships were quickly scrambled away to Haifa or sent south through the canal, their crews jeered by the troops based along its banks.

Chapter Two

The Last Chance

I

FOLLOWING the disastrous June failures Malta resigned herself to tightening her belt still further. It was hard, but very apparent that no further convoy attempts would be mounted right away; the risks were too obvious, the enemy strength too great and Britain's weakness everywhere too clear. In fact the months of June and July 1942 marked the absolute nadir, both of Britain's fortunes on land and sea, and of the whole Allied camp. Everywhere the Axis appeared dominant; everywhere it was they who held the initiative. That the pendulum would swing back was something that most people believed; with the gigantic resources of America immune from assault and getting into their stride it could only be a matter of time. But meanwhile the Allies had to hold the ring and hold it against enemy forces with their tails up and with the prospect of defeat on every front.

In the Pacific the Japanese Navy after running wild for six months had been checked at the Battle of the Coral Sea and defeated at the Battle of Midway, but although these were morale-boosting victories for the Americans after an unprecedented period of disaster, it was the Japanese who still had the forces available to continue expanding. It was not until August that the United States Marines waded ashore on Guadalcanal to begin the murderous slogging match which was finally to halt the men from Nippon.

On the Eastern front, the Russian winter had provided the check to hold back Hitler's unmatched armies, not the numerically superior Soviet forces, and with the coming of the summer months the Wehrmacht rolled forward again in unequalled efficiency and strength, penetrating deeper than ever before into the Ukraine, almost to the Turkish borders. With the Afrika Korps poised for the knockout blow in Egypt it seemed that Hitler's planned occupation of Malta, Operation 'Hercules', must surely follow.

Strangely enough the very scale of their successes dazzled the enemy leaders into believing that the basic aims of 'Hercules' could now be achieved without the necessity of going through with the occupation of Malta itself. Just to keep the island neutralised was felt to be sufficient. Thus, unknown to the hard-pressed defenders, the biggest threat was lifted from them, but in every other respect the position was grim enough.

The fact was that the Royal Navy was attempting to fight a three-ocean war with a two-ocean fleet; and they were now finding that it could not be done. The lack, both of numbers of ships and of up-to-date vessels and equipment was a handicap almost impossible to overcome, and the summer of 1942 saw crisis follow crisis at sea. The Mediterranean, dominated by the Luftwaffe, was very nearly an enemy lake. In the East a much reduced Eastern Fleet had retired hastily to East Africa after coming close to annihilation the previous spring, and in home waters the fleet was by now almost totally committed to one major task, that of fighting through convoys of war material to North Russia.

This bitter battle tied down not only the Home Fleet cruiser squadrons and destroyer flotillas but the presence of just one of Germany's modern battleships, the *Tirpitz*, meant that at least two of the Royal Navy's few modern counterparts and one carrier had to be held in readiness to operate against her.[1]

July saw the sailing of the ill-fated PQ17 convoy, 35 ships fully laden with war supplies, and no forces could be diverted to the Mediterranean until this task was accomplished. What few ships we had spare from these commitments were engaged in the occupation of Madagascar in the Indian Ocean, a move made necessary by the easy dominance of the Japanese carrier force some months before, which led to the fear that they might be allowed to bloodlessly occupy the island in the same manner that they had been let in to French Indo-China prior to their invasion of Malaya and Burma. Thrown into this operation were the bulk of Force H and two of the Royal Navy's few modern carriers, the

[1] Which of course does not say much for the battleships of the 'King George V' class, but it must be remembered that these ships were designed to conform to Treaty limitations which were ignored by other nations. *Tirpitz* was more powerful in every way. Just how powerful the *Bismarck*, sister ship of *Tirpitz*, had shown, and the Admiralty could not risk another disaster like the *Hood*'s loss at this stage of the war.

Indomitable and *Illustrious*.

Malta therefore had to undergo another reassessment of her position and the findings were not encouraging. The Deputy Governor, Sir Edward Jackson, spelled it out to the island's population a few days after the June convoys, or what remained of one of them, had arrived:

> We have received about 15,000 tons of stores from the two ships which arrived. That is something and certainly help, but it is a very small part of what we had hoped for.... Our security depends, more than anything else, on the time for which our bread will last...
>
> We knew that our present ration could not be reduced and it will not be reduced. That calculation gave us a date, which I shall call the Target Date, the date to aim at. Our next task was to see how we could make our other vital necessities last to the Target Date. We found that with some things we could not do so without some restriction in the ration, or without making a wider interval between the issues than we make now ...
>
> I cannot tell you what the Target Date is, for if the enemy came to hear of it he would learn something that he would very much like to know, but I can tell you that it is far enough off to give very ample opportunity for fresh supplies to reach us before our present stocks run out ...

These were brave words. In fact, the absolute deadline was 7th September.

II

It was the enforced suspension of the Russia convoys coupled with the easing of the situation in the Indian Ocean which gave the Navy the opportunity to assemble the forces powerful enough for the desperately needed convoy. Churchill and the Cabinet were in complete accord that the attempt had to be made. The Premier stated that the loss of Malta would be a disaster of the first magnitude to the British Empire and would be fatal in the long run to the defence of the Nile Valley. The 'fate of the island is at stake', he told the Admiralty.

The C-in-C Mediterranean, Admiral Sir Henry Harwood, was dubious, after the events of June, whether it would be worth while running another convoy, but the Governor, Lord Gort, took a more optimistic view of its chances. The Admiralty were certainly in no doubt, both of the necessity and the ability of the Navy to carry out the task, although it was feared that casualties might be heavy.

The actual date of the convoy depended firstly on the ability of the Navy to assemble a powerful enough force to guarantee its passage, a condition they were capable of meeting by mid-August, and secondly on the best timing to outwit the enemy. This was dependent to a large extent on the moonless periods so vital for the final part of the long passage, the deadly stretch of water, between Sicily and Tunisia, known as the Narrows. Therefore it was decided that the period between 10th and 16th August would be the last possible time in which to mount the operation. This would give the Admiralty the time to assemble its forces and carry out some rudimentary training and also, just as important, to plan the operation in great detail.

Indeed the detail and care of the planning was one of the major features of both sides of the 'Pedestal' operation.

As the attempt was to be made from the west, it was the Commander of Force H, the unit usually based on Gibraltar, who was entrusted to command and carry out the operation. Vice-Admiral Sir Neville Syfret, of South African extraction, had been in command of Force H since the transfer earlier of the famed Sir James Somerville. As Rear-Admiral under Somerville's command, Syfret had extensive experience of all the many practical problems of the Malta route.

He had commanded the close escort of cruisers and destroyers during the previous *big* convoy operation, 'Substance', which had been so successful in July 1941. Because the Home Fleet was so tied up in the Arctic it was his command which had been selected to carry out the Madagascar occupation and consequently he had sailed from the Rock in April aboard his flagship the battleship *Malaya*. Once this action was completed *Malaya* had returned but Syfret remained, hoisting his flag in HMS *Canton* at Takoradi.

On receiving his orders with regard to 'Pedestal' from the Admiralty Syfret left East Africa by air for London – with his Operations Staff Officer, Commander A. H. Thorold, OBE, RN – arriving in England on 13th July. At the Admiralty he met his senior commanders for the forthcoming operation: Rear-Admiral A. L. St G. Lyster, CB, CVO, DSO, who was to co-ordinate the aerial defence of the large carrier force involved, and Rear-Admiral H. M. Burrough, CB, DSO, who, as Rear-Admiral Commanding the 10th Cruiser Squadron, was to command the close escort force through to Malta, 'Force X'.

Rear-Admiral Burrough was another capable officer who knew the Malta run, having held the same command in the 'Halberd' convoy of September 1941. On that occasion, with a force of five cruisers and eight destroyers, he had led the convoy on an audacious course within miles of the south coast of Sicily, successfully throwing the enemy off the scent and delivering the ships to Malta for the loss of only one vessel by mining. In December he had made the Vaagso raid and in February he had visited Murmansk. During the spring and summer the 10th Cruiser Squadron had been engaged in acting with other Home Fleet units as cover for the PQ convoys in Murmansk, during which time the British had lost the cruisers *Edinburgh* and *Trinidad*.[1]

These officers assembled with Admiral Pound's staff at Norfolk House in St James Square and commenced the intricate planning work, which was to last for many days of that hot humid summer month.

Broadly speaking the operation was to be a repetition of the 'Harpoon' plan but this time only a diversionary convoy, not the real thing, was to be sailed simultaneously from the eastern basin. The bulk of the Home Fleet was concentrated to form the main escort, the cruiser and destroyer strengths especially, as well as

---

[1] Burrough was in fact senior to Syfret on the Navy List, but he willingly agreed to waive his seniority, to serve under Syfret, who was appointed Acting Vice-Admiral.

Victorious, leaving only the two modern battleships and the heavy cruiser squadron at Scapa to watch *Tirpitz*. This was a calculated risk, but it was thought unlikely that the Germans would sortie her out into the Atlantic because of her recently proven advantage as a threat to the Arctic sea lanes.

Admiral Syfret subsequently reported that he found it a great advantage that the planning could be done at the Admiralty because:

(a) Early decisions could be obtained and questions answered, thus avoiding signals.

(b) Communications were better and there was less chance of loss of security.

(c) General views on policy could be obtained.

(d) The advice and help of the Naval Staff was always at hand.

Based on the study of 'Harpoon's' failure it was decided that the chief needs for 'Pedestal' were, firstly, heavier air cover during the critical period when the convoy was between the south of Sardinia and the mouth of the Narrows. Secondly, a much heavier force of cruisers and destroyers was needed to complete the last stage through the Sicilian channel to the island itself in order to deter or defeat a similar intervention by enemy cruiser forces. At one stage indeed it was suggested that battleship cover should be given right the way through, but this idea was soon dropped; the risks were much too great and it was felt extremely unlikely that the Italians would venture with their own battleship into these waters.

I had hoped to be allowed to follow close down the south-west coast of Sicily [Admiral Burrough commented later] as I had done in a previous Malta convoy in September 1941. This bold course had paid us well on that occasion and only one ship of the convoy was lost. Admittedly the enemy Air Forces had been greatly strengthened by August 1942 and we should have been very close to the Sicilian Air Bases on the forenoon of the 13th, but I still felt it would be better than the narrow Tunisian Channel. However it was ordained otherwise and in the light of the information available I have no doubt that the decision was the right one.

To provide a deterrent should the enemy decide to use capital ships against the convoy, or against the carriers, some big ship support was required, and it was decided to use the *Nelson* and the *Rodney* who were then at Freetown. They were immediately sailed back to Scapa Flow. These two vessels were the most modern battleships of our elderly pre-war fleet, and were powerful, rugged ships with 16-inch calibre main armaments, the heaviest guns in the Royal Navy. They were felt to be more than a match even for the new Italian battleships should it come to a slogging match in defence of the convoy. But past experience had shown that there was little likelihood of this and with top speeds of only 21 knots the British clearly had no intention of pursuing the enemy had they in fact approached the convoy. The two battleships were there in a purely defensive role and would have to rely on the two large striking forces of Albacore torpedo-bombers, embarked in the carriers, to hit and slow down the Italian big ships whose speeds exceeded 30 knots, before they could have brought them to battle.

Another major asset was the fact that both these ships possessed very heavy anti-aircraft batteries which should prove invaluable in protecting the convoys, as well as the fact that both were fitted out for flagship duties and could thus easily accommodate Admiral Syfret's full staff.

For their main defence against the enemy bombers the convoy could call on a total of 72 Fleet Air Arm fighter planes, from eight interceptor squadrons. These would be embarked in the Force H carrier *Eagle*, which was already at Gibraltar; in the *Victorious* from the Home Fleet, Admiral Lyster's flagship; and in the *Indomitable*, which was being brought round the Cape from the Indian Ocean especially for the convoy. Nearly all the fighter squadrons involved were equipped with the Fairey Fulmar two-seater fighter/ reconnaissance aircraft, which with a top speed of under 300 mph would obviously be outclassed by the modern land-based fighters the Germans and Italians were expected to deploy.

A crash programme of replacement was put into effect whereby most, but not all, of these units had their Fulmars replaced by Sea

Hurricanes and Martlets (USN Wildcats) both of which had slightly better performance. The efficiency of these fighter aircraft depended on both their abilities and on their being vectored out to their targets in time to be effective. The most experienced pilots were in *Eagle*'s squadrons, unfortunately as it was to turn out. *Victorious* could not even strike down her Sea Hurricanes as her lifts were too small, and so she was allocated the low-level interception role in the main. *Indomitable* had one enlarged lift. While the Grumman Martlet Its provided medium altitude defence the Sea Hurricanes were to provide top cover at 20,000 feet. Eighteen fighters were to be kept in the air, with a further eighteen at instant readiness and twelve more in immediate reserve.

But if they were to be effective they had to be sent out in time and at the right heights to intercept the enemy formations. To aid in this the height-finding qualities of the Type 79B radar of *Victorious* were to concentrate on this duty while *Indomitable*'s and the cruiser *Sirius*'s Type 281 sets kept a low-altitude, all-round search pattern. The aircraft were fitted with VHF and IFF while the ships all had VHF R/T for general exchanges of information. RAF liaison officers were also embarked in certain command cruisers to vector in the RAF fighters from Malta later in the journey.

The Royal Air Force was to provide long-range escort planes from Gibraltar and Malta to the limit of their range; to ensure close cooperation between the convoy, the escorts and these aircraft both Admiral Burrough's flagship *Nigeria* and the anti-aircraft cruiser *Cairo* had been fitted out for fighter-direction duties, embarking specialist personnel and equipment to enable them to direct the fighter cover on to enemy formations picked up on the warships' radar screens.

Although the need for such co-ordination between the ships and the fighter aircraft had long been held as essential, an effective system took some years to perfect. By 1942, although improved in technique and application, the system was far from perfect. As the Official Naval Historian had since recorded: 'The whole art of fighter direction depended on efficient radar warning sets in the ships and efficient radio-telephone communications from the ships to the aircraft, neither of which existed in the early days.'

The provision then of *two* such vessels fitted with high-frequency sets was therefore something of a luxury and was yet another indication of the detailed planning of this operation. And another lesson, which had been learnt from similar convoys, to both Malta and North Russia, was the need for an oiling force to accompany the convoy and escort. The smaller warships, particularly the destroyers with their high speeds, were heavy consumers of fuel and as Malta herself was in no position to replenish any of the through escort it was essential that the final bout of fuelling should be carried out as late as possible before the final dash through enemy controlled waters. Accordingly two Royal Navy Fleet Auxiliary tankers were detailed to leave Gibraltar and rendezvous with the convoy escorts on their second day out past the straits to perform this duty. Another tanker was assigned to the carrier force to top up their escorts during Operation 'Berserk', this being a secondary operation, a sea/air exercise to be held out in the Atlantic to lick the FAA crews into a team.

The 10th Cruiser Squadron comprised three ships of similar armament, age and speed, the two brand-new 'Colony' class cruisers, *Nigeria* and *Kenya*, which mounted twelve 6-inch guns in triple turrets and a heavy anti-aircraft battery on 8,000 tons displacement; and the slightly older *Manchester*, similarly armed on a displacement of 10,000 tons. Three light cruisers of the 'Dido' class, 5,525-ton ships with primarily anti-aircraft capacity, were assigned to escort the carriers of Force Z; these were the *Phoebe* and *Sirius* with ten 5.25-inch guns; the *Charybdis*, mounting eight 4.5-inch and finally there was the old A/A cruiser *Cairo* with four twin 4-inch guns.

Great emphasis was placed on the heavy destroyer screen, no less than sixteen being sent to Force Z and ten to Force X. To assemble so many of these much-needed vessels for just one convoy was in itself another real achievement by the Admiralty, shortage of destroyers being the biggest headaches they had to face at this stage of the war. Naturally it had to be accepted that such a concentration would not comprise a series of homogeneous flotillas, this was just not possible. Therefore any available ship was assigned to the nominal command of the two senior destroyer captains, Captain R. M. Hutton, Captain (D) of the 19th Flotilla, normally a part of Force H at Gibraltar, and Acting-Captain R. G. Onslow, Captain (D) of the 6th Flotilla, a Home Fleet unit-he was standing in for Captain J. Eaton in the *Somali*, the proper Captain (D) 6, who had recently gone sick. Richard Onslow was the Senior Divisional Commander of the flotilla and was given the acting rank of captain for this and subsequent operations. He was therefore summoned to the Fleet flagship and told by Admiral Tovey that he was to issue complete orders for all destroyers and escorts. Captain Hutton of the *Laforey* was actually the senior destroyer officer but his flotilla was then in the South Atlantic and so could not be briefed.

The resulting escort proved to be a powerful force but included ships of widely varying age and ability. But far the most powerful were Captain Hutton's three '*Laforey*' class boats, brand-new ships of almost 2,000 tons displacement with heavy dual-purpose armaments. Somewhat older and slightly smaller were Captain Onslow's four 'Tribals' mounting six 4.7-inch and two 4-inch HA guns on 1,870 tons displacement. Other Fleet destroyers included the new boats *Pathfinder*, *Penn* and *Quentin*, which were standard Emergency flotilla destroyers built under the War Programme, to which could be added the recently completed ex-Turkish *Ithuriel* and the pre-war *Foresight*, *Fury*, *Intrepid* and *Icarus* from the 8th Flotilla Home Fleet.

All these vessels mounted torpedoes, which would be essential to repel surface attacks, as well as good surface and AA armaments. The other new destroyers included were seven of the small 'Hunt' class which counted heavy AA armaments as their chief weapons, but unfortunately suffered from poor fuel stowage and had no torpedo tubes. The rest of the destroyer strength was made up of older vessels some of which dated from the First World War, all of which had been converted to a primary anti-submarine role.

In addition to the surface escorts plans were made for the 10th Submarine Flotilla, recently re-established in the Mediterranean, to take up positions to intercept any Italian heavy units coming down from the north. Two of the submarines were put on normal diving patrols in the north of Sicily, one off Palermo and the other off Milazzo further east, while the other six were given alternate patrol lines south of Pantelleria, one of which they were to take up at daybreak on the 13th.

Once the convoy had passed this patrol line the submarines were to surface and proceed parallel to it as a screen. Complete freedom of action was allowed if air or surface attack developed, and in the case of the latter their task was to go for the battleships and cruisers of the enemy line. Their task was also to deter such an attempt and they were expressly intended to be seen and reported by the enemy in order to achieve this.

The Royal Air Force at Malta was to co-operate to the maximum and as a necessary preliminary over a hundred aircraft were flown in from the Middle East, which increased the RAF's nominal strength to 250 machines. However the maximum number available at any one time was about 100 Spitfires, 36 Beaufighters, 30 Beauforts, 3 Wellingtons, 2 Liberators, 2 Baltimores, 3 Fleet Air Arm Albacores and, as additional reconnaissance machines, 5 more Baltimores, 6 photo-reconnaissance Spitfires and 5 Wellington VIIIs, which meant that their role was necessarily defensive though some token strikes were planned.

Air Vice-Marshal Sir Keith Park defined the RAF's duties as follows:

(1) To locate, shadow and report all enemy surface forces in order to warn the convoy escort.
(2) To protect the convoy from air attack when in range.
(3) To destroy the enemy surface forces.
(4) To dislocate the enemy air forces on the ground by means of low-flying attacks by Beaufighters, night bombing of Sardinian bases by the Liberators and large scale night bombing by Liberators from the Middle East Command.

It was also hoped that the Army would help by staging a diversionary attack in Egypt but this they refused to do. The Army never seemed to understand the importance of Malta, although it was they who benefited whenever an Italian tanker went down with fuel for Rommel's tanks aboard. Indeed General Auchinleck, the Army Commander in Egypt, had stated that Malta's retention was not absolutely necessary to his plans. Fortunately for all concerned both the Navy and the Air Force, with the active backing of Winston Churchill and the full support of the War Cabinet, saw the true picture and made their moves accordingly.

While these complex moves were being worked out in London preliminary movements were already taking place; the *Nelson* and *Rodney*, stationed at Freetown, were brought back to Scapa, a move which Admiral Syfret described as 'fully justified':

> Assembling and sailing of ships at Scapa Flow not only enabled me to discuss the operation with the majority of Commanding Officers of ships taking part, but also gave many advantages from the security point of view. The use of a telephone fitted with a scrambler was invaluable as it enabled many points of detail to be cleared up, up to the moment of sailing.

Not all the warships had time to come back to England and a complicated routing plan was necessary to bring together all the forces earmarked at the junction east of the Straits of Gibraltar on the 11th.

In the midst of these planning moves the Chief of the Air Staff, Air Chief Marshal Sir Charles F. A. Portal, GCB, DSO, MC, told Admiral Pound that he was concerned at the high wastage of Malta's Spitfire squadrons. Of those flown in earlier only eighty remained fully effective at the end of July and losses averaged seventeen a week. Acting with typical energy Pound organised a further supply operation, code-named 'Bellows', to be added on to 'Pedestal's' already complicated procedure. The carrier *Furious* was made available to carry 40 more Spitfires out to the Mediterranean and Commander A. B. Russell's Escort Flotilla from Western Approaches was assigned to the task of escorting her back to the Rock once she had completed flying-off operations. The detailing of this flotilla brought the total destroyer strength on the British side to 32.

III

Equally complex was the organisation necessary for the assembling; loading and despatch on time of the cargo vessels, which were to form the convoy itself. As has been noted earlier, finding the fast modern vessels needed for such a high-speed convoy was extremely difficult. Losses in mercantile tonnage were running at an all-time peak in the North Atlantic battle and already many of Britain's most suitable ships had been lost. The Mediterranean had proved a heavy drain on this type of vessel with the fine ships of the Clan type being pressed into service time and time again with resulting casualties.

Knowing as they did that the enemy would try to mount a larger scale of attack than ever before against 'Pedestal' it was almost certain that a large proportion of the convoy might not get through. Malta's position was so desperate that the Admiralty decided to make ample allowances for heavy losses, even if it meant scraping the barrel for modern freighters.

Eventually twelve big ships were earmarked for the convoy and as they arrived in British ports they were hustled away to be 'combat loaded' in readiness. This was standard practice; each ship was allocated a proportion of the total cargo so that a percentage of every commodity was certain to get through despite heavy casualties. Unfortunately this system broke down when it came to the most vital cargo of all, oil fuel.

The necessary tankers with the speed required – sixteen knots – just did not exist in the British Merchant Fleet. The only people possessing tankers of this performance were the Americans, and quite naturally they wanted every one of these vital vessels for themselves. The war in the Pacific was rapidly becoming a war of logistics for them, and the Navy Department was taking over every fast tanker it could lay its hands on.

Fortunately, a far-sighted member of the Ministry of War Transport, Sir Ralph Metcalf, had already foreseen this need and had despatched a cable to Sir Arthur Salter, the head of the British Merchant Shipping Mission in Washington, detailing the type of vessel we required. In the face of some considerable opposition he managed to persuade the United States Maritime Commission of the dire urgency of our case and as a result, with typical generosity, the Americans had allocated two of their precious tankers to our needs. These were the *Kentucky* and the *Ohio*. *Kentucky* had accordingly sailed in the June convoy and had been lost, therefore only the *Ohio* remained and she became doubly precious, being then the sole vessel available to break the blockade. There was no chance of obtaining another tanker at this time and therefore everything rested on this one ship.

She was a modern tanker, built in 1940, owned by the Texas Oil Company's tanker group, Texaco. She put into the Clyde in June 1942 with a full cargo and at once her owners were informed that she had been requisitioned. She lay at her anchorage off Bowling awaiting her fate while the exact details of her take-over were being worked out. The British *Eagle* Oil and Shipping Company assumed nominal ownership of the big tanker on behalf of the Ministry of War Transport and on 10th July the American crew were disembarked, and the British crew came aboard. They were under the command of Captain Dudley Mason, who at 39 was the youngest Master in the *Eagle* Fleet. Forty-eight hours later she moved down to the King George V dock, whereupon the dockyard fitters swarmed aboard her to supplement her armament in readiness for the voyage ahead of her.

She was already fitted with a 5-inch gun aft and a 3-inch HA gun in her bows but these were augmented by the addition of a 40-mm bofors and no less than six 20-mm Oerlikons, quite the most powerful anti-aircraft armoury the mercantile crew had seen aboard one of their vessels before, and one which gave them some indication of what lay ahead. Two dozen Naval and Army gunners also joined the ship to man these weapons, and Captain Mason was joined by a Naval liaison officer, Lieutenant D. Barton.

Further work was carried out on her during the following weeks, which included the fitting of special bearings to her engines designed to reduce the shock of close explosions to her and her steam pipes were similarly protected. On 28th July the tanker moved down the Clyde to Dunglass where she was loaded with 11,000 tons of oil fuel. On completion of this she joined the bulk of the convoy already assembled and awaiting their final briefing.

All these had received similar reinforcements to their armaments and complements; every ship was heavily armed and had a Naval liaison officer embarked to assist in the complicated manoeuvring which would become necessary. Naval signallers and de-coding operators were also taken aboard. Their cargoes, totalling some 85,000 tons, were chiefly flour, ammunition and shells, although many had dangerous stores of petrol and aviation spirit in cans embarked in case *Ohio* did not get through to Malta.

Twelve big freighters had now assembled,[1] the thirteenth, the *Santa Elisa*, was something of a last-minute addition and was actually loading cargo for the States at Newport, Mon., when she was ordered to discharge and reload with war material. She arrived off Greenock on 31st July.

For secrecy the convoy was allocated a bogus 'WS' number, 5.21. These WS convoys were usually those which sailed from Britain to Suez by way of the Cape of Good Hope and had become affectionately known as 'Winston's Specials'. It is uncertain whether in fact all the elaborate precautions taken prior to sailing to keep their destination a secret were successful. For example the Convoy Commodore, Commander A. G. Venables, reported that in his opinion security had been weak.

He suggested that a small convoy would have enabled leakages to have been more readily suppressed. Lieutenant-Commander S. W. F. Bennets of the destroyer *Bicester* stated that the charts of the Mediterranean were openly issued to HM ships before the convoy sailed and that the pub-talk in the town had revealed the fact that they were assembling for Malta. In fact so common was criticism of security after the operation that a special inquiry was subsequently mounted by the Ministry of War Transport into the whole operation, after Admiral of the Fleet Lord Cork and Orrery had suggested that there was evidence of a serious leak in a speech made on 29th September 1942. Cargo clearly marked 'Malta', he

[1] Full details of the convoy are contained in Appendix I.

claimed, had been loaded on public docks.

Lord Cork returned to this theme in a debate in the Lords the following month; he rose to ask His Majesty's Government:

> Whether they consider that every possible step is taken at the ports of the *United* Kingdom to keep secret the destination of the ships loaded therein.
>
> My reason for putting the question [he went on] was that I heard at second hand of a young officer whose ship was lost in the last convoy to Malta ['Pedestal'], who had stated that cases had been passed into the ship with the name 'Malta' on them. He told my informant that this had caused adverse comment among the officers.

The Earl then quoted a letter from the manager of a large engineering firm in the north:

> *'My only son, an engineering officer in the Merchant Navy, whom I visited in Liverpool at the end of July 1942, told me that he saw cases being loaded into his ship marked "'Malta". He also informed me that several of his fellow engineering officers discussed the question of refusing to sail as an extreme protest against this culpable carelessness or worse.'*

This gentleman [continued the Earl] appears to have reasoned with his son and the other officers and was informed the next evening that out of consideration for our men in Malta they were quite ready to sail, but if they returned they would demand full investigation before sailing again as the convoy was supposed to sail under secret orders. My correspondent goes on to say, that *'the last words my son spoke to me in Liverpool on the evening of the 28th July were "Well, Dad, Jerry will be waiting for us in full force, and with our cargo we shall be trapped in the engine-room if we are hit, and it will be a miracle if we return in this suicide ship, so this is most probably our last farewell.*

It was [continued the Earl] ; the ship did not survive. She was lost with one hundred of her crew including all her officers. The gentleman who wrote the letter also tells me 'I have not the slightest doubt regarding my son's statement that cases were loaded on the ship clearly marked "Malta".'

For the Ministry of War Transport, Lord Leathers rose to soothe:

The particular case mentioned by the Noble Earl Lord Cork on a previous occasion has not been traced and indeed, by the nature of the evidence available, I cannot trace it.

Lord Cork was not easily dissuaded however:

The young officer [John C. Waine] is perfectly willing to come and be examined [he said of another witness]. He feels very strongly about it. He told me in his letter that he is only a cadet, but feels he has a mission and would be quite willing to come out in public and give his evidence.

There was strong verbal support for the Earl and finally Lord Leathers had to assure the House:

I do most sincerely give an assurance that this matter will be investigated and by that I mean a special investigation arising out of what has been said in Your Lordships' House today.

It was of course a secret session and the findings have never been generally divulged to this day. The whole episode certainly has a ring of truth; to decide whether or not this was a serious case of negligence we can turn to a statement made by the German Admiral Weichold, C-in-C Mediterranean at that time, that he had received, towards the end of July, an Intelligence report advising as follows:

A large-scale Allied operation was about to break into the Mediterranean. Large merchant-ships and fleet units were being fetched from far and wide in preparation.

It would seem clear that 'Pedestal' was not the surprise it was meant to be to the Axis.

On 2nd August, after a normal convoy conference, a special meeting was held in the aircraft hangar of the *Nigeria*, where Rear-Admiral Burrough called aboard his flagship all the masters of the convoy and explained the whole plan in great detail to them.

This was supposed to be the first occasion on which their destination was made known to them. The operation was discussed down to the smallest points using models and diagrams and Burrough emphasised the need for strict discipline if the convoy was to stand any chance at all.

At the same time, also aboard the *Nigeria*, a second special conference was under way for the W/T operators assigned to the merchantmen during which all details regarding fleet communications and procedure were fully explained. Admiral Syfret described these two meetings as invaluable.

At the conclusion of these conferences the Merchant Ships' Masters returned to their vessels to break the news to their crews. The convoy itself was due to sail that evening with only a light destroyer escort so as not to arouse suspicion; the main bulk of the escorting forces was to join up the next day well out of sight of land. Already the operation had suffered its first casualty: the destroyer *Lamerton*, assigned as part of the initial escort, had been steaming in thick fog on the morning of 31st July when at 6.25 that morning she had been in collision with the SS *Almenara*. The destroyer's bow was set back as far as the capstan so she was sent in to Londonderry. Her place was later taken by the Flotilla Leader *Keppel* already at sea on her way to Gibraltar.

The movement of this one destroyer illustrates in its own small way the manner in which our over-stretched forces had to be switched from one theatre of war to another at a moment's notice. *Keppel* had come straight from the Arctic Ocean and the disastrous PQ17 convoy and was now on her way to Gibraltar via the Azores. As Commander Broome phrased it at the time, it was a case of 'from Polar Bears to Pineapples' in a matter of days.

As dusk fell the dim bulks of the waiting freighters were becoming active as anchors were weighed and the vessel's engines set to 'Slow Ahead'. Silently and without fuss the fourteen big ships edged slowly out of the anchorage and into the darkened channel, their destroyer guardians[1] frisking around them and nudging them

---

[1] *Bicester, Bramham, Ledbury* and *Wilton*.

verbally into line and order. Very few saw them go, and those who did could not know that on this handful of men rested the fate of the island of Malta and possibly even the whole war in the Middle East. Certainly to the casual watcher it would appear to be just another routine convoy heading out into the grim wastes of the North Atlantic. Nobody could guess how few of these vessels would ever sail through the murky waters of the Clyde again.

Captain D. A. G. Dickens later served with Trinity House in a long and very honourable career. Back in August 1942 that career was just commencing and he was a young apprentice aboard the ss *Dorset*. He recorded all the momentous events as they happened and later wrote up his eyewitness account of the convoy. Seen through his young eyes the battle takes on a fresh look. He listed the assembly of the convoy and its early movements thus:

The ships that made up this convoy assembled at Gourock on Sunday, 2nd August 1942; these ships were drawn from various ports in the following manner:

Wairangi, *Empire Hope*, *Glenorchy* and *Santa Elisa*, from ports in the Bristol Channel area; *Waimarama*, *Melbourne Star*, *Brisbane Star*, *Dorset* and *Ohio* from Liverpool; *Deucalion*, *Almeria Lykes*, *Rochester Castle* and *Clan Ferguson* from Glasgow.

It will be noticed from the above list that approximately one third of the convoy was drawn from the Bristol Channel, one third from Liverpool and the remaining one third from Glasgow. Probably the idea of this was secrecy more than anything else.

Ships were mostly loaded with the same cargo, which consisted of flour, petrol, coal, ammunition, bombs, medical supplies and army equipment. Various stores such as wines, spirits, chocolate, biscuits and cigarettes were also carried but not to any great extent.

It is believed that the ships from the Bristol Channel arrived at Gourock on Friday, 31st July. The Liverpool ships, however, cast off at approximately 1400 on Friday, 31st July and anchored in mid-stream until 1000 Saturday, 1st August, when they sailed bound for Gourock. Incidentally it is interesting to recall that they hove-to to the sound of an air raid warning! These ships were escorted on this occasion by about four of HM destroyers and anchored in Gourock Roads at about 0800 on the Sunday. All that day various naval officials kept visiting the ships, these men were chiefly engaged with the ship's armaments and the fire-fighting equipment, which they inspected very thoroughly indeed. Most ships were armed in the same manner; as a typical example *Dorset* had ready for immediate use: Six Oerlikon (20mm) guns; one Bofors (40mm) gun; two Hotchkiss guns; one 4-inch (LA) gun; for FAMs (Fast Aerial Mines); two UPs (Unrotating Projectiles, nicknamed 'Pig Troughs') and four PAC (Parachute and Cable) rockets.

That Sunday in August was not a very good one from the point of view of the weather, for it was dull in the extreme, and there were several heavy storms. Towards 1700, however, it began to brighten up considerably and it was at this time that ships got the news that they could 'heave away' at 1800. Promptly at that time ship No 21, *Port Chalmers* (Commodore) got under weigh followed by the others – all steaming very slowly in single line ahead.

To any onlooker this must have presented a memorable sight – those fine merchant ships slowly but surely making weigh, while in the background lay the beautiful mountains of Scotland. From the ships themselves the land looked more beautiful than ever before – probably because the men who manned them knew what lay ahead of them and thought to themselves that they might never be there to see them again; and it was indeed not long before that came to pass for many brave men who were to give their lives in order that Malta would not starve. Before long the sun sank below the mountains and shortly afterwards the ships reached the open sea.

On board most felt confident; they knew that they were in for a rough time, but the very strength of the escort promised to them indicated that the Navy would do everything in its power to get them to their destination and back again. Before they had sailed each skipper had been handed a sealed envelope marked 'Not to be opened until 0800/10th August'. It contained the following letter from the First Lord of the Admiralty, Mr A. V. Alexander:

> Before you start on this operation the First Sea Lord and I are anxious that you should know how grateful the Board of Admiralty are to you for undertaking this difficult task. Malta has for some time been in great danger. It is imperative that she should be kept supplied. These are her critical months and we cannot fail her. She has stood up to the most violent attack from the air that has ever been made; and now she needs our help in continuing the battle. Her courage is worthy of yours.
>
> We know that Admiral Syfret will do all he can to complete the operation with success, and that you will stand by him according to the splendid traditions of the Merchant Navy. We wish you all Godspeed and good luck.

Operation 'Pedestal' was under way.

Chapter Three

Into Battle

I

DAWN on Monday, 3rd August found the merchant ships of the convoy well on their course and throughout the day more wheels of the great operation were set in motion as squadron after squadron of lean grey ships left their bases to rendezvous in the Atlantic. From the Clyde, from Londonderry, from bleak Scapa Flow, sun-drenched Gibraltar and far-distant Freetown, His Majesty's ships were beginning to assemble to form the biggest concentration of British sea-power so far brought together to protect a single convoy.

First to join WS21S was the flagship of Force X, the *Nigeria*, with the *Kenya*, *Amazon*, *Derwent* and *Zetand*.[1] They had left the Clyde at 11 pm the previous night and sighted the merchantmen at 6.30 am, first light. The destroyers *Malcolm*, *Venomous*, *Wolverine* and *Wishart*, which had been detached at Londonderry to refuel, also joined at this time.

As soon as Rear-Admiral Burrough arrived he formed the convoy into two columns and started the first of a long series of tough exercises, designed to work the clumsy freighters into as near the equivalent of a battle-fleet as was possible. It was essential that by the time they reached the Mediterranean the Merchant Navy crews should be as proficient as possible, their very fate and that of Malta would depend on their ability to carry out complicated manoeuvres quickly and accurately, in the face of heavy enemy attacks. Nothing was more alien to the captains and the men of the merchantmen; by their very nature seamen are independent and all of them loathed the tight formation and rigid orders this involved.

All of the merchantmen had been in many convoys since the outbreak of war and the majority of the seamen were no novices to the standard convoy duties, but 'Pedestal' relied, even more than usual, on good station-keeping and discipline; at fifteen knots this was the fastest convoy most of the freighters had even taken part in.

[1] The various forces comprising 'Pedestal' are fully listed in Appendix 2.

Rear-Admiral Burrough was in no doubt of the need for intensive training in the week allowed him; on their first attempt he recorded the convoy's station-keeping as 'very poor'. This was only to be expected and given the will he was sure that they would become more proficient.

Other forces already on passage were the ancient aircraft carrier *Argus*, escorted by the destroyers *Sardonyx* and *Buxton*, which had left the Clyde on 31st July. She was to rendezvous in the Atlantic with the *Victorious*, which had left Scapa the same day accompanied by the cruiser *Sirius* and the destroyers *Foresight*, *Fury*, *Intrepid* and *Icarus*. These four destroyers were to play an important part in the operation for, equipped for high-speed minesweeping, their ultimate task was to lead the convoy through the extensive minefield laid across the narrow channels between Sicily and Tripoli and known on Admiralty charts as Minefield *QBB255*. This deadly area of sea had already claimed many ships and was continually being further extended by the enemy.

As soon as she had left harbour *Victorious* embarked her new Sea Hurricanes, 885 Squadron flying aboard at first light. *Indomitable* was far to the south, forging up from Freetown with her escorting cruiser *Phoebe*, screened by Captain Hutton's three big 'L' class destroyers, *Laforey*, *Lightning* and *Lookout*. Also steaming to the rendezvous for Operation '*Berserk*', the carrier-training programme, was the oiling group from Freetown, *Abbeydale*, guarded by the corvettes *Burdock* and *Armeria*.

At 4 pm Syfret weighed anchor at Scapa and proceeded to overhaul the convoy with the *Nelson* and *Rodney* escorted by the leader of the 6th Flotilla, *Ashanti*, with *Tartar*, *Eskimo*, *Somali*, *Pathfinder* and *Quentin*. The destroyer *Penn* had minor boiler defects, which she had to stay behind to repair; she planned to overtake the rest of the force later. The two massive battleships ploughed majestically out into the Atlantic, carrying out anti-aircraft sleeve target practice in the Pentland Firth *en route*, for it was not only the freighters which required additional working-up.

Two further groups of warships had not yet sailed. The Gibraltar force consisting of the *Eagle*, *Charybdis*, *Cairo*, *Ithuriel*, *Antelope*,

Westcott, *Vansittart* and *Wrestler* were not all to take part in Operation 'Berserk' and some of these ships would remain at the Rock until the convoy passed, to husband precious fuel. *Eagle* herself was due to sail as soon as she had embarked her aircraft; space aboard the old ship was restricted and she could only assemble sixteen of her twenty Sea Hurricane B 1s – six of which had to be stowed on deck in the outriggers – and in the remaining four were parked in the forward hangar with only one wing on as reserves.

Force R, the main oiling force, was also at Gibraltar, and this consisted of the tankers *Brown Ranger* and *Dingledale*, and the tug *Jaunty*. The *Salvonia* – this was not part of the original plan – was added on the orders of Vice-Admiral North Atlantic. It was also intended that *Jaunty* should accompany the convoy right through to Malta in order to salvage any ship badly hit but capable of being brought in, another lesson learnt from 'Harpoon'.

The last-minute addition of the *Furious* called for her to sail with the convoy from the Clyde on the 2nd, but during her preparations a snag had been discovered. She had been ordered to carry out Operation 'Bellows', the Spitfire reinforcements, on 29th July and had at once sailed for Campbeltown to disembark her operational aircraft, Albacores of 822 and 823 Squadrons. These she flew off to the Naval Air Station at Machrihanish *en route* to pick up the Spitfires. In the afternoon of the 30th she proceeded to the King George V dock at Govan and embarked the 41 Mark VB Spitfires throughout the rest of that day, returning to Tail 'o' Bank on 1st August. During the passage it was realised that due to her peculiar construction, which had resulted in her having a pronounced hump on her flight-deck, the fighters, being of a new improved mark with larger propeller blades than the previous types, would not easily be able to take off, if indeed at all, from her flight-deck.[1] The Spitfires fitted for earlier trials had been fitted with 10 foot 3 inch blades

[1] *Furious* had led a very chequered life, being originally designed as a light battle-cruiser mounting two single giant 18-inch guns fore and aft. Lord Fisher had envisaged her steaming into the Baltic in 1916 to aid the Russians. She was finally completed with one gun mounting aft and a flight-deck forward. Between the wars the flight-deck was extended aft; this resulted in a hump in the centre and the deck sloped down considerably towards the bows and stern!

giving 3,000 revs at 12-pounds boost. The Mark VBs had De Havilland bracket type 5/39 propellers with an 11 foot 2 inch overall diameter, which allowed only 2,650 revs on the ground at 12-pounds boost and a hurried trial, with a take-off wind speed of 29.5 knots, proved that the Spitfire could only just clear with such a boost. The old *Furious* would be pushed to make anything like this speed and the trial was pronounced unsatisfactory.

An Air Ministry expert was hurriedly sent for and he arrived from London early on the 3rd to effect adjustments to increase the take-off boost and the revs. Alterations were made, but there was no real improvement and during a second trial the pilot misunderstood his instructions and only just got off. As a result it was decided to embark hydraulic propellers to give around 3,100 revs at 12-pounds boost.

Forty of these arrived on the morning of 4th August and they were embarked together with one spare Spitfire giving a total of 42. Loading was completed by 10.35 pm and ten minutes later she at last hurried to sea escorted by the *Manchester* and the Polish destroyer *Blyskawica*.

Throughout the next two days her maintenance crews worked full out in changing the props on the Spitfires and by the afternoon of the 8th the job was completed. Meanwhile the *Sardonyx* had joined her escort from Londonderry where she had been refuelling after escorting the *Argus* to meet the *Victorious* group, and at 7 am on the 5th a Spitfire was flown off in a successful trial. This accomplished, they set off at full speed to catch up with the convoy and escort. Fog was encountered on the night of the 5th/6th and the two destroyers were deemed no longer necessary and sent back to their bases. The carrier and cruiser finally made rendezvous at 3.10 on the 7th in 39°20'N, 17°20'W, with the *Victorious* group.

Admiral Syfret had meantime joined the convoy at 9.35 on the 3rd and the force steered west at twelve knots, later increasing to fourteen. A Sunderland escort was provided throughout the day and one of these, appearing suddenly out of low cloud, was taken for an enemy aircraft and shot down. Although the *Ledbury* was quickly on the scene only one of the crew survived. It was to avoid just such unfortunate mistakes that the convoy was drilled and drilled again in the ensuing days.

On the 4th the difficult manoeuvre of changing from four columns to two for passing through the Skerki Narrows was practised. The places of *Cairo* and *Manchester*, who were to be the column leaders, being taken by the *Ashanti* and *Derwent*. This was the danger moment of the voyage; such a change was a complicated manoeuvre for merchant ships to perform but it was necessary in order to group the entire convoy behind the four minesweeping destroyers for the passage through the Narrows on the evening of the 12th. Further drilling was carried out during the dog watch until the convoy had satisfied Rear-Admiral Burrough that it could perform the changeover satisfactorily. Unfortunately, when the time eventually came to carry out this manoeuvre, it was under circumstances that no exercises, however thorough, could simulate.

The short-range destroyers were refuelled during the day: *Wolverine*, *Venomous*, *Derwent* and *Wishart* from the *Nigeria* and *Kenya*, *Amazon*, *Malcolm* and *Zetland* from the battleships. This type of fuelling was acceptable out in the wastes of the Atlantic but for the vital final spurt through the central Mediterranean and also for the homeward journey, it was essential that all ships were fully topped up by the morning of the 12th. This was to involve the fleet in a series of very complicated manoeuvres during the next few days, refuelling both from tankers at sea and at Gibraltar. The escorts could not count on refuelling at Malta for she was without sufficient oil fuel and the risk of enemy observations of the many comings and goings of the warships to and from Gibraltar had to be accepted.

They were now passing through the dangerous Western Approaches and during the day no less than seven emergency turns were carried out due to submarine alerts. The *Penn* joined the fleet during the afternoon and at 10.34 course was altered to 186 degrees.

The 5th was much the same, the convoy being drilled in the forenoon; blind and umbrella barrages were practised by the battleships and cruisers. Both the *Nigeria* and *Kenya* were detached during the morning to fuel at Gibraltar. The following day the convoy ran into thick fog and visibility was at times down to two cables, but by afternoon it had cleared. The operating of the fleet via low-power W/T was exercised at 3 pm when course was again altered to 155 degrees. Numerous submarine alarms necessitated a further six emergency turns and because of the many such alarms a destroyer was stationed on each quarter. So far progress had been excellent, indeed they were ahead of schedule, and speed was reduced to 12 knots.

The same day the carrier forces met in position 35°N, 14°W to carry out Operation 'Berserk'.[1] Opportunity for so many carriers to work together had not occurred very frequently during the war and, in addition, the carriers themselves had come from widely differing areas of combat. Many of the squadrons were newly equipped and others had to readjust to convoy protection warfare after serving as fleet units – a very different role. 'Berserk' was designed to give them the opportunity to work as a whole group and to iron out as many problems as they could before they took on the Luftwaffe.

The *Indomitable* had had both 806 and 800 Squadrons re-equipped just prior to her leaving the Indian Ocean; 806 changing from Fulmars to Martlets – the British name for the Grumman Wildcat supplied under lease-lend – and the latter with Sea Hurricanes. Both these units had been disembarked for training, but the time allowed was brief and when they had landed aboard from Tanga airfield on 9th July one of the new fighters had already been lost. As the ship called at Durban, Capetown and Freetown on the way to the Atlantic, so the squadrons were flown ashore for further practice but this was not the best way to work up an inexperienced air group. *Victorious* had ten new pilots with no combat experience at all aboard and this lack of training was reflected during 'Berserk' when they wrote off four aircraft.

The varying standard of equipment aboard each carrier meant that to obtain maximum efficiency each ship's fighter group was allotted a specific task. It was decided to allot low cover to *Victorious*, who had the higher percentage of the old Fulmars, while the Martlets and Sea Hurricanes of the other two carriers

[1] The *Indomitable* and *Victorious* groups met at 8.20 on the 5th and the *Eagle*'s group from Gibraltar a few hours later.

were to mount high cover starting at 5,000 feet, but each carrier had to maintain its own defensive air patrol.

The three carriers were to operate independently inside the destroyer screen to the rear of the convoy and each was provided with a 'close escort' anti-aircraft covering cruiser, *Victorious/Sirius*, *Indomitable/Phoebe* and *Eagle/Charybdis*, whose sole function was to provide a heavy flak umbrella over the carrier during bombing attacks. For protection against submarines it was laid down that one destroyer was to stand by each carrier and, should it be necessary for her to leave the screen for any purpose, the two nearest destroyers would automatically attach themselves as further A/S protection.

The fighter groups spent two days carrying out high and low cover sorties, dusk landings, W/T transmissions and identification. It was feared that the high concentration of wireless signals, which resulted from, this would almost be certainly to be picked up by enemy monitoring services established in Spain. Vice-Admiral Syfret's report also reflected a bigger danger:

> Operation 'Berserk', invaluable in itself, was a further source of embarrassment from the fuelling point of view. With the efficient intelligence service which it appears the enemy now has in the Gibraltar area it may be argued that the small chance of effecting any surprise is not worth the complications and difficulties of attempting to do so. I think, however, it would be wrong to take this line. Until the enemy reconnaissance forces actually see us in the Mediterranean he cannot be sure his intelligence is correct, and any uncertainty we can create in his mind must be all to our benefit.

Fuelling indeed now began to dominate everything. The *Abbeydale* was operating with the carriers during 'Berserk' in order to replenish their destroyer escorts, but her crew was new and inexperienced and the result was complete disorder. After distributing orders to the fleet the *Intrepid* commenced oiling at 2.53. It was 5.55 before *Fury* managed to complete. Her commander reported to Captain Hutton that while the stirrup method was working all right, the rate of pumping was very slow. *Foresight* was already oiling when *Lightning* and *Lookout* were detached, and, to add to their troubles, a nasty swell was kicking up. The *Lightning* could not be secured correctly due to lack of proper hawsers but after three-quarters of an hour was satisfactorily alongside, and then almost immediately both hawsers parted. Another attempt re-secured her and then the tanker yawed as *Foresight* parted her lines and hoses, the oil spurting everywhere, and *Lightning*'s lines parted again. *Foresight* had taken on only 80 tons of oil before nightfall ended any further attempts; *Wishart* and *Derwent* therefore had to be sent into Gibraltar.

Not that things were much better there as Rear-Admiral Burrough was finding out. His flagship refuelled from the tanker *San Claudia* and found that it was a very slow affair, with an hour's delay caused by burst hoses and pumping failures. *Kenya* replenished from the Royal Fleet Auxiliary *Brown Ranger* which was much more efficient.

While the two cruisers were at the Rock opportunity was taken to hold a final conference which took place at 1 pm on the 5th with the Commanding Officers of the *Cairo*, *Wilton*, *Derwent* and *Ledbury*, all of which were to be part of the close escort.

The convoy was now approaching the Straits and the tension was gradually increasing. The freighters could now perform their complicated manoeuvres with some skill and both Admiral Syfret and Rear-Admiral Burrough commented favourably on their proficiency. At 1100 on the 7th a Catalina had made contact and from then until the 11th the RAF Coastal Command at the Rock performed a permanent rota of anti-submarine duties overhead.

This task they carried out well and on the 8th a Wellington of 233 Squadron attacked and damaged one of the three German submarines allocated for special duties against 'Pedestal', the *U-333*, east-south-east of Formentera Island. The U-boat was not sunk in this attack but her engines suffered damage, which necessitated return to her base at La Pallice for repair.

One of the fighters from *Victorious* crashed during the concluding stages of 'Berserk' and although the wreckage was found, the destroyers *Laforey* and *Fury* could not locate the pilot. Apart from this accident the day was uneventful. The *Furious* and *Manchester* joined the convoy during the afternoon and the cruiser, with the *Eskimo* and *Tartar*, were detached to refuel soon after.

The 8th saw the carriers joining up with the main force which had changed course to 092 degrees at 10.15 am. The last convoy exercises were held in the forenoon and there were anti-aircraft barrage tests by the fleet. A certain amount of difficulty was experienced tuning all 67 ships into the Fleet's waveband. On joining the convoy the fuelling difficulties encountered with the *Abbeydale* were reported which led to additional ships being added to the already complex arrangements for fuelling at Gibraltar.

Vice-Admiral Sir G. F. B. Edward-Collins and his staff performed miracles of organisation in arranging for the quick turn-round of so many ships under the cover of darkness, but it seems certain that the enemy received the first news of the approach of a convoy from the abnormally large numbers of vessels arriving at the Rock during the night hours of the 8th/10th. The Italians certainly had wind that a big operation was afoot as early as the 9th despite all the precautions taken.

The *Indomitable,* with the three 'L' class destroyers, was sent in to fuel first, arriving after dark on the 8th and sailing again to twenty miles west after first light, the *Lightning* taking the opportunity to land survivors from the Norwegian vessel *Tank Express* which she had picked up in the South Atlantic, on her way from Freetown. The *Sirius* and *Phoebe* arrived at Gibraltar just before midnight needing 850 tons of oil fuel and during the 9th the pace quickened still further.

When *Indomitable* and *Manchester* rejoined the fleet the former was still some 300 tons short of the required amount of oil, while the cruiser was 600 tons short. There was nothing for it but to send them in again with *Eagle* and *Charybdis*. Other warships sent in were the *Pathfinder*, *Penn* and *Quentin* at 8 am, the *Ashanti*, *Somali* and *Zetland* at midday, and at 11 pm the old *Argus*, which had completed fighter-direction exercises with the other carriers during the morning, was detached to Gibraltar with *Venomous*, *Wolverine*, *Amazon* and *Malcolm*; she was to play no further role in 'Pedestal'.

As one group went in to Gibraltar so the others returned to the fleet replenished; *Nigeria* and *Kenya* at 8.20 am, *Bicester*, *Ledbury*, *Wilton* and *Westcott* at 2.30 pm, but also of this force *Wrestler* was found to have a defective evaporator which meant repairs at Gibraltar; her place in the operation was taken by the *Amazon*. Between 4 and 6 pm the fleet's aircraft staged dummy air attacks and on completion of this staged a fly-past to enable all ship's gunners to familiarise themselves with their own side's aircraft. Unfortunately this was one lesson the convoy tended to forget in the heat of battle.

One young gunner on the tanker *Ohio* wrote to his wife on 8th August, the eve of the battle:

> It is 4 p.m. Saturday and have just had a shave and bath. We are at present somewhere around the Azores, each hour getting nearer our objective, how I wish that we were here on the return journey. I expect by then will have seen a little activity. Of course you don't know where we are bound, how grateful I am, at least you will not have the extra anxiety and worry.
>
> 4.30 Boat drill. 6.00 Just finished tea – Kipper, lamb chop and mash, veg salad, luncheon sausage, cheese, jam, 'New' white bread and butter. Feel like having a nap now. To get back on my course – The day after leaving, the skipper mustered all hands and told us the whole of the convoy – 14 ships – were bound for Malta. As it was imperative that the convoy arrives safely we were having the strongest naval escort that had ever undertaken such duties – 2 battleships, 4 aircraft carriers, 8 cruisers and 40 destroyers. At present we have 12 destroyers, 1 aircraft carrier (the *Victorious*) and the battle-waggons *Nelson* and *Rodney*. We are to pick up the remaining escort tomorrow on approaching the Straits of Gibraltar. In spite of the dangerous mission we are on I feel pleased at having been chosen to be in charge of the guns and, gunners on one of the most valuable ships carrying one of the most, if not the most, valuable cargoes. Each night in my prayers I ask that all ships may reach their goal to relieve Malta, which without doubt is the most distressed place in the world.

Am feeling quite fit and am extremely comfortable on board. I don't do any watches but am on duty from dawn till dusk. I have plenty to do cleaning guns, preparing ammo, training different squads for various duties. We have been free of activity up to the present apart from warnings – mostly subs in the vicinity – which the destroyers dealt with. There has been plenty of firing but only practice, the real thing no doubt will be with us soon enough.

My cabin is now looking very smart. Dave and I managed to paint it out while lying in the Clyde and have now got the brasswork looking like brass.

The weather has been a bit erratic, one day it is sweltering, the next, misty, today squally with choppy sea, the ship being more under water than above. My cabin is on the port side, which today is the weather side so the porthole has to remain closed.

It is now 8.30. Have had to leave this several times since starting. The best job was to issue the rum, which at present we get weekly. Next week I believe we are to get it daily – will need it! Everyone on board is in good spirits (I don't mean the rum) and looking forward to a good scrap, determined to get the convoy through. The soldiers are mostly Lancs lads, some of them did their training in Blackpool – Squiresgate and Bispham. As is usual with Pongoes, a bit scruffy, but nevertheless a good set with plenty of enthusiasm.

Was disappointed not getting a letter from you before we left. A few came on board the last minute. Don't expect shall have any now until we reach Good Old England, which may be within the next few weeks. Surely after this trip they will give us a break. Am now going for a drink of tea and a sandwich.

At 11 pm on the 9th Cape Spartel was abeam and they entered the Straits. Thick fog was encountered which reduced visibility to one cable at times and it failed to clear completely until first light. This was very welcome from Syfret's point of view but it had failed to shield the vast concourse of ships from the eyes of at least two

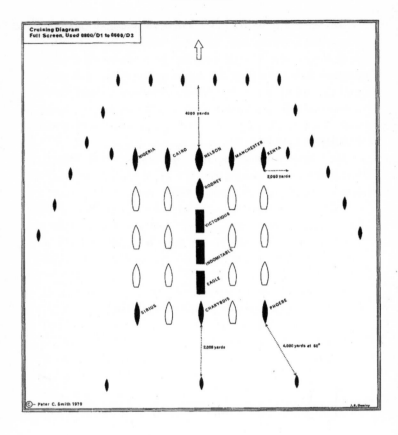

neutral vessels encountered steaming west, nor from a large number of Spanish fishing vessels which were passed between Malabata and Tarifa; Captain Frend of the *Phoebe* reckoned that the convoy passed through two lines of tunny boats between Gibraltar and the North African coast, and even though many of them might have been genuine fishing boats, they had certainly had an obvious chance to report the presence of the convoy.

The weather had dawned clear on the 10th and the convoy increased to 13½ knots. The final dispositions were now being made. Force R had sailed from the Rock at 3 am with the destroyer

Westcott as Senior Officer and during the day the rest of the warships rejoined from their refuelling missions.

At 7.45 am the *Cairo*, *Tartar*, *Eskimo*, *Quentin*, *Ithuriel*, *Antelope* and *Derwent* joined from ahead and *Ashanti*, *Somali* and *Zetland* took station soon after. The main cruising dispositions with the convoy steaming in four columns with the carriers astern in line-ahead were now formed and they settled down to what was to be their last peaceful day.

At 11.30 the *Indomitable*, *Manchester* and the three ships of the 19th Flotilla rejoined, as did the *Eagle*, *Charybdis*, *Penn*, *Pathfinder* and *Amazon* at 4pm. The day was uneventful save for two things. The first was a number of alarms caused by friendly Hudson bombers from Gibraltar on anti-submarine patrols who were not showing their recognition signals or IFF beacons.[1] This led, on two separate occasions, to the scrambling of four fighters from the *Victorious* to intercept a suspected enemy reconnaissance plane, with the resulting loss of W/T and RDF silence.

At 5.25 four Sea Hurricanes were scrambled away to find an unidentified plane but after a long chase they failed to catch it. At 6.45 the same thing happened and they found it to be a Hudson. This led to the comment that the RAF were a positive hindrance to the operation at this stage because of their lack of IFF. Signals sent direct to the aircraft or via the Flag Officer, North Atlantic and the RAF Command to the aircraft concerned produced little improvement!

Victorious had earlier flown off two surplus Albacores and one unserviceable Fulmar back to the Gibraltar airstrip to clear deck space. Despite their vigilance the disposition and speed of the convoy was soon made known to the Axis by the kindness of the French. At 5 pm a civil aircraft flying from France to Algeria passed overhead and broadcast the information that she had seen two battleships, two aircraft carriers, two cruisers and fourteen destroyers escorting twelve merchant ships, the speed and course were also obligingly given. The Italian Official Historian dryly comments that 'this interesting information proved of the greatest usefulness later'.

Already the Axis had planned their counter-moves and it only

[1] IFF = Identification, friend or foe.

needed such a sighting to set in train very detailed plans, plans which were to work almost perfectly.

II

The Italians and their German allies were in no doubt both as to the state of Malta itself and the urgent need for the British to attempt another supply convoy as soon as possible. The position of the island in relation to their own coast ruled out all but a few permutations of the same basic plan and the Axis had had two years to analyse all the alternatives available to a convoy from the west. Their basic plans were easily laid, therefore, and it was a simple matter to make slight adjustments as and when necessary.

In fact once the composition of the British force was known, Supermarina[1] considered four alternatives open to the enemy force. The most obvious was the relief of Malta and the sighting of so many transports seemed to make this almost certain. The second was a combination of this with a sortie by the main British Fleet into Italian waters in unprecedented strength to provoke a major action; the addition of the two battleships and no less than four aircraft-carriers made this type of offensive action possible. The third alternative was again a convoy to Malta, but the big covering force of warships might be intending to force a passage to the north of Pantelleria instead of turning back at the mouth of the Skerki Channel; this would be a natural reaction to the debacle suffered by the British with 'Harpoon' in June and would be to ensure that such a convoy was not again molested – it is interesting that the Italians considered this a possibility in view of its discussion and rejection by the British planners. The last alternative was a large-scale attack on Sardinia with a view to the complete destruction of its airfields and thus facilitate the passage of a convoy later.

Just as the Royal Navy had committed its greatest strength yet to force the convoy through, so the Axis, who were in the summer of 1942 at the peak of their strength, devoted their heaviest weight of attack against it.

[1] Supermarina was the Italian Supreme Command, Naval Operations.

Only in one respect was the Axis plan weakened severely; their battleships were unable to take part. This was solely due to lack of oil and the Italians waged a constant battle with the Germans to get their supplies increased but to no avail; each sortie by their main fleet was an enormous drain on their limited stocks and the Germans were in a similar position with regard to their own big ships in their Norwegian bases. Thus it was that they found themselves with only sufficient supplies to send one of their battleships out and it was decided that for her to do so alone would almost certainly risk losing her. Instead they decided to combine Admiral da Zara's light-cruiser division with a heavy-cruiser division, providing a force which they felt would be adequate to deal with the close escort.

Supermarina knew also that the heavy covering forces of Malta convoys had never proceeded right through to the island with the convoy; always, they had turned back well before the Narrows, not being willing to risk the minefields and bomber bases of that area. The close covering force, they were aware, usually consisted of only cruisers and destroyers, and their naval chiefs were satisfied that they could easily mount a force large enough to annihilate this. True, hesitancy had before allowed victory to slip from their grasp in similar circumstances, but they relied on the convoy and escort being greatly reduced before they attacked with surface forces south of Sicily and felt certain that this time they would be successful.

Well before the proposed Italian surface striking force – two squadrons of cruisers, three 8-inch and three 6-inch ships with their escorting destroyers – were destined to fall upon Force X, the convoy would have to cross no less than four major lines of defence, consisting of submarines, minefields and E-boats, in addition to heavy air attacks.

Already several submarines were at sea in the western basin, with more squadrons of boats at readiness in Sardinian and Sicilian ports. The first concentration of submarines was laid to the north of Algiers, between meridians 01'40'E and 02°40'E and consisted of seven boats, *Brin, Dagabur, Giada, Uarsciek, Wolframio*, and the German *U-73* and *U-205*. Their tasks were; first, to locate and then to attack the convoy, special targets were specified as the aircraft-carriers.

Once the convoy was found and pinpointed then it was arranged for a second concentration of submarines to form further east off the Tunisian coast, between the Fratelli Rocks and as far as the northern approach to the Skerki Narrows: these boats would be the *Granito*, *Emo*, *Otario*, *Dandolo*, *Avorio, Cobalto*, *Alagi*, *Ascianghi*, *Axum*, *Bronzo* and *Dessie*. To pick off any ships which survived the minefields and E-boats in the Narrows, yet another submarine, the *Asteria*, was stationed to the west of Malta.

Although the Germans and Italians were to co-operate in the attacks on 'Pedestal' the majority of the units of each country acted independently; close partnership in Axis terms had a different meaning from that to which the Allies were to become used – thus the German Naval Command was to write: 'Nothing is known of the number of Italian submarines at sea'. The Axis air forces were also preparing, although again the Germans were to record:

> Axis measures against the enemy convoy have begun. Five bomber groups and the aerial torpedo training unit at Grosseto are available in Sicily. Other [Italian] details are- not known to the Naval Staff.

Fliegerkorps II had been heavily committed to the desert campaign supporting Rommel but quick strategic moves were a feature of their operations and during the 10th and 11th several units, including I/Stukagruppe 3 were transferred from Libya to Trapani in Sicily. The bulk of the newly trained torpedo-bomber forces had been transferred to Norway during June and there they had participated in the near annihilation of the ill-fated PQ17 convoy the following month. They were not brought back to the Mediterranean – time would not allow this – but ten Heinkels under instruction with II/KG.26 were available.

This operation was a good example of the mobility of the Luftwaffe. I and II/LG.I, under the command of X Fliegerkorps, were based on Crete. On 11th August, however, twenty serviceable Ju88s of these two Gruppen flew to Sicily and were ready for operations against 'Pedestal' the following morning. Eight further Ju88s of these Gruppen flew to Sicily on the 12th on completion of convoy escort duties in the Aegean.

Great inter-changeability of bases was to be demonstrated in II Fliegerkorps area. Aircraft from many units were later to be found taking off from Elmas in Sardinia and landing, on completion of their sorties, at one of the Sicilian airfields. Bombers of KG 54 were taking off from Pantelleria later in the battle, although their base was at Gerbini.[1] Luftwaffe pilot Gerd Stamp told me how these moves affected his unit.

> From January 1941 onwards until the end of 1942, I, II and III/LG 1 were the only Junkers Ju88 bombers stationed in the Eastern Mediterranean. At the time of Pedestal there were only I and II Wings stationed at Herakalion, there were no other dive-bomber units in Crete and none then at Athens-Eleusis field.
>
> I was then a pilot with I/LG 1, A2- and A3-Officer also, and I remembered that we did not like to be moved to Sicily. We were happy on Crete. Any temporary moving to Sicily caused a lot of discomfort, as our technical preparedness had to be looked after by people we did not know, and who were already overworked with their own Ju88 units anyway.
>
> KGr606, which specialised in torpedo-bombing, and KGr806 were both units also equipped with Junkers Ju88s and both of them were temporarily moved from bases in Southern France to Sicily, just as we, I and II/LG 1, were ordered from Crete to Sicily.
>
> I often wondered how I/KG54 got into and out of Pantelleria. The airstrip was so short at that time – I flew over it several times in November 1942 – that I doubt that Ju88s could land and take off there. The same was true to a lesser extent to Cagliari-Elmas. I remember well that we were told not to land at Elmas, unless it was an emergency.

Lack of German torpedo-bombers was compensated for by the fact that the Italians had large numbers on hand. Long acknowledged as the foremost Air Force – as distinct from Naval Air Arm – in the

[1] St.G.3 led by Hauptmann Martin Mossdorf, Kg.26 by Major Werner Klumper.

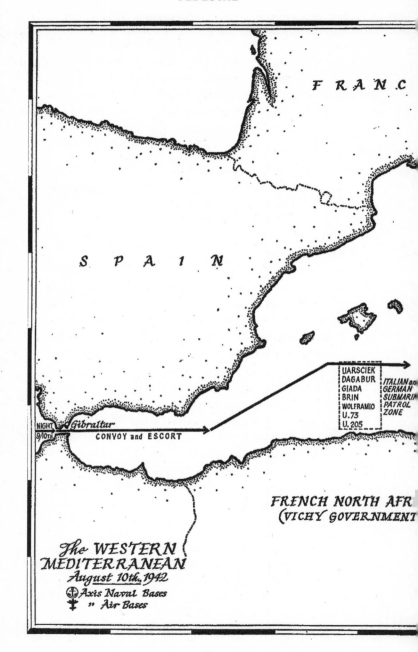

FRANCE

SPAIN

| UARSCIEK |
| DAGABUR |
| GIADA |
| BRIN |
| WOLFRAMIO |
| U.73 |
| U.205 |

ITALIAN and GERMAN SUBMARINE PATROL ZONE

NIGHT
9/10th   Gibraltar
CONVOY and ESCORT

FRENCH NORTH AFRICA
(VICHY GOVERNMENT)

The WESTERN
MEDITERRANEAN
August 10th., 1942
Axis Naval Bases
"   " Air Bases

use and development of the aerial torpedo the Regia Aeronautica had changed almost completely to this type of airborne weapon to harry the Royal Navy in the Mediterranean.

Their early attacks during 1940–41 had been made very largely with the standard high-level bombers, so beloved by the RAF, and their experience with this form of attack had shown them just how useless this was against ship targets. By the mid-summer of 1942 the majority of the crack units were equipped with torpedo-carrying Sm79s, although adaptations of other bomber types was also being tried.

The well-known three-engined Savoia Marchetti Sm79 had begun trials with the standard 450-mm naval torpedo, fitted with a 375-pound warhead, at Gorizia in 1937. Using a special rack offset from the centre-line of the plane and a newly developed launching sight, this had quickly proved successful, although later attempts at fitting their aircraft with two mountings had to be dropped as it affected aircraft performance too much. Ultimately a torpedo-training school was established and when the Luftwaffe became interested in torpedo-bombing their first squadrons were sent to a similar establishment on the north-west coast of Italy, Grosseto, and here they studied Italian methods, equipment and ideas.

The Italians had also come up with several new airborne inventions and 'Pedestal' was to be the test-bed for them. In all some 320 aircraft, fighter, bomber and reconnaissance, were available to the Italian air force for use against the convoy and during the 10th and 11th, Superaereo[1] also made its dispositions. 32 Stormo moved 1 up from Gioia del Colle to Villacidro airfield in Sardinia and 105 Stormo transferred from Pisa to Decimomannu as did 153 Gruppo of Re2001 fighters from Caselle Torinese. Into Monserrato were also flown the fighters of 2 Gruppo and 362 Squadriglia from Ciampini. To reinforce the Sicilian air strength 132 Stormo of Sm79s transferred from Gerbini to Pantelleria and 102 Gruppo of Ju87s was flown into Trapani from Gela.[2]

Both the Italians and Germans started flying long-range

[1] Superaereo-Italian Supreme Command, Air Operations.
[2] 132 Stormo led by Capitano Buscaglia; 362 Squadriglia led by Capitano La Ferla; Z Gruppo led by Magg. Scarpetta; 105 Gruppo led by Tenente Colonel Cadringher; 32 Stormo led by Colonel Leone.

reconnaissance missions into the western basin early on the 11th but it was not from these that the first positive identification of the convoy was received but from the most westerly of the submarine patrols.

III

The submarine *Uarsciek* (Tenente di Vascello Gaetano Targia) was lying submerged in her war zone with the hydrophones switched on listening for the first noises of ships' propellers on the 11th when her operators at 3.40 pm picked up a distinct contact, which they identified as turbines.

The noises grew louder and at 4 pm Targia brought his boat to the surface and proceeded stealthily west towards the contact. Some 38 minutes later, after running west at low speed, the port lookout, Midshipman Florio, distinguished a sharp, dark outline at 350 metres ahead of the submarine. It was recognised instantly from the conning tower as an enemy vessel. Targia later reporting sighting one aircraft-carrier and one battleship.

The course of the leading British vessels was at right-angles to the U-boat so Targia decided to circle around and make his attack on the carrier as he had been previously instructed. At 4.42 am in position 37'52'N, 01'48'E, he launched three torpedoes against his target. Two explosions followed his attack but almost at once he was subjected to a strong series of depth-charge attacks from an escorting destroyer. Between 4.47 and 5.04 he logged four distinct attacks, gradually receding. He dived deep and thus evaded any damage. Satisfied eventually that he had shaken off his pursuer he shaped course to track the formation.

Commenting on this attack later the Italians found it surprising that the British post-war accounts largely overlook the incident; it is not even mentioned in the Official History, although it did represent the first accurate contact between the enemy and units of 'Pedestal'. The only confirmation of the attack is made by the corvette *Jonquil* (Lieutenant-Commander R. E. H. Partington, RNR). She reported hearing four depth-charge patterns ahead at 5 am – she was with the oil tanker force astern of the main groups – but stated that no alarm was heard, or apparently given, by the ship involved.

Dawn found the convoy formed up and steaming steadily eastward approaching the latitude of the Balearic Islands. The fog had long since cleared and visibility was excellent; at 6.45 the final fuelling programme was commenced. The destroyers *Ashanti*, *Foresight*, *Ledbury*, *Zetland*, *Wilton*, *Bramham*, *Bicester* and *Derwent* closed with the tankers of Force R to replenish. Meanwhile the cruisers *Sirius* and *Phoebe* joined the fleet as did the tug *Jaunty*. The latter reported her best speed to be only 12 knots and this led to her being dropped from the original plan; instead of accompanying the convoy through to Malta she was later sent back to join the fuelling force.

From now until 8.30 that evening the two oilers were continuously in use as all the ships of the destroyer screen and three of the cruisers were topped up. By nightfall the tanker *Brown Ranger* had been reduced to a mere one hundred tons of fuel oil and a further thousand tons was transferred to her by the *Dingledale* the following morning to ensure that both vessels would be available if further oiling requirements became necessary.

Vice-Admiral Syfret commended the extreme efficiency of the two oilers in carrying out this difficult, tiring and dangerous job, under enemy observation and in submarine-infested waters. He also made the point that good fortune with the favourable weather conditions and light winds contributed much to the success of the refuelling operation. This had certainly proved an improvement on the previous replenishment and showed what could be done with experienced crews. *Cairo* completed her fuelling in an hour and a half and considered that the tanker did well. The average time for destroyers was two hours but the 'F' and 'I' class boats needed more oil and took longer.

That the oilers accompanying the fleets had up to that time led charmed lives was emphasised when the corvette *Coltsfoot* (Temp-Lieutenant The Hon. W. K. Rous, RNVR) reported at 8 am sighting two torpedoes breaking the surface. The *Uarsciek* was tailing the convoy in the same position and at 8.39 she surfaced well astern of

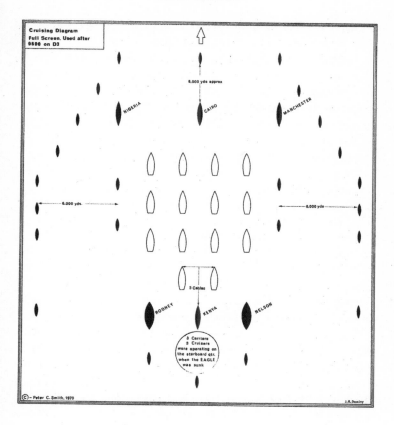

the fleet and reported its speed, composition and position to Rome, who received it at 9.30 and put out an 'all units and stations' alarm. This was picked up at Gibraltar and passed on to the convoy at 10.55.

Enemy snoopers were soon on the scene, the first radar contact being obtained at 8.15. Although our standing air patrols were constantly vectored out to make interceptions, they found the enemy planes very elusive targets. Five actual contacts were made and one enemy bomber was claimed as destroyed. According to enemy records, however, the Germans, who had long-range Ju88s over the fleet at this time from I(F) 122 unit, were able at 10.10 to report three aircraft-carriers, three battleships, twenty cruisers and destroyers and twenty merchant-ships moving at speed on course

90 degrees in position 38°08'N, 01°56'E, which was slightly in error but near enough to home other units on to it.

The carriers had been having some difficulties with their aircraft, *Victorious* reporting that one of the planes which had been embarked the day the ship left Scapa nearly flew into the sea; it was found that the engine had been wrongly assembled. One of her Fulmars was seen to fire a red Verey light and it was found that her port wing was on fire, apparently an old incendiary had ignited. This aircraft was forced to ditch but the pilot was rescued unharmed by the *Wishart*.

Four of *Indomitable*'s Sea Hurricanes of 800 Squadron intercepted a Ju88 and claimed to have destroyed it, but Lieutenant J. G. S. Forrest, RNVR was hit in return by their victim and had to force-land; he too was rescued by a destroyer.

At 11.28 another submarine attack was reported, both the *Nelson* and the *Charybdis* claiming to have sighted disturbances on the surface of the sea about three miles from the convoy-an officer aboard *Charybdis* reported one as like a torpedo breaking the surface. The fleet submarine officer aboard *Nelson* described them as exactly similar to the torpedo discharges of a carelessly handled submarine.

An hour later, with the convoy steaming in four columns with the heavy ships close around it and the destroyer screen of thirteen ships ahead, the *Furious*, screened by *Lightning* and *Lookout*, moved out to the port quarter to carry out the subsidiary Operation 'Bellows'. The previous day she had made trial runs of all her Spitfires and one plane had been found faulty; this still left her thirty-eight which would be a very welcome addition to Malta's defences. At 12.29 the first flight of eight was flown off and at 1.09 she commenced flying off the second group.

All was proceeding smoothly when the enemy struck, dealing the fleet a severe shock, all the more hard because of its unexpectedness. Everyone was tensed and ready for the first sight of Axis aircraft but it was from beneath the waves that the first serious attack materialised.

The *Eagle* (Captain L. D. Mackintosh, DSC) was stationed well over on the starboard quarter of the convoy, with the *Charybdis* (Captain G. A. W. Voelcker) keeping close station on her. She was steaming at thirteen knots, on the starboard leg of a zigzag. She had a four-plane patrol of Sea Hurricanes aloft at the time, who were sharing this duty with four from the *Victorious*. At 1.15 observers saw four explosions along her port side and she immediately began to list to port.

The shock of this attack is vividly described by a young Sea Hurricane pilot, at the. time strapped into his cockpit on the *Indomitable*'s flight deck awaiting take-off:

> The wind was chancy, and we were to be boosted off. I was in position on the catapult, engine running. The flight deck engineer waggled the ailerons to draw my attention to something or other, and I looked out over the port side to see what he wanted. And, as I did so, I stared in shocked surprise beyond him to where *Eagle* was steaming level with us, half a mile away. For as I turned, smoke and steam suddenly poured from her, and she took on a heavy list to port, and the air shook with a series of muffled explosions.
>
> There had hardly been time to assimilate the fact that she had been hit before she had capsized and sunk; and when I took off a few minutes later, my mind was still numbed by what I had seen. It had come so completely without warning. It was as if, at any moment, our own ship might stagger and lurch and list, and our aircraft go slithering down the deck into the sea.

A similar picture was seen from one of the escorting destroyers:

> We watched, hypnotised by the speed of events, for her list was rapidly increasing. By the time she had swung ninety degrees to starboard she was right over on her beam ends, with the port side of her flight deck in the water. Then she disappeared into the cloud of smoke and steam which hung around her.

In fact the first torpedo had struck the *Eagle*'s port quarter and was followed in ten seconds by three more. All hit between her P2 and P3 6-inch guns. After the first hit she heeled to five degrees to port and this increased to fifteen degrees after the final hit. All explosions occurred in the vicinity of the port wing engine room; no immediate damage was caused in the centre or starboard engine-rooms. A, C and D Boiler Rooms in the centre were flooded and in each case the port wing bulkhead collapsed. She finally settled bodily at thirty degrees and sank within six minutes in position 38°05'N, 3°2'E.

What was it like aboard the *Eagle*? Three survivors have given me their eyewitness impressions. Henry Rathbone was a Visual Signals rating aboard her that day.

There had been several air raid alerts during the forenoon but eventually I was able to return to the communication messdeck for dinner and hopefully a nap in my hammock. I should explain that our messdeck was situated one deck lower than the main messdeck and towards the bows of the ship. My first impression when the *Eagle* was hit was that we had been bombed, but in seconds the ship was turning violently to port and listing badly. Some emergency lighting came on and I managed to scramble up the ladder to the main messdeck.

By that time the angle of the list had increased and it was becoming difficult to walk on the deck but for the fact that most of the mess tables were securely fixed to the deck and we used them as handholds. I climbed towards the starboard ladder leading to a platform projecting from the ship's side. A leading hand had found a rope to assist those of us who were climbing out from the messdeck and was shouting words of encouragement. I was fortunate in that I could swim and my lifebelt was in good condition. I remember how the *Eagle* was by then practically on her side and I was able to walk into the sea climbing over what I understood to be the 'torpedo bulge' (what happened to the ones on the port side?).

A number of seamen escaped from this platform and I then became aware that the flight deck commander complete with gold cap was swimming beside me. We exchanged a few words but both of us were intent on putting as many yards as possible between ourselves and the sinking ship. However, when it came, the end of the old ship seemed very peaceful with no great suction to pull us down.

By now the destroyers were active and dropping depth charges, I hoped they would not come too near as I did not take kindly to being thumped in the stomach after each explosion. Fortunately the sea was warm and fairly flat and after about three-quarters of an hour I was picked up by the tug *Jaunty*. I found a large blue flag in her signal locker and dried myself with it. I was one of the lucky ones.

Les Owen's story is similar:

It was when we dropped astern of the convoy to take on our returning aircraft that we got hit amidships by four torpedoes. I can't remember hearing the order to 'Abandon Ship' but it was obvious as she immediately started to go down on the port side, the aircraft began sliding overboard and a lot of the ship's company as well, including one of my close shipmates, Ginger Gerhard, the ship's barber, never to be seen again.

I think that from the time that we were hit she was gone in seven minutes. The ship was at action stations at this time and my station was on the forward multiple pom-pom. Before going over the ship's side I tried to close an ammunition locker to stop shells coming out so they would not hit my mates coming up the flight deck. When I thought it was time to go I almost walked down the ship's side on to the bulges with a lot more of the ship's company. There I blew up my lifebelt, took off my sea boots and jumped in. At first I was drawn down by the suction of the ship sinking, then I came to the surface and managed to get to a messdeck stool floating by and, with about six other shipmates, we got fairly shook up by the depth-charges being dropped by the destroyers.

After some time, it seemed like hours, we were picked up by a boat lowered by the tug *Jaunty* and from there taken aboard the destroyer *Malcolm* which later landed us at Gibraltar.

E. Kenward had joined the *Eagle* in July 1939 as a seaman attached to 824 Squadron and had been with the ship continuously since.

I was on duty on the flight deck when there were four large explosions on the port side and the ship listed over immediately. Because we had been bombed so many times previously I thought it was yet another air attack, but as the ship failed to come upright again I knew then it was no bombing. In no time the flight deck was under water on the port side and aircraft were sliding into the water.

I managed to get to the edge of the flight deck and scramble down the drop into the sea. I was a reasonable swimmer and managed to get away as far as I could. On looking back I saw the ship was upside-down and sinking fast, many people were still visible on the upturned bottom as she went down and I can only assume they were non-swimmers as I found that apart from the oil on the water, the biggest hazard was non-swimmers asking for help.

After what seemed an age I was picked up by the destroyer *Laforey* and then transferred to the *Keppel* and eventually arrived back in the UK aboard the carrier *Argus*.

This skilful attack was carried out by the German submarine *U-73* (Kapitänleutnant Helmut Rosenbaum), a 750-ton, type VIIB U-boat operating out of Spezia. She had detected the approach of the convoy by the sound of advancing propeller noises and had at once come up to periscope depth and made her approach. A quarter of an hour later Rosenbaum sighted the masts of a destroyer approaching and at the same instant he caught sight of an aircraft-carrier. The speed of the carrier he estimated at twelve knots, she was zigzagging with six escorts around her and she passed the submarine some four miles away. Cursing his misfortune Rosenbaum continued his course.

An hour passed then another destroyer came up at high speed, passed close by *U-73*'s position and continued in the direction taken by the carrier group. When almost out of sight she started signalling and then returned the way she had come again passing almost over the submarine without detecting her.

The German waited until she had passed and then took another look through the periscope and at once sighted the convoy approaching him from the west. He counted eight freighters, a battleship, two cruisers and eight destroyers. Working up to full speed he closed the target and identified a carrier as the last ship in the starboard line.

Rosenbaum counted seven destroyers between him and his target which he correctly identified as the *Eagle*. Undisturbed by the fact that his boat was operating at less than full efficiency – defects in the *U-73* included an unserviceable direction-finding aerial, a leaking exhaust cut-out, leaks in the bilge pump and periscope – her captain at once went into the attack. Rosenbaum made a text-book approach on the carrier closing, undetected by the destroyer screen, to within five hundred yards of her before firing a full salvo of four bow torpedoes.

In making her approach the submarine had passed between two destroyers with under four hundred yards to spare on either side. How this was done without detection by the screening vessels is uncertain. Certainly there had been no slackening of vigilance on the part of the destroyers as the frequent earlier alarms had proven. One theory put forward was that there must have been a layer of cold water of differing density above the U-boat which shielded it from the probing beams of the asdics of the screen. The Mediterranean had already been found to contain such layers and it had often proved a frustrating problem before.

Whatever the reason the *U-73* escaped unscathed although the escorts in the immediate vicinity of the sinking carrier at once went into action. Only thirteen destroyers were actually with the convoy and Force F at this time, the others being with Force R some miles away. No torpedo tracks were seen and it seems probable that the German vessel passed under the third and fourth columns of the convoy after diving under the screen. Kapitänleutnant Rosenbaum's instructions were specific: the carriers were his targets, not the merchantmen.

The submarine dived deeply, flooding the bow tanks with all spare hands crowded for'ard, as four explosions were heard and twelve minutes later the roar of the carrier's boilers blowing up under water shook the vessel. Only then did the first depth-charges arrive.

The flotilla leader *Laforey* was ordered to stand by the stricken vessel and she was joined in rescue operations by the *Lookout* (LieutenantCommander C. P. F. Brown, DSC) returning from refuelling, and the tug *Jaunty* (Lieutenant-Commander H. Osburn). Although the ship went down very quickly these vessels succeeded in rescuing 67 officers and 862 ratings, including her captain, out of a total complement of 1,160.

Both *Lookout* and *Charybdis* steamed over the probable position of the submarine dropping depth-charges, but neither ship obtained a contact. Meantime the rest of the convoy was taking violent defensive action in a series of emergency turns and gradually drew clear of the area.

The four aircraft she had in the air at the time she was sunk were Lieutenant-Commander R. Brabner and Sub-Lieutenant Hilton of Red Sub-Flight and Sub-Lieutenant MacDonald and Sub-Lieutenant Hankey of Yellow Sub-Flight and they were brought down eventually on the remaining two carriers, MacDonald on *Indomitable* and the others on *Victorious*. One of these pilots who had to make an emergency landing signal, circled until his companions and the returning patrol from *Victorious* had landed. His windscreen was covered with oil and his petrol was almost exhausted, but fearing that he might crash on landing he waited lest by encumbering the deck he should prevent the others from following him until the wreckage was cleared away. He got down safely but 'Pedestal' was now denuded of some 20 per cent of its fighter strength, only 60 serviceable machines remaining.

For about an hour and a half after this sinking numerous sightings of submarines and torpedoes and asdic contacts were reported. The rescue ships were joined at 2.29 by the destroyer flotilla sent from Gibraltar to escort *Furious* back, the *Keppel* (Commander J. E. Broome), *Malcolm*, *Venomous*, *Amazon*, *Wolverine* and *Wrestler*, and Captain Hutton ordered them to carry out an anti-submarine search. This they did but without success. Lieutenant-Commander Gretton of the *Wolverine* described the little tug packed with survivors as '... an astonishing sight. She had so many men on board that some were even up the rigging. She was literally hidden by a mass of bodies.'

Meanwhile the *U-73* had crept away at 500 feet depth, her hull creaking frighteningly at such unaccustomed pressures. All her auxiliary machinery was stopped and the bilge-pump stationary, with the water leaking in through the defective cutout and periscope. For three hours Rosenbaum stayed at this depth but no further depth-charges arrived so the submarine was brought carefully to the surface. Oil leaking from her hull was mingled with that from the sunken carrier successfully hiding her whereabouts. Rosenbaum signalled to Admiral Kreisch, C-in-C German submarines in the Mediterranean, the composition, speed and bearing of the convoy, adding that he had sunk the *Eagle* and was himself undamaged. At ten o'clock the same evening the *Deutscher Rundfunk* broadcast a special news bulletin. Rosenbaum was awarded the Knight's Cross of the Iron Cross for this brilliant attack.

Thus passed the old veteran *Eagle*. As the Official Historian wrote later: 'If we were to lose her it was appropriate that her grave should be in the Mediterranean, whose waters she had known so well.'

Indeed the *Eagle* had spent the major portion of the war in these waters. She had served with Admiral Cunningham's Main Fleet at Alexandria during 1940 when the British Mediterranean Fleet had swept all before it and her aircraft had served well at the battles of Calabria and Taranto as well as in the Desert campaigns and the Red Sea.

Her ancient hull strained by successive near misses from the scores of bombs aimed at her during these months, she had been replaced by the new *Illustrious* only to reappear in the western basin in 1941 and 1942 when she made several convoy runs and no less than nine aircraft ferrying trips despatching in all 183 fighters to Malta. Although the American carrier *Wasp* made two such trips and was awarded a blaze of publicity, the anonymous old *Eagle* certainly did far more to save the island.

IV

At 3.45 Commander Broome's destroyers rejoined and were told to take aboard the sunken carrier's survivors, those having been picked up by *Laforey* being transferred to *Keppel*, those by *Lookout* to *Venomous* and those in *Jaunty* to *Malcolm*.[1] The *Amazon*

---

[1] Actual numbers of survivors thus embarked were *Keppel* – 9 officers and 186 men; *Malcolm* – 13 officers and 185 men; *Venomous* – The Captain, 48 officers and 487 men, plus one pressman.

(Lieutenant-Commander Lord Teynham) was then told to take the *Jaunty* under his orders and join Force R to replace the *Wrestler*. The rest of Broome's flotilla formed screen on *Furious*.

The flying off of the Spitfires was continuing, the last three flights being despatched between 1.47 and 3.12. In all 38 Spitfires were flown off, of which one developed trouble with the newly fitted propeller while airborne. After some anxious moments the young RAF pilot put his aircraft safely down aboard the *Indomitable*. Despatching had begun at a range of 584 miles from Malta and the final group were sent off at 555 miles. Vice-Admiral Sir Ralph Leatham at Malta later signalled that all 37 had arrived without further mishap. This completed Operation 'Bellows', but *Furious* and her escorts were to score yet another success.

This took place while they were steering west just after midnight on the night of the 11th/12th. It was a dark night with no moon. The five screening destroyers were on the port leg of a zigzag at a speed of 21 knots when at 0054 the *Wolverine* (Lieutenant-Commander P. W. Gretton, OBE, DSC) obtained a radar contact at 5,000 yards bearing 265 degrees. Immediately the depth-charges were prepared and B gun, already manned, was trained round on the bearing, but Gretton did not open fire lest this forewarn his victim.

Excitement mounted on the destroyer's bridge as, with the range down to 800 yards, the contact was identified as a submarine. Full speed was rung down to the engine room, three boilers being already lit, and Gretton brought his ship's bows round to catch his target amidships. 'Crash Stations' was sounded as the *Wolverine*'s knife-edge bows rapidly closed the U-boat at 26 knots. The submarine was struck squarely abreast the after end of the conning-tower and rolled over and sank at once in position 37°18'N, 01°551'E.

At once the engines were stopped aboard the destroyer and Gretton signalled to *Malcolm* that he had rammed the enemy amidships.

The destroyer passed over the submarine and two deep underwater explosions were heard. As no depth-charges were dropped by either of the British ships, it was thought that these were torpedo warheads exploding as the U-boat went down. The *Wolverine* had lost way at once and stopped in the midst of a spreading pool of oil.

The submarine was the Italian *Dagabur* (Tenente di Vascello Renato Pecori) a 700-ton boat built in 1937, operating out of Cagliari. She was obviously caught unawares being in full surface trim, proceeding steadily at an estimated ten knots and she had made no attempt to dive. There were no survivors and although shouts were heard in the water by *Malcolm* (Commander A. B. Russell) they had no opportunity to effect a rescue.

Wolverine herself had not escaped unscathed, severe damage was done to her bows by the collision and an auxiliary steam pipe was fractured which necessitated the evacuation of the engine-room. Steam was shut off from the boiler rooms.

> The Stoker POs in the boiler rooms showed great coolness in a most terrifying situation [Gretton wrote later]. At high speed these huge spaces, filled with the roar of rushing air and separated from the sea by only a thin sheet of steel, were awe-inspiring to the most unimaginative mind. The first sign of trouble was the ringing of the alarm gongs, which warned them to stand by for a crash of some kind. After the bump, which was particularly shattering below the waterline, the men were unable to get in touch with the empty engine room; but steam was calmly shut off, and a stoker sent up on deck to report that the boilers were undamaged.

Gretton attributed much of his success to the Type 271 radar with which his vessel was fitted at the time, which had held the contact down to six-hundred yards' range, and was still working perfectly after the shock of the ramming. He also said that the high speed on contact which brought about the damage was due to a determination not to miss.

The carrier had meanwhile pressed on ahead with the remaining three escorts but *Malcolm* stood by while *Wolverine* was got under way on her starboard engine, eventually working up to six and eventually eleven knots, at which speed her shored-up bulkheads still held firm. The *Malcolm* was finally detached to assist the *Nigeria* late the following day but the corvettes *Burdock* (Lieutenant-Commander E. H. Lynes, RNR) and *Armeria*

(Lieutenant M. Todd, RNR) came out from Gibraltar to assist and *Wolverine* made harbour at midday on the 13th.

Furious went straight into dock to embark a further 23 Spitfires for Malta which she flew off on the 17th. Her docking back at Gibraltar led the Italians to mistakenly believe that either *Uarsciek* or *Dagabur* had hit her.

V

Around the convoy after the departure of the *Furious* and her consorts, the outlaying wolf-packs closed in to the attack. A few minutes after *Eagle* had been sunk a torpedo track was reported crossing the bow of the *Victorious* and during the afternoon the force made several emergency turns. Despite this Vice-Admiral Syfret concluded in his report that there was no conclusive proof of a second U-boat being in the vicinity during this period.

In fact there are no reports of any U-boat making an attack during the afternoon of the 11th, although *Uarsciek* was still trailing the fleet, but Albacores from the carriers kept her at a discreet distance. *U-73* was still far behind lying doggo. The *Brin* reported sighting a destroyer at 2,000 metres and steered well clear of her.

The enemy air force continued to make probings of the convoy defences, and at 2.20 pm radar warning of the approach of a formation was received. These planes flew over the force at a great height, approaching from the starboard beam, and were not visible from the ships. The high-angled batteries of the two battleships barked hopefully away for a few minutes in a controlled barrage, but this was merely a gesture and there is no indication that the enemy were troubled by it. It was thought that these planes were carrying out a photographic reconnaissance, and although they could be heard above the fleet for some time, no attack followed. Nor did the standing air patrols have the height to intercept. The Germans state that only one aircraft, a specially converted Ju88, was used, and she did indeed carry out photo reconnaissance at this time.

One of the British fighters was forced to ditch some 23 miles from the fleet after an abortive attempt at interception and the *Westcott* (Commander I. H. Bockett-Pugh, DSO) was detached from the screen to search for it. This mission was successful and the pilot of the Martlet was picked up after a Fulmar had guided the destroyer to the spot. *Westcott* joined Force R's screen at dusk. The pilot reported that ammunition had exploded in the wing of his plane which had then rapidly caught fire.

Enemy reconnaissance continued unabated.

> The speed and height of the Ju88s [Vice-Admiral Syfret wrote] made the fleet fighters' task a hopeless one. It will be a happy day when the fleet is equipped with modern fighter aircraft.

Also at this time a signal was received from the Flag Officer North Atlantic informing them that intercepted wireless signals indicated that the enemy planned air attacks which could be expected to develop at dusk.

The fleet was at this time at second degree HA readiness and Vice-Admiral Syfret ordered Captain Onslow, Captain (D) 6 in *Ashanti*, to open up the destroyer screen preparatory to an air attack. This manoeuvre required the leading wing destroyers moving out to increase their distance from the convoy to six thousand yards, while certain 'Hunt' class boats moved in close astern of each of the four columns of merchant ships. In this position they could provide an umbrella of 4-inch shells to deter flank dive-bombing runs down the lines of freighters, a favourite German technique. The two remaining carriers turned into the wind and scrambled away as many additional fighters as they could. Each ship had a section parked on deck in readiness and these were quickly boosted off and climbed to 20,000 feet while being vectored out to the north.

Several destroyers were still absent from the screen when the alert was given; these, including *Laforey*, were still fuelling from the two tankers astern. On receipt of the air raid warning they disengaged as quickly as possible, and, at high speed, rejoined the fleet just as the first bombers were sighted. Just previous to this, Captain Hutton, as Senior Destroyer Officer, had enquired of

Brown Ranger's skipper as to how many destroyers had completed fuelling. Captain Ralph had replied that *Laforey* was the thirteenth!

If Captain Hutton was superstitious now was the time to be apprehensive, for as *Laforey* took up her position on the screen some fifteen minutes from sunset, the destroyers out on the port bow opened up with a distant crack of 4.7-inch guns and within seconds the heavy ships had joined in.

Diving in from 8,000 feet towards the port side of the convoy came 30 Junkers Ju88s in shallow bombing runs, while much lower down, skimming in across the waves in a synchronised assault could be seen the evil forms of six 11/KG26s Heinkel 111 torpedo-bombers.

These latter were severely shaken by the barrage put up by the destroyers and did not press home their attacks with sufficient determination to be dangerous; although a few torpedo tracks were seen approaching the convoy they were easily avoided. The Junkers nosed around the fringes of the convoy while their commander looked for a weak spot and the others picked their targets. The warships followed them round with a 'spectacular' barrage but this did not usually deter the enemy who were experts in this type of attack. However the *size* of the barrage on this occasion was evidently much more than they had ever had to face before and the majority of them made somewhat ineffective strikes.

The Wing Leader, accompanied by another, was made of sterner stuff and these two planes selected the *Victorious* as their target, attacking her together from astern. The carrier swung round, keeping the planes silhouetted against the sunset where they stood out sharply and all guns engaged them with heavy fire. Both these aircraft were hard hit and were claimed as shot down; two bombs dropped by one of them fell close astern of the carrier without causing damage.

In all, the fleet claimed to have destroyed three aircraft by gunfire. Some of the Junkers, discouraged by the wall of flak, tried their hands at the less well protected tankers of Force R, one of them scoring a near miss with a stick of bombs which fell between a tanker and one of the corvettes. Another dived on the *Jaunty*, which was on her own returning to the convoy from Force R at her best speed. The tubby little vessel showed herself to be no push-over and drove her attacker away with spirited bursts of Oerlikon fire and reckoned she had damaged him.

The cruiser *Manchester*, in common with the other 'Town' class ships, normally carried two Walrus amphibious floatplanes in a hangar abaft the bridge structure. For 'Pedestal' one of these had been put ashore to decrease the bogey of aviation fuel fire risk. *Southampton*'s loss by fires after bombing in January 1941 may have highlighted this defect. Even this one Walrus scout plane was not used, for in this attack it was hit while still in its hangar by bomb splinters, and so would appear to be the only casualty suffered by the fleet and convoy from this raid.

Although fully engaged with aircraft during the attack the destroyer *Quentin* (Lieutenant-Commander A. H. P. Noble, DSC) out ahead of the convoy in position 'A', obtained a positive asdic contact and dropped aside to make three determined attacks. No results were forthcoming and Noble reluctantly left the scent to hurry on after the receding convoy, which he rejoined at 9.40 pm.

Anthony Kimmins, the famous wartime broadcaster on naval events, was aboard the *Nigeria* and he later described this attack very vividly in a broadcast:

By the time the attack had developed the sun was setting in a big red glow, and the barrage put up by our ships was one of the most staggering things I have ever seen. Tracers screaming across the sky in all directions, and overhead literally thousands of black puffs of bursting shells. The din was terrific but through it all you could hear the wail of the sirens for an emergency alteration of course to avoid torpedoes, and the answering deep-throated hoots of the merchantmen as they turned in perfect formation. Then suddenly a cheer from a gun's crew, and away on the port bow a Ju88 spinning vertically downwards with both wings on fire and looking like a giant catherine wheel. More cheers and over to starboard another Ju88 was diving headlong for the sea, with smoke pouring out behind. At about five hundred feet the automatic pull-out came into action, and she flattened out and crashed on her belly, with a great splash of water. Against the sunset you could see the parachutes of her crew as they drifted slowly downwards.

So it went on, right up to darkness; the gunfire never easing up for a moment, and the great columns of water as bombs dropped between the ships.

The air attack had died away some ten minutes before *Quentin* rejoined, the last of the bombers droning away to the north-east. They claimed later to have hit a carrier, a cruiser and a merchant-ship, but this was not so, although both *Victorious* and *Manchester* were near-missed. This first raid was, however, a mere probe, a test for the big attacks planned for the morrow.

The solid bulks of the merchantmen plodded steadily eastward into the darkening sea, their numbers undiminished. Their first test had not been a crucial one but at least now they had been under fire and knew what to expect. As usual, it was found that, after such a raid, there was a tendency for the gunners in the convoy to be very 'trigger happy'.

The fighters scrambled out from the carriers had been unsuccessful in their attempts to break up the bomber formations before they reached their targets. A flight of Sea Hurricanes from *Indomitable* made contact in the fading light but the Ju88s simply put their noses down and left them standing. Dispirited, the Fleet Air Arm pilots returned to the fleet to land and to their horror were greeted with a furious barrage.

> The sight we saw took our breath away. The light was slowly dying, and the ships were no more than patterns on the grey steel plate of the sea; but where we had left them sailing peaceably through the sunset, now they were enclosed in a sparkling net of tracer and bursting shells, a mesh of fire. Every gun in the fleet and convoy was firing, and the darkening air was laced with threads and beads of flame.
>
> We moved round the fleet, and the bursts of fire followed us; and the truth could no longer be disregarded. They were firing at anything that flew.

Eventually with fuel supplies failing, the Sea Hurricanes managed to land on *Indomitable*, after Captain Troubridge had turned the carrier into the wind, put on all the deck lights and steamed a straight course at 26 knots far beyond the destroyer screen. Even so returning fighters were fired on by their own ships as they landed. One pilot, his tank empty, had to crash-land aboard *Victorious* while that ship was turning under full helm.

With the coming of night came also some respite for the ships, while from Malta itself the RAF was preparing to take a hand in the proceedings.

VI

From dawn until dusk on the 11th a strike force of fifteen Beauforts had been held at instant readiness, parked out on their airstrips. They were all those available from 39, 86 and 217 Squadrons, and were led by Wing Commander R. P. M. Gibbs, DFC. With an escort of fifteen Beaufighters led by Wing Commander Ross Shore, AFC, drawn from 235 and 253 Squadrons, this force was ready to go into action against any Italian surface forces, which might sortie out against the convoy.

In addition small raids were made on Sardinian and Sicilian airfields in an attempt to take some of the pressures off the ships the following day. Two Liberators out of a strike force of four from Middle East Command bombed Decimomannu, the other two failing to find their targets. A lone Wellington was despatched to Catania as a special diversion later in the night.

The heaviest raid was carried out by nine Beaufighters of 248 Squadron led by Wing Commander Pike, DFC. These were sent out to make dusk attacks on Elmas and Decimomannu airfields. On their way in to the target they passed low over three Italian submarines leaving port to take up their positions against the convoy. Altogether six sailed from Cagliari that evening, *Axum*, *Avorio*, *Otaria*, *Cobalto*, *Dandolo* and *Emo*.

The Beaufighters' attacks were unsuccessful at Elmas, as the submarines had given early warning of their approach, but at

Decimomannu complete surprise was achieved, no aircraft was airborne and the British planes were able to strafe many bombers parked on the runways. They claimed to have destroyed six Italian bombers on the ground and badly damaged others. Study of enemy records reveals that they knocked out one Savoia at Elmas in the face of heavy flak, and that they destroyed four Savoias and a Ca164 at Decimomannu, damaging eleven others and destroying two torpedoes.

It was while returning from this raid that the flight made the most important discovery of all, for as they returned over Cagliari they sighted the two light cruisers and two destroyers of Admiral da Zara's 7th Cruiser Squadron which had just sortied out from the harbour and was steering east.

This was the first positive news the British had received that the Italians were apparently going to use their heavy ships and it was bad luck on da Zara's part to have been sighted by chance almost before his ships' mission had commenced. The Beaufighters circled the group for a short period but had to break off due to lack of fuel. They reported in to Malta and at last light Wellington 'O for Orange' was despatched to take up the watch.

At 11.55 pm Orange made an ASV sighting at 2,500 feet and reported locating four cruisers and eight destroyers steering east. She then shadowed the ships into the Tyrrhenian Sea. As yet this squadron, strong though it was, did not present an immediate threat to the convoy which still had its powerful escort. Once Force Z turned back the Italian cruisers would be able to overwhelm the convoy. Therefore plans were made to shadow them. The Wellington made an ineffectual bombing attack at 1.30 am on the 12th before returning to Malta.

Nor were these air attacks the only diversions laid on from Malta to protect 'Pedestal'. On 9th August the submarine *Una* (Lieutenant D. S. R. Martin) had slipped quietly out of Valletta harbour as if on a routine patrol. In fact she carried a small band of men, comprising three officers, an NCO and two soldiers of a Special Boat Party, under the command of Captain Duncan, RA.

It has originally been the intention of this raiding party to attack

Comiso and Gela airfields and destroy Axis aircraft and installations. Discussions determined that these targets were too far inland to make success certain and the plan was revised to be a raid on Catania, which was closer to the coast, although it had the disadvantage of being far more heavily guarded.

The force was put ashore safely at a point a little to the south of Simeto around midnight on the night of the 11th/12th. Unfortunately the whole plan almost at once went awry. An initial explosion, which blew up a pylon carrying cables between Syracuse and Catania, although successfully cutting the link, alerted the defences. Almost at once the NCO was captured by two soldiers in the vicinity and by seven o'clock the following morning the rest of the party was discovered by local fishermen and arrested before even reaching the airfield.

Una returned to the rendezvous on the nights of the 12th and 14th but when nobody turned up it was evident that the scheme had gone wrong and the submarine returned to Malta on the 19th. A similar raid on German airfields in Crete earlier in the year had scored some slight success, but, despite the bravery of the little groups involved, the forces available to the Axis were so vast that, even had they have reached their target it is doubtful whether they could have accomplished much against the well-defended airfield.

The final diversion was carried out by the sadly depleted Mediterranean fleet under Admiral Harwood. This consisted of a large bogus convoy, MG3, which was sailed in two groups from Haifa and Port Said respectively with the intention of sortieing into the Eastern Basin as far as the longitude of Alexandria in an attempt to lure out the cruiser squadron the Italians had at Navarino and also keep tied down German air units in Crete. In fact the German aircraft had already been redeployed and the Italian cruisers eventually stayed in harbour, but the attempt had to be made.

Three merchantmen sailed from Port Said at dusk on the 10th escorted by the cruisers *Arethusa* and *Euryalus*, the destroyers *Aldenham*, *Pakenham*, *Paladin*, *Hurworth*, *Dulverton*, *Beaufort*, *Jervis*, *Kelvin*, *Hursley* and *Eridge* and the escorts *Antwerp* and *Hyacinth*; one merchant ship escorted by the cruisers *Cleopatra* and *Dido* and destroyers *Sikh*, *Zulu* and javelin, under the overall command of Rear-Admiral Sir Philip Vian, left Haifa at 0300 on the 11th.

Both forces made rendezvous early on the 11th and steered west until dusk the same day when they turned back as planned and dispersed. Although they drew no fire they were sighted early and kept under observation. A much graver view of the intentions of this force was at first taken by the Axis than a mere diversion. According to their Intelligence reports of the 11th there were several loaded steamers at Alexandria which were ready to sail to Malta on the 12th. This coupled with several sightings of British submarines off Italian and Greek harbours led their High Command to record that 'the operations in progress aim at something more than merely supplying Malta'.

To prepare for this, the movement of Axis shipping in the Aegean area was suspended and the only other German submarine available in the Eastern basin, the *U-77*, was redeployed. Despite this and extended air searches the enemy appear to have lost track of Vian's force during the night of the 11th/12th.

In contrast to the savage opposition which was to meet the main convoy, Force Y, the returning remnants of the 'Harpoon' Convoy, passed through the Sicilian Channel this same night almost uneventfully. This was fortunate for the two merchant ships – *Orari* and *Troilus* – and their pair of escorting destroyers – *Matchless* and *Badworth* – the last remaining survivors were in no fit state to offer much in the way of defence had they been seriously opposed. Indeed they were only just about seaworthy. During their enforced stay of 54 days at Malta the dockyard had suffered no less than 289 air raids. All the ships had been mined on their way in, as has been related, and in between the air raids and warnings the dockyard had endeavoured to patch them up sufficiently to make the breakout back to the west.

The freighter *Orari* had been mined on the port side in her No 4 hold and when she had entered the dock it was found not to be possible to pump it out and effect repairs because the caisson had been damaged by bombs. The ship was instead heeled over by filling her starboard ballast tanks and emptying those on her port side.

The mine which had damaged *Matchless* had torn a hole some ten feet by seven feet three in her starboard side with severe indentations over some 36 by 19 feet. Many bulkheads had been badly buckled and two destroyed. Her lower deck had been holed, beams and girders destroyed in the path of the explosion, fire mains, suction and vent valves in the stokers' mess were riven by the blast and some damage was sustained in the number one shell room.

Despite this, the Malta dockyard got all four vessels ready for sailing by 10th August, although anti-aircraft ammunition and fuel aboard the two destroyers was very limited. It was hoped that the enemy would be too preoccupied with 'Pedestal' to devote any attention to them.

All of the ships displayed Italian markings until they were clear of the Narrows; red, green and white strips were painted on their decks, in the hope of deceiving the enemy aircraft. They sailed at 8.30 pm.

The War Diary of the German Naval Staff for 11th August records that on the night of the 10th August their radio intelligence reported intercepted messages from what appeared to be enemy cruisers about 150 miles east-south-east of Malta; searches were flown to locate them.

These sweeps by the Luftwaffe met with no success and the Axis concluded that the squadron must have entered Valletta. Subsequent attempts to find out whether or not this was so were foiled by the smoke screen laid down over the area by the British defences. So the Germans later came to the conclusion that the original reports were unreliable.

This was a lucky break for Force Y. While the enemy were searching for the mythical cruiser squadron to the east, they plodded on to the west and remained undetected. By the night of the 11th they were almost through the Narrows. Earlier they had sighted three unidentified torpedo-bombers which approached to within three miles of them before making off to the north, but these were probably British, for no sighting report was noted by the Axis at this time. The *Troilus* and *Orari* pushed on through the channel with *Matchless* ahead and *Badsworth* stationed astern.

At 8.45 pm on the 11th the *Matchless* (Lieutenant-Commander

J. Mowlem) sighted a darkened vessel ahead and at once illuminated it with starshells and searchlights; she was identified as a French minesweeper of the *Elan* type. Thinking herself under attack the unknown ship replied with two ineffectual salvoes from her for'ard guns and displayed three vertical green lights as a recognition signal. Once her identity had been established, no further action was taken on either side.

This vessel was not in fact a French ship, but the Italian destroyer *Malocello* and a somewhat different account of this encounter is given by Bragadin and the Italian Official Naval Historian.

On previous occasions, solitary British ships had slipped through the gap in the Italian minefields by using French territorial waters and because of this the Italians had despatched the destroyer *Malocello* (Commandante Pierfrancesco Tona) and the *Mas.533* (CWO 2nd Class Luigi Riccardo) to lay a minefield to the south of Cape Bon. In order not to clash with the Vichy by causing losses in the area after the battle the mines lain were of a type fitted with a self-destruction device, a time mechanism which would render them harmless after 72 hours. The two Italian warships were busy about this work when Force Y, about which of course they knew nothing, came upon the scene.

Also present were two other MAS boats, *MAS 552* and *MAS 553*. The commanding officer of the former vessel was Rolando Perasso and he told the author, 'We were there to signal a position to the *Malocello* and we saw the convoy.'

In Bragadin's account, the *Malocello* sighted the British units proceeding westwards and, while engaged in her task, could not attack them. There was an exchange of fire with no consequence for either side. He concludes that, in failing to attack, the British destroyers lost a good opportunity because *Malocello* would have been at a great disadvantage in any engagement. No mention is made, however, of her use of Vichy recognition signals or of the fact that she fired first. It certainly seems that her ruse worked very well and completely deceived the British escorts, but it is equally obvious that, with two damaged merchant ships under his care and in French waters, the British commander could not have engaged what he took to be a French ship.

After this incident the small force was not further molested, although the barrage put up by Force F against the air raids on the 12th could clearly be seen from their bridges as they left the Narrows behind them, and steered west. Dawn also brought renewed enemy air activity and several planes flew close to the convoy endeavouring to make up their minds whether or not to attack. Vice-Admiral Syfret came to the conclusion that the enemy was "mystified".

It is doubtful whether this was in fact so as *Badsworth* on one occasion opened fire on an aircraft which ventured too close. Indeed a study of the German papers made it clear that the Axis was in no doubt both as to the composition and the identity of this group. Their reports show that air reconnaissance early on the 12th reported that two destroyers and two steamers were proceeding on a westerly course south of Galitia Island. The last sighting report received was timed 8.30 pm on the 12th, and Force Y is correctly described as being some 30 miles west of Galitia Island at that time. An entry in the Naval War Diary for 12th August clearly states that in the Germans' opinion this group of vessels, which was still under observation, had 'presumably departed from Valletta where they had been staying since the last convoy operation in June'.

No air strikes were directed against them and the group arrived safely at Gibraltar on 14th August.

VII

It is not certain whether Admiral da Zara knew that he had been sighted on the evening of the 11th/12th, but having left Cagliari at 10.30 pm he held on his course with the cruisers *Eugenio di Savoia* and *Raimondo Montecuccoli* of the 7th Division and their escorting destroyers *Gioberti* and *Oriani*. The plan called for a rendezvous at 7 pm the next day to the north of the eastern tip of Sicily, with three other naval formations. These were the two heavy cruisers of the 3rd Division under Admiral Parona, *Gorizia* and *Bolzano*, which were to sail at 9.40 am on the 12th; the light cruiser *Muzio*

Attendolo of da Zara's own division which was to leave Naples at 9.30 am the same day after hurriedly completing a refit; and the heavy cruiser *Trieste* which was coming down from the north.

Once the concentration had been effected this combined squadron, three 8-inch cruisers, three 6-inch cruisers and eleven destroyers, was to steer on an intercepting course throughout the night of the 12th/13th and fall upon the remnants of the convoy and their escorting Force X at first light to the south of Pantelleria, the scene of the inconclusive action of June. This time the Italians were assembling a surface force powerful enough to put the issue beyond dispute if ably handled and they could be fairly confident of a successful outcome to the encounter.

Only one issue was still undecided and that was the question of fighter cover for da Zara's ships on the 13th. With so many powerful formations available in Sicily it was not a problem which need have caused the Axis any trouble, but events were to prove otherwise.

Chapter Four

The Long Day's Dying

I

THE convoy was unmolested during the night, but first light on the 12th found it approaching the chief danger area, fifty miles north of Bone and within a biscuit toss of the Sardinian airfields. As the day progressed they would penetrate even deeper into the waters of 'Mare Nostrum' and here lay concentrated another large group of enemy submarines. From this point on they could expect round-the-clock attentions from every aircraft the enemy could send from Sicily as well as Sardinia, and by noon the bombers could rely on fighter escort to help penetrate the fleet's fighter defences.

Although the Royal Air Force's attentions of the night had caused the enemy a few losses and, from the Italian viewpoint, a sleepless night, the bombers and submarines would have the whole long day ahead of them in which to get organised and do their worst. To aid them in this the day was another gloriously sunny one, with a smooth calm sea and visibility absolutely perfect. Not surprisingly therefore they were soon located by Axis reconnaissance planes. The enemy had arranged pre-dawn sweeps to cover the area between meridians 6 and 9 degrees east and at 6.20 am a German aircraft reported sighting 50 units in latitude 37°50' longitude 6°50'. Very soon other units, Ju88s and Cant Z1007bs, had homed in on this report and several aircraft were soon located on the fleet's radar screens.

The two carriers flew off a standing air patrol of Fulmars and Sea Hurricanes, two planes from each ship, at 6.30 am and later a standing air patrol of twelve fighters was constantly airborne with all the other serviceable units at instant readiness. Once again they found they had not the speed to intercept the shadowers and despite their vigilance the screen was never completely clear of enemy aircraft.

Nor were the enemy submarines any less attentive. The fleet had received a warning report of a possibly strong wolf-pack to the north-west and north-east of Galitia Island. Accordingly the destroyer screen was pulled in tighter to give better cover ahead of the convoy. The escort was at full strength now and an attack from any quarter was liable to meet with a warm reception. The *Uarsciek* and *U-205* moreover were still in contact from the previous day and *U-73* was also following their route and all these submarines from time to time surfaced and transmitted further details of the convoy's passage to supplement the reports of the aircraft. The Axis High Command in Rome therefore had no difficulty in directing their increasing scale of attacks throughout the whole day.

It was the Luftwaffe which made the first probe and at 9.07 a big formation of bombers was picked up approaching from right ahead. It actually consisted of nineteen Ju88s which had left their airfield as soon as the first certain reports were received of the convoy's position that morning. The fleet's fighters were vectored out and additional aircraft were scrambled away. Sixteen of them made interceptions. The Sea Hurricanes, Fulmars and Martlets were soon in among the powerful German bombers and, although handicapped by lack of speed and cannon fire-power, they claimed to have despatched four of the enemy. One pilot, Lieutenant R. H. P. Carver, claimed two certains alone. Some of the enemy jettisoned their bombs on coming under attack, but only a few, the majority continued on towards the convoy.

Lieutenant Carver and Sub-Lieutenant Hankey were flown off *Victorious* but were unable to gain sufficient height to make interceptions before the enemy had dropped their bombs. Instead they had to attack planes breaking away from the convoy. *Indomitable*'s planes intercepted some twenty miles from the fleet. The Junkers were powerful aircraft and Sub-Lieutenant Hankey was lost in this raid.

The surviving bombers arrived over the convoy and carried out individual shallow dive-bombing attacks on selected targets from out of the sun. Heavily engaged by all the ships, two were claimed shot down by the fleet's gunfire, one by *Pathfinder*'s pom-pom and the other by the *Deucalion*'s 4.7-inch gun, which was being very enthusiastically manned by an Army officer who happened to be taking passage in her to Malta. Captain Brown, *Deucalion*'s master, claimed that his ship most certainly hit one of the bombers which was seen to crash. As every other ship in the area was blazing away perhaps this was a little optimistic, but nevertheless a total of six Ju88s failed to return from this raid, a very bad return for the Germans, who, in spite of their claims to have sunk one cruiser and two merchant ships, had in fact inflicted no damage whatsoever. The carriers' fighter pilots were soon landing on their carriers full of excited claims of kills. Enemy losses were put at eight "certains" and three "probables" but this was a wild over-estimation; only four bombers fell to their guns, but even so it was a grand start.

A further minor success came soon afterwards when, after patient manoeuvring, planned in great detail after the previous day's frustration, two Fulmars were carefully and unobtrusively directed up-sun of a shadower. The two fighters, from 884 Squadron, then pounced before the enemy could dive away and escape and they were rewarded with the sight of a Savoia Marchetti Sm79 flaming down into the sea within half a mile of the North African coast.

At 9.40 two more Fulmars were similarly directed against another Sm79 hovering on the horizon. He was a more wary bird and spotted them in good time. During a long chase his gunners so damaged the Fulmars that they were forced to give up and return to their ship.

There was a long lull before the next raid came in; the enemy had planned a mass assault for around midday and were preparing for this maximum effort from the Sardinian airfields. The snoopers remained, sometimes growing a trifle bolder and – evading the fighter patrols– slipping in towards the convoy. At intervals, when this happened, the destroyers nearest the enemy would let fly with their main armaments, the crack of the guns being followed by ugly black bursts around the intruder, upon which he would wobble, turn, and put a more respectful distance between himself and the outer screen.

The convoy was now entering the main area of submarine strength and the morning was punctuated frequently by asdic reports and emergency turns as these hidden enemies attempted to pierce the guarding lines of destroyers and attack the merchantmen. Already, at 7.41, the *Kenya* had sighted two torpedo tracks about two cables ahead of her, crossing from port to starboard. She altered course and as she did so sighted a third track one cable's length away passing down her port side.

At 9.20 the *Laforey* out ahead of the fleet gained a contact and having confirmed it put in an immediate depth-charge attack. The submarine dived deeply under the convoy and about twelve minutes later was detected by the *Fury* (Lieutenant-Commander C. H. Campbell) on the starboard wing. Joined by her sister ship, *Foresight* (Lieutenant-Commander R. A. Fell), she carried out a hunt, dropping several patterns. The recipient of their unwelcome attentions was the *Brin* (Tenente di Vascello Luigi Andreotti). She had left Cagliari on the 1st for her patrol area 30 miles north-west of Algiers and she was pursuing the convoy when she was located. Other destroyers joined in the hunt but by a rapid deep dive Andreotti's boat escaped destruction.

The convoy plodded on past her and Captain Hutton recalled the ships. There was no time to allow for a prolonged hunt for every gap in the screen was a potential danger; many of the destroyers were therefore denied the satisfaction of a likely kill. Provided they kept the submarines at bay they were doing the job required of them.

At 9.22 the destroyers *Bicester* and *Ledbury* were ordered by Captain Hutton to take up station astern of the guides of the fleet to act as reserves during U-boat hunts. It was not only the vigilant destroyers which made the Axis submarines wary, danger threatened them from the air also. In addition to a standing patrol of Albacores provided by the two carriers, long-range aircraft from Gibraltar and Malta carried out sweeps far ahead of the convoy route seeking out further concentrations of the enemy boats as they began to assemble. One of these, Sunderland TK7R from Gibraltar, found the Italian submarine *Giada* (Tenente di Vascello Gaspare Cavallina) as she cruised some 70 miles to the north-west of Algiers in a position to intercept the convoy.

The big flying-boat delivered a very accurate attack on her at 9.34 am, dropping two depth-charges which exploded close alongside the submarine. Although the blow was not a fatal one Cavallina reported that the concussion had damaged all the control instruments, compass and rudder; in addition it had caused severe seepage through her plates. Despite these handicaps he took the

Giada down to 140 metres and thus escaped. *TK7R* signalled at 0950 that she had damaged a submarine in position 37°23'N, 1'2'E.

The leakages increased and it was obvious that the *Giada* would never make her base unless some temporary repairs were carried out; accordingly Cavallina surfaced and steered for the nearest neutral port, Valencia. Progress was slow and painful and being surfaced for such a prolonged period had the inevitable result that she was spotted again, by another Gibraltar Sunderland, *TK7C*, at 1.45 pm. It was impossible to dive so Cavallina decided to fight it out as best he could on the surface.

The Sunderland made an initial run-in and dropped a four-stick pattern, which severely shook the already dangerously unbalanced vessel. As the aircraft circled in readiness for the kill the Italians manned their guns and prepared to meet the attack when it developed. While circling, the Sunderland sent out a message timed 1345 which was received at Gibraltar stating that she had severely damaged the submarine in the bows and had killed two members of the crew. She gave her position as 37°45'N, 1°0'E. Having done this the huge aircraft commenced its second attack. The Italian submarines engaged with their puny weapons and scored a devastating series of hits. The Sunderland crashed with a large explosion close-by to the cheers of the incredulous crew of the *Giada*. After this spectacular finale they were not further attacked and limped into Valencia soon after midnight. Sufficient repairs were effected to enable her to reach La Maddalena on the 14th-but another of the pack had been safely removed from the convoy's path.

Meanwhile the *U-205* (Kapitänleutnant Franz-Georg Rerchke) approached the convoy at 11.35 am from the port bow. Unfortunately for him the destroyer *Pathfinder* (Commander E. A. Gibbs) was in this position and her asdic crew located him. The destroyer dropped a heavy depth-charge pattern, which promptly made the German skipper forget his approach and concentrate on extracting himself. The *Zetland* (Lieutenant J. V. Wilkinson, DSC) had been stationed to act as reserve destroyer for just such an eventuality, and she swiftly sped to Commander Gibbs' assistance. For fifteen minutes they plastered the unhappy U-boat before she shook them off and crept dispiritedly away to carry out repairs. Once again the hunters settled back in their appointed positions and the fleet pushed on.

At midday more Axis bomber formations were detected, coming in towards the convoy in several large groups. This was the main Italian effort mounted from their Sardinian airfields and was heavily escorted by fighters. Our own interceptors were soon heavily embroiled with this mass.

The Italians' attack was a cleverly designed one, in which Superaereo had combined all available forms of attack into one devastating combined assault, designed to cause maximum damage to convoy and escort. The object of the first phase of these co-ordinated attacks was to throw the escorting warships into confusion by forcing the convoy to take avoiding action, thus breaking up the formation and allowing heavy torpedo-bomber assaults to penetrate through to the convoy.

To achieve this the Italians started to attack with a force of ten S84 bombers of 32 Stormo each carrying two *Motobomba FFs*. This was a new weapon for which the Italians held great hopes, not so much for the success it would score but for the diversion they hoped it would cause. These weapons were described as circling mines, and were dropped by parachute ahead of the target. On contact with the water an automatic pressure device activated a propeller which drove the mine around in a circle of about 15 kilometres' radius.

To co-operate with the minelayers was a squadron of Fiat Falcon fighter-bombers, which were to carry out low-level attacks on the ships of the destroyer screen to further ease the task of the following torpedo-bomber formations. These Cr42s were stubby little biplanes, roughly the equivalent of the British Gloster Gladiator. The arrival of Spitfires and Hurricanes in the Western Desert area had decimated the Italian fighter squadrons which were equipped very largely with this obsolete plane and consequently the Italians had tried to make use of them in the tank-busting role. Now they were trying them against warships, but the light weapons which comprised their main bomb loads, two 200-lb bombs, were of little effect even against destroyers. Their only value proved to be in the diversionary role.

Both the bomber groups, minelayers and fighter-bombers, were given a powerful escort of fourteen sleek Macchi Mc202 fighters of 153 Gruppo based at Decimomannu, which were the equals, if not the betters, of the FAA Sea Hurricanes.

The first wave arrived over the convoy around 12.15 but fortunately for the British the following waves did not keep to the strict timetable required and the convoy was thus afforded enough respite to deal separately with each wave as it approached instead of a combined assault which would have been far more dangerous.

Colonel Leone was the commander of 132 Stormo based at Bari, which consisted of 24 S84s each capable of carrying either ten 100-Kg bombs; four 250-Kg bombs; two 500-Kg bombs; or two 1,500-Kg torpedoes. An alternative load was two *motobombas* of 400-Kg each. Leone describes the *motobombas* as a *naval* weapon which was dropped perpendicularly by parachute and on impact on the water the parachute automatically released itself. A gyroscopically controlled motor then started and at three metres depth a syphon of mercury started the motor and fins which would drive the bomb forward in a spinning motion, without leaving a wake. They were self-destructive and had a maximum time allowance of twelve hours.

On the 11th Leone's Stormo was transferred to Villacidro airfield in Sardinia where they refuelled and loaded their *motobombas*. Soon after this they were ordered against the convoy and at midday were on their way at an altitude of 3,000 metres. Visibility was good, 80 to 90 kilometres, and they were sighted and engaged by three Fleet Air Arm fighters from one of the carriers.

The Italian formation pressed on towards the convoy and at a range of about three kilometres ahead of the leading ships they dropped their bomb loads as planned, despite heavy anti-aircraft fire. On completion of this the aircraft returned on a northerly course for Sardinia. Two of the S84s were lost and every single one of the others was damaged, which meant that the Stormo was unable to take part in further attacks.

The ten S84s were intercepted by defending fighters who destroyed one of them and the blazing trail he left was sighted by the destroyer *Ashanti* (Captain R. G. Onslow) ahead of the fleet. The remaining nine were then at once brought under heavy fire by the leading ship and consequently their minelaying was more

Diagram showing the positions of the merchant ships 0800/D.1 to 0600/D.3 before the loss of the "Deucalion"

DEUCALION

(Commodore)
PORT CHALMERS

ALMERIA LYKES

GLENORCHY

CLAN FERGUSON

MELBOURNE STAR

OHIO

SANTA ELISA

ROCHESTER CASTLE

DORSET

BRISBANE STAR

WAIRANGI

WAIMARAMA

EMPIRE HOPE

© Peter C. Smith. 1970

J.R.Dominy

112

hurried than accurate. Nevertheless it had the desired effect for on sighting these 'black canisters' being dropped, the whole fleet made an emergency turn 45 degrees to port and back again to starboard to avoid them. The *motobombas* were heard exploding harmessly some fifteen minutes later.

As the ships turned, three of the Fiat Cr42 Falcons roared in over the screen at mast-head height, strafing and bombing as they came. These three were the only survivors of the eight of 160 Gruppo. They had been intercepted by Martlets from the *Indomitable*'s 806 Squadron who had effectively broken them up. The remaining three very bravely pressed on to follow their instructions but they scored no hits, although *Lightning* (Commander H. G. Walters, DSC) was near-missed.

It was while the convoy was in the middle of its avoiding action that the second wave of the Italian assault was designed to strike, but it was slightly delayed. It consisted of two groups of torpedo-bombers, 33 Savoia Marchetti Sparrows (Sm79s), from 160 Gruppo and 105 Stormo and ten S84s of 130 Gruppo, which were also equipped as torpedo carriers. These bombing formations were provided with fighter cover in the form of 26 Reggiane Re2001s, a very powerful interceptor.

The defending fighters managed to keep 130 Gruppo at bay but the Sm79s pressed on towards the fleet. Their late arrival had spoilt the well-laid plan; the attentions of the defending planes, despite the efforts of the Italian escorts, was too much for them. By the time the torpedo-bombers reached the destroyer screen they had become split up into groups of five or six planes as they came in from the port bow, port beam and starboard quarter. Thus the destroyers were presented with scattered bunches of low-lying aircraft, their favourite targets, and they punished them severely. Admiral Burrough later wrote that the Italian torpedo-bombers turned away as soon as fire was opened, but this was not quite correct; in fact many of the Sm79s were steered most gallantly through the wall of flak into the heart of the convoy. Although many released their torpedoes 8,000 yards from the nearest merchant vessels, others were undeterred by the

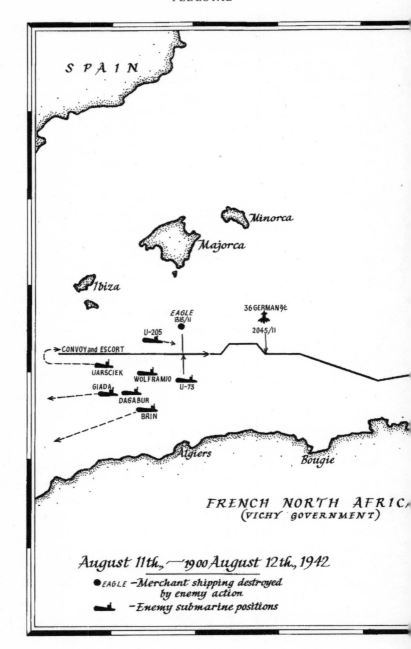

SPAIN

Minorca

Majorca

Ibiza

EAGLE
1315/11

36 GERMAN ╫c
2045/11

U-205

CONVOY and ESCORT

UARSCIEK

WOLFRAMJO

U-73

GIADA

DAGABUR

BRIN

Algiers

Bougie

FRENCH NORTH AFRICA
(VICHY GOVERNMENT)

August 11th., — 1900 August 12th., 1942

● *EAGLE —Merchant shipping destroyed*
by enemy action

— *Enemy submarine positions*

115

terrific defensive fire, which included the *Rodney* laying down an awe-inspiring splash barrage with her 16-inch guns.

An eyewitness aboard the freighter *Waimarama* saw one torpedo-bomber coming right into the convoy and apparently making for the *Nelson*. It had already been hit and its engines were actually on fire before the torpedoes were released; both of them missed their mark. A minute later the aircraft crashed into the sea.

Although this was not the only gallant deed performed by these Italian pilots, all their bravery availed them nothing and they scored no hits on any ships, although as usual returning planes subsequently claimed to have sunk two merchantmen and a destroyer, and to have damaged a battleship, three cruisers and two further steamers. Considering the scale of the attack their casualties were light; only one Sm79, two S84s and one escorting Re2001 were lost in this attack, although others were damaged; they had achieved no success.

The carriers' fighters had protected the convoy well, but they were now to face a more severe test; in conjunction with further Italian assaults with special weapons, the Germans laid on a heavy dive-bombing raid by 37 Junkers Ju88s from Sicily and these were now spotted approaching as the Italian torpedo-bombers began to disperse.

A Fulmar from 809 Squadron, from *Victorious*, intercepted a group of sixteen of them at 11,000 feet and made a quarter to stern attack on two of them. One bomber at once jettisoned his bombs and dived away. The pilot of the Fulmar tried to follow and managed to fire off seven more bursts before heavy anti-aircraft fire drove him from his target.

The air fighting was confused and desperate. In all, four Fulmars from 809 and four Sea Hurricanes from *Indomitable*'s 885 Squadron were scrambled away to intercept this raid. The Junkers approached in loose gaggles of four and twelve at heights ranging from 10,000 to 15,000 feet. The large group attacked by the four Fulmars broke up, four of them jettisoning and breaking away. Some of the Sea Hurricanes didn't have the height to intercept and had to wait and attack aircraft leaving the fleet after they had dropped their bombs. Sub-Lieutenant Wood found a lone Sm79 with its nose down for home on the fringe of the convoy and attempted to attack, but again the fierce barrage from the fleet drove him away and the Italian escaped.

About twelve of the Ju88s penetrated the destroyer screen and at 1.18 broke through the barrage, crossing the convoy from the starboard side and commenced their dives from 3,000 feet to deliver accurate attacks on the merchant ships and escorts on the port wing. This proved to be by far the most dangerous assault so far, the Germans pressing home their attacks, scoring near misses on both battleships while the *Cairo* and several merchantmen were straddled.

The *Deucalion* (Captain Ramsey Brown) proved to be the Germans' solitary success. She was no stranger to the Malta run and had successfully made the trip before without damage. In addition to the usual cargo of war supplies she was carrying a large complement of passengers to Malta and she also had eighteen Army and six Navy gunners manning her anti-aircraft weapons, three Naval signalmen and a Naval wireless operator.

She was the leading freighter of the port-wing column and became the target for one of the German bombers who planted a four-bomb stick almost on top of her. Three of these were very near misses, one to starboard and two to port, but the fourth scored a direct hit on No 6 derrick and, penetrating No 5 hold, came out of the side of the ship above the water line and exploded. Seriously disabled, she slowed down and the rest of the convoy picked their way past her. Thinking she was mortally hit, some of the crew panicked and two of the ship's lifeboats were swung away as they abandoned ship. Vice-Admiral Syfret ordered the destroyer *Bramham* (Lieutenant E. F. Baines) to stand by her and the two skippers held council. Captain Brown reported that No 1 hold was flooding and that No 2 hold had already flooded completely, but that he had hopes of still getting her in. After twenty minutes' delay while the lifeboats were recovered and their sheepish crews hauled aboard, the freighter's engine-room reported that they could restart the engines and eventually she worked up to eight knots.

At this speed it was obviously impossible for her to catch up, or stay with, the convoy which was still maintaining almost twice that speed, so *Bramham*'s skipper was told to attempt to use the inshore route through the Tunisian narrows and shoals. Listing, and at her best speed, the crippled ship followed the destroyer south, but they were not unobserved. Late in the afternoon the Luftwaffe was to find them again.

Meanwhile the Fleet Air Arm fighters continued to harry the Junkers. Lieutenant Patterson attacked a retreating enemy bomber over Galitia but he was jumped by enemy fighters and severely shot up. The same fate overtook Lieutenant R. L. Johnston, who was badly wounded in combat. He glided his plane back to the *Indomitable* and down on to her flight deck, but his arrestor hook carried away; the stubby little Martlet fighter went over the side and sank like a stone. The CO of 806 Squadron, he was a great loss.

Other Martlets from 806 chased a group of four Ju88s west of the fleet but they escaped. After abandoning the chase they found a consolation prize in the form of a Cant Z1007b shadower at 9,000 feet, quite oblivious of their approach from this unexpected quarter. They made astern attacks on him from above and soon his starboard engine and wing caught fire. Two of the bomber's crew managed to jump with parachutes before it plunged solidly into the sea.

The third wave of the Italian assault was also cleverly planned and thought out. It consisted of two Special Combat Units, both intended as nasty surprises for the two surviving British carriers. The first was the brainchild of the Italian General Raffaelli and amounted to what was one of the first flying-bomb concepts.

A standard Sm79 bomber had been especially converted and filled with tons of high explosives. This flying inferno was piloted off the ground in the normal way by a very brave pilot and taken to its cruising altitude. As soon as the aircraft was set on its predetermined course towards the fleet the pilot baled out and an attendant aircraft, a specially fitted Cant Z 1007b 11, took over control by radio and steered it towards its target. These two planes were given an escort of five G50 fighters.

There can be little doubt about the appalling destruction such a concentrated amount of high explosive would have caused aboard a carrier or battleship had this aircraft hit its target – consider the near loss of the battleship *Warspite* off Salerno in 1943 after a single hit by a radio-controlled bomb or the carnage inflicted on Allied carriers in the later stages of the Pacific war by the Japanese suicide planes, the *Kamikazes*. It was very fortunate for the fleet then that once again things went wrong for the Italians. *En route* to the fleet the controlling pilot's radio gear developed a fault and the Sm79 droned on until it ran out of fuel.

It finally crashed on the slopes of Mount Klenchela on the Algerian mainland where it exploded. Considerable dismay was caused on both the French and the Italian sides by this accident. The French, understandably, visualising the effect of such an explosion had it occurred in the heart of one of their North African cities and the Italians fearful that their secrets would be discovered. On 14th August the Italian Armistice Commission[1] visited the still smoking crater and was able to report that the plane had been utterly destroyed.

This phase of the scheme had gone awry but the second, minor phase was brilliantly successful, although not as destructive as the Italians had hoped. Two Reggiane Re2001s were to have been equipped with yet another newly developed weapon, an armour-piercing bomb capable of being dropped at a low height by specially adapted fast fighters in sneak attacks. Again faults were found in the weapon prior to the attack, but the basic surprise tactic was retained, the two fighters being equipped instead with antipersonnel fragmentation bombs. It was hoped to catch the carriers after the main raid as they were landing on their aircraft when these weapons could cause devastation among the deck crew and parked aircraft.

Having beaten off the bulk of the mid-day raid so well, the Fleet Air Arm fighters were starting to land on their carriers around 1.45 pm. Two Sea Hurricanes had touched down on *Victorious* and there were apparently three more circling round, awaiting their turn. Suddenly two of them detached themselves, dived down off the carrier's port quarter and roared over the flight deck just a few feet up. Everyone thought that they were Sea Hurricanes showing off in a burst of exuberance after their

[1] Set up after the French defeat in June 1940.

victories, but as they zoomed over both released bombs which bounced along the deck like a couple of cricket balls.

The two daring Italians had in fact achieved complete surprise but their bombs, estimated at no more than a hundred pounds each, had little effect on the armoured deck of *Victorious*. One broke up on the deck and, knocking a starter trolley flying, showered the deck with small splinters as it had been designed to do. The other slid across the flight deck and exploded fine on the carrier's bow.

The Re2001s both escaped unharmed from the stream of flak which followed them from the surprised British gunners. Their daring and audacity certainly earned them such a respite. Four officers and two men were killed and two men slightly wounded aboard the ship. This was the last act in the Sardinian raid. It was expected that more severe air attacks would be mounted from the numerous bases in Sicily but these were not expected to develop until later in the afternoon.

II

With the air attack over, the submarines again closed in.

> The following two hours brought innumerable reports of submarine sightings [Vice-Admiral Syfret later wrote] and asdic contacts. As an additional anti-submarine measure I ordered Captain (D) 19th Destroyer Flotilla to arrange for a depth charge to be dropped by a destroyer on each side of the screen every ten minutes between 1400 and 1900.

The *Tartar* (Commander St J. R. J. Tyrwhitt) sighted a submarine on the surface, which at once dived. The destroyer dropped a depth charge pattern to keep it down. At 2.17 pm the 'Hunt' class destroyer *Zetland* (Lieutenant J. V. Wilkenson, DSC) suddenly altered course and sped southwards, signalling as she did so that she had sighted a submarine on surface on the horizon bearing 200 degrees.

As this submarine was too far away to be a threat to the convoy the racing escort was curtly recalled to her former position. A warning was passed to *Bramham* and *Deucalion*, in whose path she lay, to be on the alert.

At 4.16 the *Pathfinder* confirmed another asdic contact off the port bow. Commander Gibbs estimated that the submarine was shaping up in a position in which he could torpedo either the battleships or the leading merchantmen and, increasing speed to twenty knots, he dropped two 5-charge patterns to throw the submarine commander's aim out. These hurriedly delivered depth charges were more accurate than had been expected. After the resulting explosions the *Pathfinder* lost contact. Joined by the ever-eager *Zetland*, she continued to send down patterns until the convoy was clear.

Her target was the Italian submarine *Cobalto* (Tenente di Vascello Raffaele Amicarelli) and she had been very badly damaged by the first two patterns, being driven down until her crew started bleeding at the ears and nose. Fighting to regain control she was over-trimmed and broke the surface astern of the convoy.

At 4.40 her periscope and part of her conning tower were sighted by vigilant lookouts aboard the *Ithuriel* (Lieutenant-Commander D. H. Maitland-Makgill-Crichton, DSO) on the convoy's port quarter. As the submarine went down again the destroyer counter-attacked with a heavy group of depth charges. Pounded by these, the *Cobalto* again broke surface well out of control behind her assailant. *Ithuriel*'s skipper was taking no chances, turning his ship in a tight circle he brought her racing in at high speed with the for'ard 4.7-inch guns blazing, and rammed the submarine abaft the conning-tower.

A boat's crew was quickly away, but although they managed to land on the upper casing of the submarine she sank before they could get inside to retrieve documents. Her bows pushed back as far as the foremost collision bulkhead, the *Ithuriel* stopped to assess the damage. While doing so she picked up three of the *Cobalto*'s officers, including the captain, and 38 ratings. *Cobalto* had been a fairly new boat of some 750 tons operating from Cagliari.

Although pleased at the despatch of an enemy submarine Vice-Admiral Syfret later commented:

> The submarine when it came to the surface after being depth-charged was obviously 'all-in' and I thought the

expensive method chosen by the Commanding Officer of HMS *Ithuriel* to sink it was unnecessary. Moreover I was disturbed at the resulting absence of the *Ithuriel* from the screen when an air attack was impending.

This verdict might appear to be rather harsh to anyone examining the action, bearing in mind the many frustrations suffered by the naturally keen destroyer commanders, who had been necessarily held back on a short leash. But it was the protection of the vital merchant ships which was uppermost in Syfret's mind and he was determined that this must take precedence over all else – and that included the destruction of the enemy, no matter how tempting.

While rejoining the fleet at 5.50 the *Ithuriel* at least had the satisfaction of drawing some of the fire from the convoy for, presenting as she did a solitary target, she was brought under attack by a Ju88 and four Cr42 fighter-bombers. Although her speed had been reduced by twenty knots her captain skilfully steered her through the towering bomb splashes unscathed. Her prisoners, having already had a very trying day, having been depth-charged, fired on and rammed, were by no means happy during these attacks as their airborne compatriots made many determined runs and planted several bombs close along both sides of the destroyer.

The destruction of one of their number had no effect on the remaining U-boats for their probings grew more intense. Next to try was the *Emo* (Tenente di Vascello Giuseppe Franco). At 4.04 he had sighted the convoy through his periscope, counting 29 ships including sixteen freighters, an aircraft carrier, probably a battleship and numerous escorts. The convoy's speed he estimated at 14 knots, course 70°. He decided to attack the carrier.

Some twenty minutes later, as he had almost completed his run in, the convoy suddenly changed course which brought a cruiser and some destroyers between him and his chosen target. He decided to go for the cruiser instead and at 4.33 he launched all four bow torpedoes at her from 2,000 metres' range. Some minutes later he heard the explosion of one torpedo and at ten-second intervals later two more. Feeling certain that he had sunk the cruiser he was jubilant. In fact he had missed and these explosions were probably the torpedoes exploding as they crossed a ship's wake. The torpedo tracks, however, were sighted by the *Tartar* and she followed them up to deliver an attack.

Emo had already started to withdraw when at 4.37 the first two shocks and concussions from depth charges rocked the Italian boat. The destroyer *Lookout*, stationed astern of the *Tartar*, had spotted the submarine's periscope just before she dived and both British ships dropped two more patterns. Franco reported frequent depth-charge explosions growing gradually more remote during the hour which followed but his ship escaped undamaged. Many of the explosions that he heard were in fact not directed against his boat at all, but were aimed at the next submarine of the wolf-pack to venture into range.

This was the *Avorio* (Tenente di Vascello Mario Priggione), who had spotted the convoy at 5.08. Priggione also counted several lines of steamers and destroyers and also three battleships and an 'American-looking' carrier.[1] His hydrophones were not functioning correctly but another look through the periscope revealed two destroyers at 12,000 metres, two freighters at 15,000 metres and a battleship at 18,000 metres. The conditions for an attack could not have been worse from a submarine commander's viewpoint, calm sea and smooth water making an undetected approach very difficult. He decided to attack the battleship and shaped course to bring this vessel in line.

As he continued his cautious approach towards the battleship he observed two destroyers leave the formation and steam towards him. Thinking that he could not have been detected at that range he

[1] Priggione was not alone in mistaking one of the British aircraft-carriers for an American vessel. The German Naval Staff War Diary is full of similar reports from the attacking airmen which led the Axis to believe that the USS *Wasp* was escorting 'Pedestal' and the *Indomitable* was frequently reported as the *Wasp* in subsequent air attacks. The US carrier had certainly received ample publicity during her two runs to fly off Spitfires to Malta earlier in the year which would give the Axis some excuse for assuming her to be present on this occasion. Also, the whereabouts of the *Indomitable* was probably not known to them at this time, although it would have been easy for them to have learnt that *Victorious* had left Scapa. *Indomitable*'s lighter colour scheme, acquired during her period in the Indian Ocean, might have further misled them, as until that time British warships operating in the Mediterranean or Home Waters had a darker paint scheme. Whatever the reason, the Germans were convinced that they were attacking the *Wasp*.

continued with his attack but the two destroyers continued to close him at high speed. At 3,000 metres there could no longer be any doubt that they had located him, but Priggione held his course, taking the *Avorio* down to a greater depth.

At 5.30 the submarine was badly shaken by four depth charges which exploded close alongside and the screws of the destroyers were heard passing overhead. Priggione promptly gave up all ideas of going on with his attack plans and instead took his boat down another 100 metres. The destroyers continued to paste the area with depth charges but they were not dangerously close. Nevertheless the submarine was forced to lie doggo for the next five hours. The hydrophones were not working and Priggione had no idea at all whether or not the destroyers were waiting quietly above him. At 10.25 he was finally forced to surface. He went up into the conning tower and swept the area with his night glasses, but the horizon was empty, the convoy had long since passed him by. Priggione steered north at a slow speed, recharging his batteries, which were much depleted, as he did so.

The attacks continued without respite. At 4.35 the *Dandolo* (Tenente di Vascello Giovanni Febbraro) located the convoy and by 6 pm was close enough to identify numerous merchant vessels, a cruiser and a battleship. He could also see no less than five destroyers between him and his nearest target. He was unable to fire due to frequent alterations of course by the escorts and the convoy and at 6.30 he was subjected to a prolonged depth-charge attack which drove him away.

As the convoy and escort fought off this succession of attacks they were steadily approaching the point where the heavy covering force would have, perforce, to turn back, and Vice-Admiral Syfret began making his dispositions accordingly. The destroyer *Wilton* (Lieutenant A. F. Northey) was added to Force X to replace *Bramham*, by now far astern. The Admiral also notified all ships that he planned to turn back with Force Z at 7.15 pm.

For over half an hour reports were being received from the fighter patrols and radar plots of a very heavy build-up of enemy aircraft. Mixed formations were arriving from Sicily in droves and circling some 20 to 30 miles from the convoy in readiness for another attack. The two carriers managed to get some 22 fighters airborne in time to carry out distant interceptions as this big raid developed. This was made more difficult by the fact that the *Victorious* had been experiencing difficulties with both her lifts throughout the day which meant considerable delay in striking down planes to be refuelled and rearmed and in ranging new patrols.

With everything now depending on these two ships and their few remaining fighters, conditions aboard were frenzied as every available plane was made ready. An eyewitness aboard the *Victorious* describes the scene:

> The pilots snatched meals as they could and rushed back on deck to take their places on the revolving wheel of readiness. And in the hangar the maintenance crews worked like men possessed to make the aircraft serviceable as they were struck down. They were coming on now with battle damage to be repaired as well as the normal troubles of oil-leaks, coolant leaks, sprained oleo-legs and what-not. The hangar itself was a shambles as aircraft were ranged, struck down, stowed, refuelled and rearmed at top speed; and the hangar-deck became more and more slippery with oil.

It was much the same aboard the *Indomitable* and in the fleet in general there was the feeling that, with evening rapidly approaching, the enemy was liable to make this final big effort his most fierce and determined. Guns' crews, already tired from twelve hours continuously at action stations, braced themselves for a last big effort to ensure that the thirteen remaining merchantmen of the convoy came through this final air assault under their protection, in one piece.

III

The Axis had indeed planned to pull out all the stops in this attack in an endeavour not only to damage as many merchant ships as they could, so that the submarines could finish them off in the morning, but to knock out the big ships of Force Z, especially the carriers, so that they would be unable to intervene when the Italian cruiser squadrons closed with the remnants of the convoy south of Sicily the next day. For this, both the Italians and the Germans mustered strong forces, although the main attack was chiefly an Italian affair, the German raids being organised in two separate groups but timed to merge with the whole.

The Italians' original plan was for a massed assault under a co-ordinated attack by all arms of the Regia Aeronautica to saturate the fleet's defences. It called for an attack force comprising 22 torpedo-bombers heavily escorted by fighters, 14 dive-bombers also with fighter escort and 40 high-level bombers similarly guarded; and these were all to arrive over the fleet at the same time.

Yet again however a good plan was to be spoilt by various failures before the attack itself got under way and the details had to be modified at the last minute. The escorting fighters, nine of each were to be supplied to cover the dive-bombers and the high-level bombers respectively, were to have come from the Re2001s of 2 Gruppo which had flown as escorts for the torpedo-bomber attacks of the midday raid from Monserrato in Sardinia.

These had returned to Monserrato and were due to be replenished and then flown to Sicily in time for the second attack, but it was belatedly realised during the afternoon that due to mechanical faults, combat damage and other related problems, such a manoeuvre would place a great deal of stress on the pilots. The fighter cover was therefore cancelled and it was decided that one section of the planned assault would have to be dropped and the high-level bomber attack was cancelled, as it had become increasingly obvious that this was the least effective means of attacking ships. It was decided to transfer instead the dive-bomber Gruppo from Trapani to Pantelleria where they could be covered by the fighter escorts laid on for the torpedo-bomber strikes. This latter force, 102 Gruppo, was the only Italian dive-bomber force in the area at this time, and was equipped with German Junkers Ju87s, the famous Stukas. Italian pilots had been trained by the Luftwaffe who themselves had used this aircraft with such success to smash their way through the Low Countries, Greece and into the Soviet Union with unparalleled rapidity. Dive-bombing and torpedo-bombing had soon proved the only effective ways of inflicting casualties on warships and this transfer had been reciprocated by the training of the German torpedo-bomber pilots at Grosseto by the Italians.

However the commander of 102 Gruppo was far from keen to commit all his precious Ju87s – called *Pichiatellos* in the Regia Aeronautica – without much stronger fighter cover than was laid on and he succeeded in reducing the number used on this sortie to nine, holding the others in reserve for a more favourable opportunity.

Nor was this the end of the sorry tale, for of the planned 22 torpedo-bombers, six of them were converted S84s which were not exclusively used in this role. Some difficulty was found in the mounting of their torpedoes; which meant that these S84s were also deleted from the force. The remaining sixteen were the well-tried Sm79s of 132 Stormo including elements of 278 and 281 Squadriglie, led by the famous ace, Capitano Buscaglia.

Rather than waste the Re2001s of 2 Gruppo, they were despatched with eight of 160 Gruppo Cr42s from Sardinia to carry out a diversionary raid prior to the main assault. It was planes from this group, which found *Ithuriel* on her own as has already been mentioned. They also reported attacking the convoy in position 37°35'E, 9°30'N and scoring a hit on a merchant ship, but in fact they caused no damage at all and one of their escorting fighters was lost.

The German first wave was designed to coincide with the Italian attack and for this twenty Stukas of 1/St.G.3 left Trapani escorted by a heavy formation of Messerschmitt Bf109s and 110s including those of Jagdgruppe 53.

These groups made rendezvous adjacent to the target area and were the first contacts made by the carriers' fighters. Heavily defended as the bombers were, the FAA pilots had no easy job getting through to them and all our interceptors were soon heavily embroiled in a wide-ranging series of dogfights.

Aerial fighting seriously commenced at 6 pm when the first fighters from the fleet located the incoming torpedo-bombers. These were Sea Hurricanes of *Victorious*'s 885 Squadron and they mistook the Sm79s for Cants. Lieutenant B. Patterson intercepted a formation of four bombers and closed one straggling and lagging behind the other three. At 150 yards he saw his tracers hitting and the starboard engine of the enemy bomber caught fire and it lost height. The return fire from the formation damaged Patterson's rudder and he had to break off the attack.

Another pilot from 885, Sub-Lieutenant A. J. Thompson, found a group of four Stukas with light brown and green camouflage approaching the fleet at 4–5,000 feet. He came up astern of one of them from 6,500 feet, dived and pulled up under them giving one a six-second burst. It trailed black smoke, turned over on its back and went into the sea. The other three jettisoned their bombs and dived away.

As Thompson broke away the escorting Bf109s came screaming down to protect their charges. Several of these, seven or eight in all, with yellow spinners, yellow leading edges to their wings and a yellow band on their fuselages, jumped him.[1] By very skilful flying Thompson turned the tables on one and gave it a short burst whereupon it dived towards the ocean. The others were all around him but luckily more of the British fighters appeared and engaged them, getting him out of a very tight corner.

Such a heavy fighter escort effectively prevented the carrier pilots from reaching the main bomber groups which at 6.35 got through to the convoy. The first enemy formations sighted from the ships were the torpedo-bomber groups, which had split up into two formations. The first came in from the starboard side of the convoy where they were met by a heavy and accurate barrage from the

[1] It is a singular coincidence that all the Fleet Air Arm fighters for 'Pedestal' were deliberately painted a brilliant yellow on their tail-fins and on the leading edges of their wings to prevent mistaken identification by the ship's gunners. Luftflotte II had just come from the Russian front where the Operational Theatre markings of the Luftwaffe were also yellow and evidently the fighters encountered over the convoy had retained their old markings in their new war zone.

ships on the destroyer screen. Several thereupon turned away after dropping their torpedoes at 3,000 yards from the nearest ships. Others kept coming but, although their torpedoes crossed ahead and astern of several ships, none struck home.

With its nine Ju87s 102 Gruppo had formed up some eighteen miles to the north-west of Cani before making their way in to the attack. Intercepted by fighters they were saved from annihilation by the intervention of their 28 Macchi Mc202 escorts of 25 and 155 Gruppo who later claimed to have shot down seven British fighters in the ensuing dog-fight. Two of the Italian Stukas were lost during the raid and the group claimed to have hit a battleship, several cruisers and four merchantmen.

An eyewitness account of their attack was later given in an Italian newspaper:

The formation reached the convoy at 1840 hours, eighteen miles north-east of Cani Island. The dive-bombers were divided into two large sub-formations each commanded by a Capitano. The British warships put up a formidable barrage of fire, and, in addition, the Italian aircraft were forced to fly with the sun in their eyes. Moreover, owing to a sudden change in the weather conditions, a low mist had arisen over the sea so that it was not easy to locate the vessels. The Italian aircraft threaded their way through a rent in the mist, when the formation leaders, estimating their position on time factors, reckoned that they had reached the convoy, and that it would be a waste of precious time to search further.

The dive was made from heights varying between 3,000 and 4,000 metres. Each formation very rapidly chose its own targets. One Capitano, an OC of a squadron, had a most unfortunate experience, as he had a faulty oil pipe which although it did not interfere with navigation continually sprayed oil over the windscreen. He made the dive with his head sticking out of the aircraft about the windscreen and one may imagine under what conditions in view of the very high speed. During a critical stage of the attack an AA shell passed clean through one of the propeller blades without doing any worse damage although it might very well have been fatal. The pilot released his bombs at a very low height, setting one of the ships on fire. In the confusion of the moment, the smoke and clouds et cetera, the Capitano flattened out and found himself in the smoke from the funnels of a cruiser and had to manoeuvre rapidly to avoid a collision.

The *Rodney* was attacked by one of the Italian Stukas, which approached from ahead in a shallow dive. The captain of the *Rodney*, Rivett-Carnac, ordered starboard full rudder and the bomb, which failed to explode, fell into the sea abreast of X turret and some twenty yards off the port side. Almost at once the battleship was engaging the first group of ten torpedo-bombers approaching from the starboard beam. She reported that many did not press home their attacks although some flew right across the convoy and made off to port.

Lieutenant B. Ritchie of 800 Squadron had just taken off from *Victorious* when he spotted a Stuka at 400 feet, which had just carried out its attack. He chased it for a mile through thick flak before carrying out a beam attack at 100 yards. Part of the Ju87's cowling broke off and as he got even closer he saw the rear gunner double up and the enemy aircraft began to smoke and flame. One wing dropped and it went into the sea from 200 feet; there were no survivors. This kill was confirmed from *Victorious* whose crew had a grandstand view throughout. Ritchie's plane was undamaged.

The Italians admit the loss of two Ju87s but no figures are available as to the number of Sm79s lost in this raid. A common report among British sources is of several enemy aircraft laying mines ahead of the fleet at this time but there is no documentary evidence of this in the Italian records and in their Official History it is denied that this took place. Nevertheless, in the midst of the assault the fleet did execute an emergency turn to port to avoid what they thought to be such a threat; in the middle of such confusion, a mistake like this is understandable.

As the bomb bursts straddled some of the ships and the water, churned up by the scudding wakes of the manoeuvring vessels, was torn into a boiling cauldron of explosions and spray, torpedoes scythed in from a fresh angle as the second group of Sm79s made their attacks. They launched a total of twelve in all and claimed to have struck a cruiser and two freighters; in fact no torpedoes actually found their mark on any such ships. But out on the edge of this furious mêlée the destroyer *Foresight* (Lieutenant-Commander R. A. Fell) was struck and slewed round to a halt, signalling as she did so that she had been hit by a torpedo on the starboard side aft.

The torpedo had in fact hit abreast the steering compartment, the ship's back was broken and her stern dropped by two feet. Immediate flooding took place below the lower deck compartments abaft the engine-room. The main engines were undamaged and usable but with great vibration at all speeds. Her steering gear was completely wrecked.

Immediately the *Foresight* was hit, the *Tartar* was detached to stand by her. As the convoy surged on Commander Tyrwhitt signalled to Rear-Admiral Burrough and asked permission to retain the destroyer *Penn* under his orders as she was nearby, in order to provide an anti-submarine escort. Rear-Admiral Burrough had to reply that, regretfully, he must keep her himself.

In the midst of this bedlam some twelve German Ju87s of 1/Stg.3 appeared suddenly from up-sun and out of a smoky blue sky. Peeling off at between 10,000 and 9,000 feet at two-second intervals, they made a concentrated assault on the *Indomitable*, some of the German pilots coming down to a thousand feet, or less, so intent were they on achieving hits.

All the carrier's guns opened up in a desperate attempt to deter the plummeting planes, but astern, her cruiser protector, the *Phoebe* (Captain C. P. Frend) was fully engaged with her main armament of 5.25-inch guns against several of the Savoia Sm79s, who were working their way aft. The cruisers close-range weapons engaged them, but brushing aside this fire and also the heavy barrage of the carrier and near-by destroyers, the Stukas pulled out of their dives and their 1,000-pound bombs 'rained down in concentration onslaught'.

From the other ships *Indomitable* became obscured by splashes and smoke was pouring from her flight deck fore and aft as she circled painfully in a wide circle at slow speed. She was turning

131

away from the wind in an endeavour to master the fires, which swept her hangar decks.[1]

Here again in operation was the Luftwaffe dive-bombing technique. Its potency had been graphically demonstrated before and once again it had proved that the fleet had developed no real answer to it. In January 1941 these inverted gull-winged aircraft had made a similar assault on the *Illustrious* off Malta and had hit her six times, putting her out of the war for months. Even before the badly damaged carrier had limped out of the Mediterranean to safety, the Stukas had turned their attentions to a cruiser squadron, sinking the *Southampton* and damaging her sister ship the *Gloucester*. The lesson thus imparted was a grim one and was soon repeated. Off the bitterly contested island of Crete the following May ship after ship went down beneath the blows of the Stukas, and another aircraft carrier, the *Formidable*, was badly damaged and had to be withdrawn. Now it was the *Indomitable*'s turn to feel the wrath of these crack units.

One bomb landed near her for'ard lift and perforated the upper gallery deck and exploded above the main hangar deck. A hole some twenty feet by twelve was blown in the upper deck. Severe structural and splinter damage was caused between the flight deck and the lower gallery deck. The for'ard lift was canted up by five feet on the starboard side and stuck. A fire was started in the hangar as the ready-use ammunition for A1 and A2 4.5-inch turrets ignited.

The second bomb hit abaft the after lift, went through the upper gallery deck and exploded just above the upper hangar deck. Twenty feet of the upper deck was destroyed and a hole was blown through the flight deck. The hangar was destroyed for a width of sixteen feet. The lower gallery deck and lift structure sustained minor damage. A fire broke out near the torpedo room, but the warheads did not explode.

[1] One post-war published account of this assault describes the German aircraft as 'screaming black winged Stukas', but the Ju87s of 1/St.G.3 were painted in desert colours, light and dark brown. The screaming sirens – or 'Trombones of Jericho' – had been removed from most operational Ju87s during 1941 as the Luftwaffe felt that by this time they had lost their psychological effect. It is doubtful whether the Stukas used in this attack, being of the D series, were ever fitted with this device anyway.

In addition to these two direct hits there were three near misses. The first grazed the port pom-pom director and exploded five feet from the hull at upper hangar deck level. The side plating between the upper and lower gallery decks was destroyed and structural and splinter damage extended for 52 feet inboard.

The second near-miss exploded 25 feet underwater to port, abreast C. 2 oil fuel tank, blowing in the side of the ship over an area 40 feet by 20 and causing minor internal damage. The wing compartments in the vicinity of the explosion were flooded causing a heel of eight degrees to port which was corrected by counter-flooding.

The third near miss exploded underwater off the port quarter and caused minor structural damage and a few splinter holes in the hull above the waterline. By the time the last Stuka had vanished through the flak-rent sky, the *Indomitable*, as a fighting unit, was finished for the rest of the operation. The for'ard lift, A1 and A2 4.5-inch guns and B Director were written off, while the after lift was temporarily out of action.

This was only the material damage, but the carnage aboard the carrier was terrible. The wardroom had been filled with off-duty pilots and observers of the Albacore 827 Squadron and one of the near-miss bombs had wrecked it killing every man there. In all casualties amounted to six officers and 44 men killed and a further 59 seriously wounded. The men killed included the Royal Marine detachment manning the port guns; they had suffered particularly when both turrets were destroyed.

> Two huge columns of black smoke suddenly blossomed from her flight deck [wrote an eyewitness] and from our position in the van of the screen it looked as if she could not possibly survive. The last we saw of her she was on a westerly course and we could still see the columns of smoke until the darkness hid them.

David 'Rocky' Royle aboard the cruiser *Charybdis* had a grandstand view of this attack, as he was later to record:

> I saw a group of black dots overhead. They started to peel off, one after the other in vertical dives. I realised they were

Ju87s (Stukas) and they were diving on the carrier *Indomitable*; although *Charybdis* was too far away from the *Indomitable* for our close-range fire to be effective I opened fire with the single port pom-pom, hoping the tracer would warn *Indomitable* and her closer escorts. Heavy AA fire started at once but these Stukas were the Luftwaffe's special anti-ship dive-bombers.

Smoke was billowing out of her hangar lifts and what I thought was the flight deck, dripping molten metal. [This was actually blazing aviation fuel.] The *Indomitable* was temporarily out of control, and *Charybdis* circled her ready to go alongside if need be.

Arthur Lawson was a leading telegraphist aboard *Indomitable*. He told me:

Round about 1930 the attacks were being concentrated on the carriers and *Indomitable* was under continuous bombing, while fighting back tooth-and-nail. Suddenly the ship shuddered from stern to stern and one had the strangest feeling of great resistance being exerted by the whole vessel to stop herself being pressed underwater. A strange hush prevailed immediately following the hits, followed by the bedlam of the damage control parties going about their grisly work. My most vivid memory of that moment was seeing an officer finishing a drink he was having with half his head blown away!

Another telegraphist was Charles McCoombe aboard the *Sirius*, who related to me:

Partially hidden under a pall of smoke, *Indomitable* looked in a right mess, with the flight deck rolled up under the extreme heat. She was hit by several bombs and looked like an old-fashioned sardine can with the lid rolled back on the key! A funeral service for the dead was a moving experience as many other warships gathered round her to pay their last respects.

The *Charybdis*, and destroyers *Lookout*, *Lightning* and *Somali* were detached by Syfret to protect and assist her as best they could. At 7.14 *Lookout* (Lieutenant-Commander C. P. F. Brown) closed the stricken vessel to assist in fire-fighting. Despite the dangers of blazing aircraft fuel cascading from the flight deck the little destroyer ran alongside and manned hoses. By 7.30 the situation was in hand and Captain Troubridge of *Indomitable* was able to signal Vice-Admiral Syfret that she was able to steam at 17 knots.

Soon she was reporting being able to steam at 20 knots and by 8.30 had worked up to 28, a magnificent achievement. Meanwhile those of her fighters, which had been airborne, had to land aboard *Victorious*, and this was to cause another fatal delay. Between 6.50 and 7.30 *Victorious* landed-on twelve of the *Indomitable*'s planes in addition to her own. One Martlet ran out of fuel waiting to land and was forced to ditch but happily the pilot was rescued by the *Zetland*.

Deck space aboard the *Victorious* was now at a premium and all manner of planes littered the flight deck. The Sea Hurricanes could find no spare space as her outriggers were full to capacity with her own aircraft and most of those badly damaged were unceremoniously dumped overboard. It had been planned to fly off a four-plane cover for the fleet from one carrier and another of similar strength to escort Force X once they had taken their departure but this proved impossible for some time.

Meantime the last Axis aircraft gradually cleared from the radar screens, winging their way back to their bases in Sicily. Once more they had failed to hit a single merchant ship and now the promise of dusk seemed to indicate safety from further air attacks. At 6.55 Vice-Admiral Syfret turned his heavy escort about leaving the convoy and Force X to continue alone. Wishing them 'God Speed', Force Z hauled round to the west. The time for this turn had been brought forward by twenty minutes because Vice-Admiral Syfret felt that in view of the scale of the last enemy air attacks the Axis would not have the capacity to mount another against Force X before nightfall.

He was also concerned by *Indomitable*'s damage and by the fact that the violent manoeuvring of *Rodney* had accentuated a defect in her boilers, which ultimately reduced her best speed to 18 knots. At

6.20 *Victorious* finally managed to fly off four Fulmars to cover the convoy but these soon became involved with a few remaining enemy fighters. In the brief scrap which followed before the Germans broke off the action to return to their bases, the Fulmars shot down one of the enemy but lost one of their own number. They were thus short of fuel and ammunition and had to withdraw from their original task. At 8.07 the final launch put four Sea Hurricanes up as a standing patrol over the main fleet but the approach of darkness led to their landing-on some forty minutes later.

It is appropriate here to summarise the achievements of the Fleet Air Arm and these were truly great. Their strength reduced by almost a quarter with *Eagle*'s loss early the previous day, the young pilots had flown their obsolete fighter without flinching into the heart of the massed enemy formations throughout the 12th. Frequently frustrated by the superior speed of the German and Italian bombers and completely outclassed by the Bf109Gs, Bf110C-4s, Mc202s and Re2001s, they had nevertheless managed to break up numerous flights of incoming bombers and their very presence caused others to lose their cohesion and discipline.

Contemporary claims made of 39 enemy aircraft shot down for certain plus many 'probables', have of course since been found to be in error,[1] but they can still claim to have inflicted the lion's share of casualties on the enemy air units and must be credited for ensuring that the convoy reached the edge of the Narrows almost intact, despite all the enemy air forces could do.

The bulk of Force Z was to cruise off the North African coast and so to be on hand to strike should the Italian fleet offer battle, but at 11.15 the next day the group of cripples, *Indomitable*, *Rodney* and *Ithuriel*, were detached to return to Gibraltar screened by the destroyers *Amazon*, *Antelope*, *Westcott*, *Wishart* and *Zetland*. Force R, the oiling group, also continued to cruise in the western Mediterranean.

[1] The Italians claim that only seventeen aircraft were lost on the 12th but this may be Italian aircraft only. Total losses for the whole three-day period they give as 42 (21 German and 21 Italian). According to the report made by the US Ambassador in Tunis seven planes made forced landings in Tunisia alone and he quoted one German pilot as saying that 'he had never seen such AA fire as that encountered over the convoy'.

As the main fleet set course towards the setting sun, the convoy with its slender escort of cruisers and destroyers slid towards the lethal waters off the Skerki Bank. The enemy failed to notice the splitting of the force for some time but by 7.30 pm it was clear to them. The reduced squadron, unscathed save for the *Deucalion* – and she was still afloat-steamed steadily on, and all concerned felt a great swell of elation that so great an enemy effort should have produced so little. Alas for all their hopes, for shortly after they had parted company from Force Z the convoy was beset by a series of disasters which were rapidly to escalate into near defeat. Already, at 7 pm, the dark shapes of over 35 Junkers and Heinkels were lifting off from their Sicilian runways, as were further Italian torpedo-bomber strikes. In quite reasonably judging that the Luftwaffe had shot its bolt for the day Vice-Admiral Syfret was in error for another wave was on its way. More submarines were gathering and so were flotillas of E-boats. And at Malta, Rear-Admiral Leatham received further sighting reports of the two Italian cruiser squadrons, now dangerously close at hand and apparently concentrating.

IV

The Royal Air Force at Malta had been fully extended since first light, stretching its meagre resources to the limit to keep track of the enemy cruisers, hamper his submarine patrols and provide early warning of his intended movements.

A Baltimore and a Maryland maintained a search over areas *H* and *J* in the Ionian Sea to cover the exits from Taranto, while other Baltimores made five sorties on a patrol line between Sardinia and Sicily. In addition the six PRU Spitfires flew twelve sorties photographing the major Italian harbours. It was one of these, returning from its mission over Naples, which at 10 am discovered that the Italian 3rd Cruiser Squadron had left Messina. A search to the north-west of the Sicilian Straits was unsuccessful due to heavy cloud, but in fact the Italians were steering a more northerly course to effect the planned rendezvous with the 7th Division and the *Trieste*.

A Maryland sent out to make further searches had to return after a short while with engine trouble but a relief Baltimore eventually found one cruiser and five destroyers at 6.54 pm. She again reported this group at 7.06 but a quarter of an hour later she was sending in details of four cruisers and six destroyers steering south at twenty knots. Except for a short period when the Baltimore was replaced by a Wellington, this force was kept under constant surveillance.

Much of the credit for this can go to the pilot of the Baltimore Pilot Officer Munro. Although fully extended to keeping in touch with the enemy to the limit of his endurance, he asked to be allowed to remain on patrol until dusk to avoid too long a gap, even though this would mean for him a night landing, for which he had had no experience or previous training. Despite this he got down safely.

Striking forces were also prepared but the number of aircraft available was pathetically small, and to mount even the smallest raid, the bottom of the barrel had to be scraped. For example, in order to send in two pinprick raids on Comiso an old Wellington IC which had crashed at Malta earlier while in transit to the Middle East was hurriedly patched up and made ready. Pilot Officer Sheppard, with no operational experience at all up to that time, volunteered to take this aircraft out on two sorties during which he dropped delayed-action bombs on the target. Unhappily this bravery was not rewarded, for on the second run over Comiso the plane was hit by flak and although Sheppard got her back to Malta the old plane crashed on landing and exploded.

The main striking force of fifteen Beauforts and fifteen Beaufighters was held overnight and throughout the day at instant readiness despite the obvious danger from enemy air raids on the aircraft thus exposed. In order to have this force ready to strike at the enemy naval forces should the opportunity present itself the number of spare planes left available to carry out any other offensive sorties on the evening of the 12th was only seven, all Beaufighters, four from 248 Squadron and three from 252.

These were despatched, under the command of Wing Commander J. M. N. Pike, to shoot up Pantelleria airfield but only three of 248 Squadron located their target at all. These three, led by Pike, claimed to have strafed only one aircraft and set it on fire. This then was the extent of the Malta air strike forces, although the Fleet Air Arm at Hal Far still had two Albacores serviceable for a night torpedo attack.

It is ironical that the Italian Supreme Command had by this time convinced itself that the potential air strike capacity of Malta was so overwhelming as to prevent their big ships operating at all to the south of Sicily without massive fighter protection.[1]

In fact compared with the huge air attacks encountered by 'Pedestal' throughout the 12th the Italian cruiser squadrons had little or nothing to fear from the twenty or so torpedo-bombers which was all the British could muster. This somewhat unwarranted fear was to have large repercussions, which were ultimately to decide the fate of the convoy.

Up until that moment the Axis were generally well pleased with the way things had developed, but the chief reason for their satisfaction was the exaggerated reports of the bomber pilots and the over-optimistic results read into their own intelligence reports. They thought that two of the British carriers had been seriously damaged on the evening of the 11th – a conclusion which was reinforced by the fact that the *Furious* had returned to Gibraltar; but as noted, this was because she had completed her flying off operation. On the 11th German Naval Command reported that at 7.55 am an aircraft carrier with five cruisers or destroyers and one steamer had been sighted proceeding on a south-westerly course 77 miles north of Algiers; 'evidently a damaged aircraft carrier which had turned back under escort', the German report concluded.

[1] For example, Bragadin records: 'In view of the increased strength of Malta's air forces over what it had been on the 15th June it was absolutely essential that this time the Italian naval group be given cover.' He puts the number of planes available to the British at 180, which is a fairly accurate figure, but most of these were fighters and *not* strike planes.

Once they had sold themselves on this idea then each new report they received only added emphasis to the assumption that *Furious* had indeed been damaged. Their spy network at Gibraltar was so efficient that on the 12th they had details that the *Furious*, 'listing slightly', and escorted by three destroyers, entered Gibraltar from the east. One destroyer was noted as having landed 200 to 250 men who had probably been shipwrecked. When on the 13th they received further information to the effect that *Furious* had entered dry-dock,[1] they were almost certain of their 'facts'.

When the Admiralty had announced the sinking of the *Eagle* on the 12th the Germans and Italians became almost certain that, in all, four carriers had been sunk or severely damaged during the battles of the 11th/12th, which, they jubilantly recorded, 'represents an all-time high'.

> The aero-naval battle is in progress [Ciano wrote in his diary on the 12th]. For the time being details are lacking.
>
> Fougier and Casero[2] are not too well pleased. The Germans have announced the sinking of the English aircraft carrier *Eagle* but there is considerable doubt about this.
>
> By dawn tomorrow a naval engagement is expected.

Despite Ciano's scepticism over the claim of his German allies, there was no doubt that *Eagle* had been sunk; perhaps he was actually referring to a claim by the Italian air force that the torpedo-bombers had sunk *Eagle* and not the German U-boat. Such a claim has been repeated, despite all the relevant facts having long been made public, in some British reference works on Italian aircraft published since the war, and Ciano, at the time, might reasonably have far more justification than post-war British air historians, to believe such a version. Such pettiness between allies and services operating against a common enemy did much to save the convoy from final annihilation on the 13th.

---

[1] Which she had, but only to embark further Spitfires for Malta.

[2] General Rine Corso Fougier was commander of the Italian Air Force and Casero was its Chief of Staff whom Ciano called, 'my old faithful'.

V

In the Eastern Mediterranean basin, Rear-Admiral Vian's diversionary force, having turned back at dusk on the 11th, dispersed according to plan. The bulk of the force then proceeded back to Alexandria but the Admiral took the cruisers *Cleopatra* and *Arethusa*, and the destroyers *Sikh*, *Zulu*, *Javelin* and *Kelvin*, to carry out a further move by bombarding targets on Rhodes. This was done at longer range than planned because of searchlights and the attentions of three E-boats. The Italians were not caught napping and their records confirm that no damage was caused by this raid.

The German submarine *U-83* reported sighting four cruisers and ten destroyers on a westerly course and made an attack on them in a position some 150 miles north of Port Said. This attack was unsuccessful and although the *Javelin* counter-attacked for a long period and reported pools of oil and floating debris, the U-boat was also unharmed. Vian's force returned to base after this operation.

There was no reaction to the raid from the Axis side. Their 8th Cruiser Division[1] remained in harbour, with four destroyers, at Navarino and made no attempt to sortie out to intercept Vian. The Germans withdrew the destroyer *ZG3* from convoy duty and sent her there to reinforce the Italian group. The only other submarine in the area[2] had lost contact and air searches flown on the 12th also failed to find the British force. Local convoys were held up and the sinking of the *Ogaden* by the *Porpoise* – which had just completed a mine-laying mission – on the evening of the 12th, also meant that shipping along the North African coast was suspended. Ship traffic between Italy and Greece was reported to be at a standstill. These numerous measures were purely defensive and it would appear that Operation MG3 failed on the whole to draw much fire from 'Pedestal'. Although the submarine *Turbulent* was left on watch off Navarino, nothing further was expected to develop from the Eastern Mediterranean.

[1] The 6-inch cruisers *Aosta*, *Abruzzi* and *Garibaldi*.
[2] *U-77*.

VI

Back at the Operations Room at Malta, Sir Keith Park and Vice-Admiral Leatham were keeping a worried eye on the Italian cruiser squadrons as nightfall approached. At 7 pm the entire Axis naval force had joined up and was proceeding south through the central Tyrrhenian Sea with the object of engaging Force X at dawn in the sea south of Pantelleria.

The shadowing Maryland reported the junction of the groups at 7.18. There could be little doubt in Admiral Leatham's mind that their objective was the convoy. He felt, however, that Force X could prove more than a match for them.

Whether this would have in fact been the case no one will ever know for one brilliantly executed submarine attack was to throw all the odds strongly in favour of the Italian Admiral da Zara.

Chapter Five

A Fateful Night

I

THE axis had prepared a strong series of defensive zones to bar the Convoy's route through the dangerous Sicilian Channel. The southern part of this deep-water route was narrow and wound between the sandbars of the Skerki Bank to form a funnel through which the deep-laden ships must pass. The shoals and coastal hazards of the Tunisian coast formed a natural point of ambush; the shallow water and shifting banks of sand providing almost ideal conditions for the light forces the Italians now deployed under their pre-arranged plan. The small draught of the E-boats allowed them freedom of movement, which the merchantmen lacked. Radar watch was made difficult by the close proximity of the coastline and the asdics of the escorts would have difficulty detecting enemy contacts because of the natural obstacles of the coast.

During the morning of the 12th five Italian submarines had taken up positions at the northern approaches of the channel; they were the *Granito*, *Ascianghi*, *Bronzo*, *Dessié*, *Axum* and *Alagi*. At nightfall on the 12th they were reinforced by a second line, consisting of the motor torpedo boats of the 2nd, 15th, 18th and 20th Flotillas, nineteen boats in all, which the German Naval Command planned to reinforce with boats of their 6th Flotilla from Crete, six of which were speeding at top speed to reach the battle zone.[1]

These lithe vessels, armed with torpedoes and light weapons, would be almost undetectable against the black coastline and the Axis expected good results from them. The Italian 2nd Flotilla was a brand-new unit equipped with a larger type of boat and not yet fully worked up but nevertheless they were committed to the battle.

---

[1] Two of these were subsequently held at Mersa Matruh to operate in the Eastern Mediterranean against the diversionary force *MG3* from Alexandria, MG3's only success.

At 7.46 Force X commenced their manoeuvres to take up the convoy's new cruising disposition to enter the northern end of the Narrows. Some ten minutes earlier the first submarine lying in wait had made her attack. This was the *Dessié* (Tenente di Vascello Renato Scandola). She had sailed from Trapani on the 11th and had reached her operational zone at 5.22 am on the 12th where she cruised and waited. Some fourteen hours later Scandola made out ships' masts and smoke through the periscope, and some minutes later had closed the convoy and was watching it zigzagging towards him.

He estimated its strength as 24 vessels, fourteen steamers and ten destroyers and, as he watched, it changed course in loose order, with three destroyers snaking on the bow of the formation and two more on the port side and towards the stern. Two further destroyers were on their own to the north. The sea was calm and he estimated the speed of the main group at 15 knots. He steered to attack.

At 7.38 at a range of 1,800 metres he launched his four bow torpedoes at two large steamers at intervals of three seconds in position 37°38'N, 10°25'E. He described his targets as steamers of 10,000 and 15,000 tons respectively, two of a group of eight modern vessels, with raking bows and cruiser stern. He identified their engines as turbines.

In spite of his firing position and angle, his first torpedoes missed by 40 metres, which he blamed on the current. Taking his submarine down to 40 metres' depth he disengaged and one minute and forty seconds later he heard two explosions but it was impossible to make out by hydrophone if any ship had stopped. He decided to return and attack using his stern tubes but destroyers dropping depth charges kept him away. It appears that the torpedo attack was not noticed and the British destroyers were merely dropping random charges as a deterrent against just such an attack.

This probe, although inflicting no damage on the convoy or Force X, should have forewarned them of the presence of enemy units but the attack is not mentioned in any report on the operation.

As the ships of the screen moved to take up the new screening formation [see Diagram 4], they were again caught unawares by

Admiral of the Fleet the Lord Lewin
(Crown Copyright)

Rear-Admiral Sir Harold Burrough
(Imperial War Museum)

Vice-Admiral Sir Neville Syfret
(Imperial War Museum)

Operation '*Berserk*': the carriers *Indomitable* and *Argus*
(Imperial War Museum)

The convoy passes into the Mediterranean *(Imperial War Museum)*

The *Eagle* after being hit by four torpedoes
(Cdr C. C. Crill)

The sinking *Eagle*
(Cdr C. C. Crill)

Short-range guns crew aboard the *Manchester*
(L. McDonald)

Captain Drew of the *Manchester*
(L. McDonald)

Pom-pom crews aboard the destroyer *Pathfinder*
(J. G. Buchan)

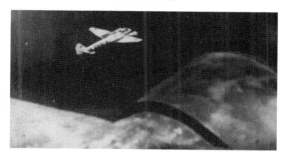

The Junkers Ju 88 dive-bombers of LG 1
(Nicola Malizia)

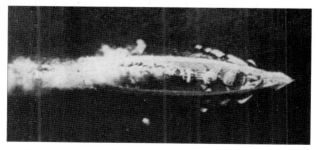

Rodney in action against dive-bombers *(Ufficio Storico, Roma)*

Bombs fall alongside the *Clan Ferguson*
(Cdr C. C. Crill)

Bombs in the convoy lanes
(Cdr C. C. Crill)

Manchester turns to meet an attack from an Italian torpedo-bomber *(*Top)
An Italian torpedo-bomber attacking at close range
(Admiral Burrough)

Bombs explode in the wake of a merchantman
(G. F. Jones)

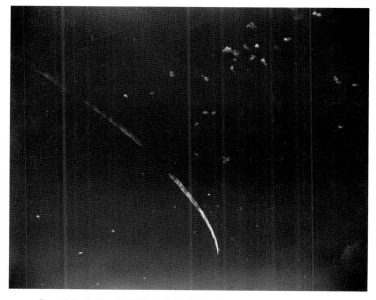

One of the Italian Ju.87 Stuka's is hit by the warships anti-aircraft fire
and plunges into the Mediterranean
(Imperial War Museum, London)

Ithuriel closing the Italian submarine *Cobalto*
(Crown Copyright)

Ithuriel rams *Cobalto*
(Crown Copyright)

Cobalto seconds before she sank
(Crown Copyright)

Italian ground crew load torpedoes in Sicily
(Ufficio Storico, Roma)

Savoia Marchetti SM79 torpedo-bombers approach the convoy
(Ufficio Storico, Roma)

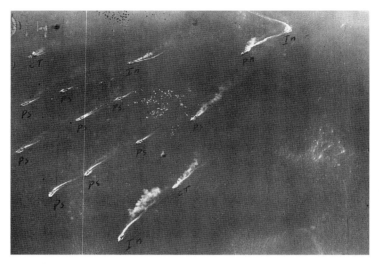

An Italian aerial reconnaissance photograph of the convoy and escort, August *12th*
(*Imperial War Museum, London*)

A squadron of Italian Sm.79 torpedo-bombers from the 132 *Stormo* approach the
convoy which can be seen in the distance
(*Imperial War Museum, London*)

Italian Sm.79 torpedo-bomber of 132 *Stormo* seen approaching the convoy to
make a low-level torpedo drop
(*Imperial War Museum, London*)

The destroyer H.M.S. *Foresight* seen from a sister ship under torpedo-bomber attack
(*Ufficio Storico, Roma*)

A Junkers Ju 87D dive-bomber over the Mediterranean coastline
(National Archives, Washington)

A Ju 88 escorting an Italian cruiser
(Hanfried Schliephake)

Heinkel 111T on a Sicilian airstrip
(Franz Selinger)

Sea Hurricanes aboard *Indomitable* during the battle
(Arthur Lawson)

The ordeal of *Indomitable*
(Arthur Lawson)

Indomitable's forward starboard guns receive a direct hit
(Arthur Lawson)

XIV

Indomitable sailing through a hail of bombs
(Imperial War Museum)

Indomitable lies enshrouded in a pall of her own smoke
(Arthur Lawson)

Ohio receives what should have been her death blow
(Cdr C. C. Crill)

The Italian submarine *Axum*
(Ufficio Storico, Roma)

The Italian E-boat *MASS 563*
(Ufficio Storico, Roma)

Nigeria after the torpedo attack in the Narrows
(Admiral Burrough)

The Merchantmen under attack
(Ufficio Storico, Roma)

The final blows
(Ufficio Storico, Roma)

SM79's circle the funeral pyre of several proud ships *(Ufficio Storico, Roma)*

XVIII

The damaged *Kenya* under heavy air attack
(Cdr C. C. Crill)

Kenya in dry-dock *(Cdr C. C. Crill)*

Port Chalmers arrives at Malta
(Imperial War Museum)

Brisbane Star limps in
(Imperial War Museum)

The *Melbourne Star* safely in
(Imperial War Museum)

The welcome given to the *Rochester Castle* as she entered Grand Harbour
(*Lieutenant H. E. Cook*)

The *Rochester Castle* unloads her precious cargo
(*Imperial War Museum*)

Two of the ships of the convoy busy discharging the invaluable cargoes into
lighters alongside during Operation *Ceres*
(*Imperial War Museum, London*)

Operation *Ceres*. All the stops were pulled out to unload the valuable cargoes
from the ships that got through before the Luftwaffe returned to destroy them.
Amazingly no attempts were made by the Axis to disrupt this vital work
(*Imperial War Museum, London*)

Nursed along by the two of the British destroyers which had fought so hard to save her, H.M.S. *Penn* (left) and H.M.S. *Bramham* (right), the tanker *Ohio*, barely afloat, approaches the entrance to Grand Harbour, Valetta, with an Admiralty tug in attendance astern (right) (*Imperial War Museum, London*)

The damaged tanker *OHIO* being 'nursed' into harbour
(*Sgt. Deakin*)

The *Ohio* never sailed again, but her badly-damaged hulk was used as an floating accommodation base for light forces at Malta in the years that followed. She is seen in that, still-useful, role in October, 1943, surrounded by corvettes, minesweepers and boom defence vessels. The Allied invasions of Sicily and then Italy had made Malta a backwater, events only made possible by the heroic efforts of this tanker, which the media, typically, labelled "The ship that wouldn't die!"
(*Imperial War Museum, London*)

the submarine *Axum* (Tenente di Vascello Renato Ferrini). The *Axum* had actually sighted the convoy much earlier. She had left Cagliari on the 11th and taken up her operational area some 25 miles north-west of Cape Bon, early on the 12th. At 6.21 pm in position 37°37'N, 10°21'E, she sighted a dark object at a great distance which she took to be a steamer or a tanker. Ferrini decided to submerge and approach it to identify. As he drew nearer he could see two columns of smoke from the east. He was submerged at 20 metres and continued to approach the contact.

At 7.27 he had closed to within 8,000 metres of his target and he risked a look through his periscope. Satisfied that it was indeed the convoy he adopted the same course and speed and tailed it to assess its strength. Although the convoy twice changed course he was able to maintain his position parallel to it and studied it carefully.

Ferrini logged that it comprised fifteen steamers, two cruisers and numerous destroyers. They appeared to be steaming in three lines or a wedge-shaped formation, with the merchantmen in three lines with two cruisers leading the centre and with the destroyers scattered around in an outer line. The sea was calm and visibility good. At 7.37 he had closed to within 4,000 metres estimating the convoy speed at 13 knots and he turned to attack.

Ferrini checked his target. At close range was the cruiser of the second line, overlapping her ahead and astern was a destroyer [actually the *Cairo*], and a large steamer. 7.55 pm! He launched all his bow torpedoes, firing tubes 1, 4, 3 and 2, in that order; 1 and 2 were set straight and 3 and 4 with a set angle to overlap. The distance to the first line of ships he had estimated to be 1,300 metres and the cruiser 1,800 metres.

After 63 seconds Ferrini heard the first explosion and at 90 seconds two more close by. The latter of these he deduced to have sunk the cruiser and the other the second ship in the line. After four and a half minutes depth charging began. A minute after he had fired the darkening sky was lit up by a succession of flashes and explosions as every torpedo hit home.

This attack, carried out in position 37°40'N, 10°06'E, hit Force X with the suddenness of a thunderbolt.

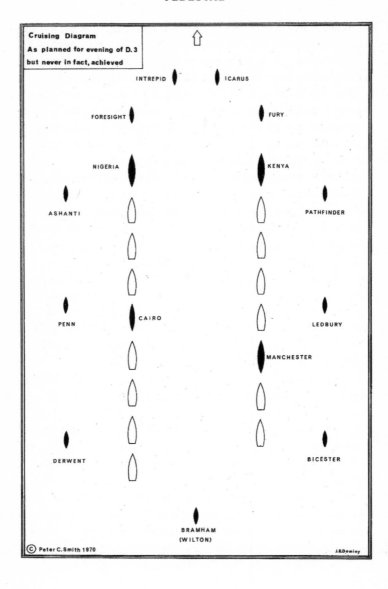

Cruising Diagram
As planned for evening of D. 3
but never in fact, achieved

INTREPID   ICARUS

FORESIGHT   FURY

NIGERIA   KENYA

ASHANTI   PATHFINDER

PENN   CAIRO   LEDBURY

MANCHESTER

DERWENT   BICESTER

BRAMHAM
(WILTON)

© Peter C. Smith 1970   J.R.Dominy

Rear-Admiral Burrough's flagship *Nigeria*, the anti-aircraft ship *Cairo*, and the vital solitary tanker *Ohio* were all struck by this brilliant salvo and all three slewed to a halt, throwing the hitherto orderly lines of the convoy into some considerable confusion.

The *Nigeria* leading the port-wing column was the first to be hit. She was travelling at fourteen knots when she was struck on the port side, abreast the foremast and below the platform deck. Severe structural damage between her keel and upper deck extended along her port side for some 40 feet. The side armour was heavily damaged and all compartments near the impact, including the forward boiler rooms, were flooded to lower deck level. Casualties were heavy, four officers and 48 men killed plus two seriously injured. H. J. Chester was range-taker in the starboard HA director:

> The convoy was reforming and *Cairo*, *Nigeria* and *Ohio* happened at that moment to be in line diagonally so we were all hit at the same time. Our hit was on the port side abreast the forward funnel.

Bad as the damage and casualties were it was the loss of the only ships fitted out for fighter control that was to prove the biggest enemy gain from this attack. J. F. Bleasdale made this point to me:

> I was the naval Fighter Direction Officer seconded to the *Nigeria* for the operation. The RAF insisted on seconding one of their controllers as well – a charming little chap called John Kemp – fearing that a naval type would vector their Spits or Beaus into mid-Med until they ran out of juice.
>
> As it happened some Beaufighters from Malta had just got within VHF range as I was pressing the tit to call them when the torpedo hit *Nigeria* and all the electrics went off so contact was never established. How different things might have been if *Axum* had been less accurate in her attack … or less lucky, for it is fantastic to get four hits in a spread of four.

The stricken cruiser at once assumed a list to port of fifteen degrees, which rapidly increased to seventeen degrees, and she circled painfully to port. All the electrical power failed for three minutes and the steering gear jammed. Small fires broke out in the

ERAs' mess, which were quickly brought under control. Swift action by counter-flooding brought the ship's heel down to four degrees and within fourteen minutes she was under control.

She had been severely damaged, however. The lower steering position, the 6-inch main armament T/S, switchboards and telegraph exchange, 1 and 2 transmitting rooms were all out of action. The 6-inch and the 4-inch guns were still workable but only by local control. Eventually a speed of sixteen knots was achieved using the two outer shafts. Clearly *Nigeria* could not carry on to Malta in this condition and Rear-Admiral Burrough and his staff reluctantly decided that they must leave her.

The destroyers *Ashanti*, *Bicester* and *Wilton* had closed her as soon as she had been hit and at 8.15 pm Rear-Admiral Burrough transferred to the *Ashanti*, sending his damaged flagship back to Gibraltar escorted by the two 'Hunts', *Wilton* and *Bicester*; Admiral Burrough later recalled that it was 'an unpleasant experience to have to leave my crippled flagship, but it was made easier by my grand company of officers and men who showed me in no uncertain fashion that they were as fully alive as I was where my duty lay'.

> I had a hell of a time getting alongside *Nigeria* [wrote the captain of *Ashanti*, Richard Onslow], as her engines were still going slow ahead and her rudder was jammed hard-a-port, so she was steaming in a circle with me chasing her on the outside edge. Eventually we managed to disembark Rear-Admiral Burrough and some of his staff; we had served with him in the Arctic and already greatly admired him.

The other cruiser victim, the *Cairo*, had been moving at eight knots when two of *Axum*'s torpedoes slammed into her port side right aft. The ship's stern, including the port propeller, was blown off, the after 4-inch gun being tossed right over and finishing up with its barrel buried in the quarterdeck. She lost way at once and settled by the stern with a slight heel to starboard and the upper deck was soon awash up to the after superstructure. Some flooding occurred in the machinery spaces and the after compartments.

The ship seemed obviously doomed, the starboard engine being

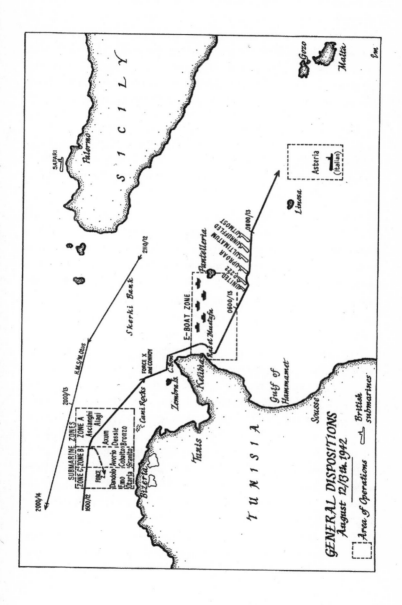

GENERAL DISPOSITIONS
August 12/13th. 1942

- - - Area of Operations
⌐ British submarines

unserviceable. No ships could be made available to tow her back to Gibraltar as losses were already beginning to mount and an air attack was impending. Twenty-three of her crew were lost and the wounded numbered two. These, and the remaining survivors, were taken off by the two 'Hunts'. The destroyer *Pathfinder* was then instructed to sink her. This proved to be a much more difficult job than one would have expected of a small 23-year-old vessel:

> *Cairo* lay quietly, with her stern deep in the water [wrote an eyewitness aboard *Pathfinder*]. Her bows were riding high. We must obviously sink her and rejoin the convoy again as quickly as possible, so we chose what seemed the quickest way of carrying out our thankless task.

The destroyer fired four torpedoes, one at a time, of which the first three missed the stationary target. This was due to a fault in their steering mechanism and gave them some food for thought as to what would have resulted had they fired them in desperation at enemy cruisers. The fourth torpedo hit the little ship under the bridge. 'But as the smoke cleared we saw that the only visible result of this was to bring her bows down and her stern up and she was now floating on an even keel again.'

Not wishing to waste any further torpedoes Commander Gibbs then steamed his destroyer close past the cruiser and dropped a depth-charge pattern hoping to blow in her hull under water. But still the little old lady refused to go down. The destroyer *Derwent* now appeared and closed them. *Pathfinder* sped off after the convoy and *Derwent* finally disposed of *Cairo* by gunfire before hastening off westward to reinforce *Nigeria*'s escort back to Gibraltar.[1]

The third victim of Ferrini's attack, the *Ohio*, was struck level with the pump-room. The deck on the port side was ripped and laid open back to the centre-line and a column of flame shot up to masthead height as her cargo ignited. The pump-room became a shambles and was laid open to the sea. The main steering gear telemotor pipes were wrecked and the lids of the kerosene tanks

---

[1] *Cairo* was a 4,290-ton cruiser of the 'Capetown' class built by Carnmell, Laird in 1918. They should be proud of their workmanship.

were blown off and buckled. The fire spread rapidly, the engines were stopped and the men brought up from the engine-room.

Chief Petty Officer Murphy, Rear-Admiral Burrough's steward, was at action stations on the bridge of the *Nigeria* and described the tanker at this time as a burning inferno; the heat could actually be felt aboard the *Nigeria*, it was so intense.

The torpedo had punched a hole 24 feet by 27 in *Ohio*'s side amidships and through this gaping aperture poured the sea. Ironically this proved far more effective in quenching the flames than the foam extinguishers and by 8.15 the fires were brought under control.

The young naval gunner aboard the *Ohio* later recorded these events in a letter to his wife thus:

The main portion of the fleet had just left us when three terrific explosions took place – the first on the *Nigeria*, second *Cairo* and the third us. We had been tin-fished aft of the bridge and were on fire. A rush was made for the boats expecting that the ship would go up any second. The skipper ordered the crew to stand fast and endeavour to put out the fire. This was accomplished. In the meantime one of the boats had been lowered and capsized, two gunners and two stewards being lost. We then had another terrific air attack in the closing light of day. The convoy had split up, the merchant ships and cruiser *Manchester* being grouped together, the other naval vessels in attendance on crippled cruisers, our ship being on her own the engines stopped. In this engagement three ships were blown up, how any others survived I cannot yet imagine. After about an hour we managed to get the engines started being escorted by one destroyer, which led us through the Straits off Pantelleria at a speed of 17 knots.

The convoy had become very strung out due to the confusion caused by the submarine attack. The *Brisbane Star*, astern of the *Ohio* when that ship was hit, had to reverse her engines to avoid a collision. On the bridge of the minesweeping destroyer *Intrepid* Commander E. A. de W. Kitcat received a decoded signal, which instructed him to leave the convoy!

Fortunately Commander Kitcat had the good sense to interpret it as *lead* the convoy – and with *Icarus* and *Fury*, the other ships fitted for minesweeping, set her TSDS at 40 foot depth and took up position ahead of the leading vessels. This clumsy equipment was the bane of the destroyer skippers whose ships were equipped with it, added to which the path it actually swept was quite narrow and it was easily carried away by any violent manoeuvre of the ship. *Intrepid* now steered the remains of the convoy towards the narrowest part of the channel and through the gap of the Cape Bon-Kelibia Light area. Her accuracy in penetrating this difficult route was due in no small way to Lieutenant-Commander J. T. Powell, RN, who had been lent to *Intrepid* from the Staff of Rear-Admiral (D) Home Fleet, especially for this task.

The Senior Engineering Officer aboard *Kenya* was Commander (E) C. G. Crill. He describes what the tensions of such prolonged action had on the men who were always below the waterline.

> My action station was the after engine-room but my duties involved regular visits to all the machinery spaces. *Kenya* was an exceptionally happy ship and in action this showed. Determination prevailed.
>
> *Ohio* was hit as the heavy escort left us and I well remember, as Senior Engineer, going round the machinery spaces at about 2015 to see how the incoming watch were, most of them having seen *Nigeria*, *Cairo* and *Ohio* hit presumably by the same submarine, a few minutes before they themselves came on watch. One of my chief stokers had a terrible twitch, poor man, but he stuck it like everyone else.
>
> When *Nigeria* was hit and turned back for Gib, Rear-Admiral Burrough and staff transferred to *Ashanti*. In *Kenya* we thought he was wrong not to come to us because *Ashanti* did not have adequate radio communication equipment. Later that night the Commodore of the convoy suggested to *Kenya*'s Captain A. S. Russell, that the convoy should turn back, so many ships were being sunk: our captain's reply

was simply, 'The convoy will carry on to Malta.' At that time Admiral Burrough was out of touch and we always felt that Alf Russell had saved the operation.

During the middle watch I heard the torpedo strike *Manchester*, in her after engine-room: had we not had our bows, and consequently paravanes, torpedoed, we would have been in the lead and would have been hit in her place.

By this time Vice-Admiral Syfret was well to the westward of the convoy, but on learning of the damage to the *Nigeria* and *Cairo* he at once despatched the *Charybdis*, *Eskimo* and *Somali* to reinforce the depleted escort; at 10.15 these vessels passed *Nigeria*'s group at high speed on opposite course.[1]

Meanwhile immediately after the submarine attack the convoy was edging away to starboard, away from the general direction whence the torpedoes had been launched; without their two column leaders and with several of their guiding destroyers busy astern with rescue work, the two lines of merchant vessels naturally began to lose some of their order. Liaison officers aboard some of the merchantmen later described the convoy in their reports as being very badly dispersed. Vice-Admiral Syfret subsequently described this opinion as exaggerated, but be that as it may there can be no doubt that there was considerable lack of cohesion at this time and it was due to this that, around 8.35 pm, the day's final air strike found them still some twenty miles west of the Skerki Bank. The *Ashanti* had by this time caught up with the tail-end of the convoy and, together with the *Penn*, had attempted to shield her charges before the attack started by laying a smoke screen, but this was insufficient to prevent the Axis airmen from scoring several successes.

Their timing was perfect; the elongated lines of the convoy were caught silhouetted against the final light on the western horizon. The 30 Junkers Ju88A-4s and the seven supporting Heinkel 111H-6 torpedo-bombers, each of which was carrying two 1,686-pound

[1] Failure to similarly reinforce the close escort during 'Harpoon' had been said to have contributed to its partial failure. This lesson had obviously been appreciated by Syfret but unfortunately *Charybdis* was only an AA cruiser whose heaviest guns, 4.5-inch, were no match for the Italian 6-inch and 8-inch cruisers, had it come to the test.

LTF5b torpedoes, were, by contrast, indistinct blurs as they filtered in from the north-east at 8.38 pm.

Such conditions were ideal for the torpedo-bomber crews and the pilot of II/KG.26 made very good use of them as did the accompanying dive-bombers. In the Heinkels with which this unit was equipped, the torpedoes had to be released by the aircraft mechanic on instructions from the observer. This was a disadvantage as it caused a slight time lag during which conditions might change. The torpedo had to be released at least 600 metres from the target and flying at this distance from the objective and at a height of 40–50 metres, the aircraft had not time to turn before reaching the target. The usual tactic was therefore to go down to sea level and to turn only after having flown past the bows or stern of the ship. At such times the aircraft were extremely vulnerable and so it was with great delight that they found the merchantmen lumbering along in effect unprotected. The six patrolling Beaufighters of 248 Squadron from Malta had just a few minutes earlier returned to their base after failing to make wireless contact with the convoy. According to their report they had tried VHF at first to make contact but had to abandon this as the fighter-direction ships had gone. They had then tried High-Frequency but this too proved unsatisfactory. W/T was also used without success; the ships would not answer. Fired on by the convoy and without direction there was little they could do so they withdrew. No sooner had they disappeared than the German bomber groups arrived.

The Luftwaffe pilots took this heaven-sent opportunity and made the best of it. The *Ohio* had shored up her damaged keel and restarted her engines, but it was then found that she could only manoeuvre sluggishly in circles. Eventually a hand-rigged steering position was set up aft and at 8.30 she again started to move at seven knots. The compass and gyros were unserviceable and it was with some relief that Captain Mason sighted the *Ashanti* with Rear-Admiral Burrough aboard closing from astern.

> *Ashanti*, after a lovely bit of bomb and torpedo dodging at full speed, closed the damaged *Ohio* [wrote Captain Onslow later]. During this action a very near miss also caused a

blowback in one of our boilers while we were at full speed and a dangerous fire developed in the boiler-room. The Chief, K. M. Symonds, arrived on the bridge in the middle of the battle to report that there was a serious fire in the boiler-rooms. My First Lieutenant, E. A. S. Bailey, told me that I replied 'Thank you, Chief; put it out please'. Half an hour later, covered in smoke and oil, soaked in sweat, and his overalls singed and burnt away in places, he arrived again on the bridge to report that the fire was out. I am reputed to have replied 'What fire?' I do remember we were rather busy. Tony Kimmins, aboard to report for the BBC, was hanging about and getting underfoot on the bridge, so Bailey put him in charge of an Oerlikon gun on the lower bridge where he thoroughly enjoyed himself.

On coming alongside, Burrough asked Mason if he required a tow, to which the tanker's skipper was able to reply in the negative, but he did ask for a guide ship to lead them through the Narrows as he was now far astern of the lead group; soon the destroyer *Ledbury* (Lieutenant-Commander R. P. Hill) made contact. She rigged up a blue signal lamp on her stern post and by following this the tanker soon began to catch up with the remainder of the convoy.

Her crew were still valiantly fighting the fires when the first bombers arrived and she was near-missed but not seriously damaged. Four of her crew were already missing. Two Army gunners, W. Hands and E. Smith, went to their allocated lifeboat positions and they were joined in the boat by an assistant steward, Mr R. V. Morton-who had been manning a Browning machinegun on the boat deck-and by a young galley boy, M. Guidotti. Before they realised what was happening and that the ship was not in fact immediately sinking, the boat was tipped up throwing them all into the water. Hands, who could not swim, was saved by Guidotti who kept him afloat. Happily the destroyer *Bicester*, searching for any of *Nigeria*'s crew who might have been lost overboard, found them soon after and picked them up. Their absence was not noticed aboard *Ohio* until the following day.

The bombers attacked in pairs and singly for over half an hour and many ships had close shaves.

The signal to form two columns was still flying when the air attack commenced from the port side. Lieutenant-Commander Hill took his ship through the convoy to the engaged side, but was still between the columns when the attack developed. *Ledbury* engaged torpedo-bombers on two separate occasions but failed to deter them from making good attacks and each plane managed to drop two torpedoes. The minesweeping destroyer *Icarus* sighted a torpedo approaching from the starboard beam; the helm was put hard over and full speed was rung down. She leapt ahead and the torpedo track crossed her wake mere feet astern. Others were not so fortunate.

The *Empire Hope* seemed to have been singled out for special attention and, during the following thirty minutes, no less than eighteen near-misses were counted around the vessel. Her Master, Captain Gwilym Williams, had commanded her since her completion and he steered her brilliantly through these vicious attacks while her crew fought back as best they could. Then at last her engines were disabled after an attack which blew a fifteen-foot hole in the ship's side and she slowed to a stop. The stationary vessel drew still more bombers and attack followed attack. Many of her gunners were wounded and injured by the blast of the bombs – and some were actually blown overboard from their gun-pits. Her luck finally ran out at 8.50 when the after part of the ship was struck by two direct hits.

No 4 hold, which contained explosives, was pierced and the explosion and fire which followed rapidly spread to the bridge deck where it ignited the high-octane spirit stowed there. Soon the whole after part of the ship was a raging inferno and Captain Williams decided to abandon her. Many of the ship's boats had been destroyed, while others were found to be half filled with coal blown into them when the bombs struck.

While lowering the motor boat it was found that the plug had become dislodged and it immediately began to fill. Without hesitation Cadet David McCallum slipped down a line into the sinking boat and fixed the plug. Subsequent bailing enabled it to be used in the rescue of several injured men. For this act McCallum was awarded the BEM.

The aviation spirit had cascaded over the ship and spread across the surrounding sea in a blazing curtain of flame. All the pumps were smashed and there was no alternative but to leave the ship. She turned in a wide circle well ablaze, her wheel jammed by the near misses earlier. Despite this all aboard got safely away including Captain Williams. They had pulled some four hundred yards clear of the ship when they heard shouts from her. On returning they found Second Officer Sendall searching for Captain Williams who he feared had stayed behind.

Soon after 9 pm the *Penn* (Lieutenant-Commander J. H. Swain) closed them and picked up all the crew before finally torpedoing the blazing ship as she pulled away. Captain Williams was awarded the DSC for the manner in which he handled his vessel – one of the first of such awards to a Merchant Navy officer. When *Penn* finally left, the *Empire Hope* was still burning furiously and apparently sinking.

A He 111 caught the *Brisbane Star* (Captain Frederick Neville Riley). The torpedo hit her stem, tearing a huge rent in her bows and blowing in her for'ard bulkheads. She started taking water and slid to a standstill. Under the inspiring leadership of her 46-year-old Master, her crew soon got to work and within twenty minutes had shored up her bulkheads and effected other repairs. The engine-room reported being able to steam at five and later at eight knots.

Commander Gibbs in *Pathfinder* closed her and they decided that at such a speed *Brisbane Star* would have no opportunity of rejoining the convoy. It was decided that her best bet was to head south and to try and make her way past Kelibia in the cover of Tunisian coastal waters. Trusting to luck that they would not be spotted, the helm was put over and she limped away in the darkness on her own.

Commander Gibbs increased speed to help other vessels. At 9.02 pm the German airmen scored another success and an aerial torpedo hit the ammunition ship *Clan Ferguson* (Captain Arthur Robert Cossar). She was steaming at fifteen knots approximately seven miles north of Zembra Island when a signalman on watch saw the torpedo approaching from the starboard and shouted for the helm to be put over. This was done but the ship did not respond quickly enough and she was hit. A colossal explosion took place, which led all that witnessed it to believe that she had blown up without survivors. The sheet of flame which followed set fire to the after part of the vessel and she began to rapidly settle by the stern. Many of the lifeboats were set on fire but most of the crew managed to get away on rafts, some using the steel helmets as paddles to get away from the blazing fuel on the sea. The Italian writer Bragadin in his account says she was 'abandoned by her escorts' but as can be seen that was just not true.

Aboard *Brisbane Star* young Officer Cadet Waine was in the thick of it:

Brisbane Star was torpedoed in attacks from starboard by Savoia Marchetti SM79s. I saw it happen. *Clan Ferguson* was hit around the same time as we were drifting with her and I remember her blazing and seeing men dying on her decks in the flames. *Empire Hope* had already gone and was a blazing hulk some distance away. We had to reverse at three knots to clear the *Clan Ferguson* and continued astern until damage was assessed and had problems clearing *Nigeria* and *Cairo* in the narrow swept channel.

The action around 9 pm in the narrows was a shambles and I have a clear mental picture of events which I recorded at the time. I am sure many other accounts were made up in retrospect so it is difficult to get a clear picture from the records. As my job was to observe and record from the bridge of the *Brisbane Star* I probably saw more than most people of the action. I also shot a film for the RN liaison officers and I had a very clear sequence of the Stuka demolition of *Indomitable* as it happened in the next column on our port beam. I never discovered whether their film survived the war or not.

Captain McFarlane was the strong man of the action and a fine gentleman and captain. It was a pity he died on his next voyage when the *Melbourne Star* was torpedoed in the West Indies on her way to Australia. I was intrigued to find that the German official time-scale for the action slipped a day from the British account. I always wondered how I lost a day in my private account but find it agrees with the

German. I still puzzle over that lost day.

Aboard one escorting cruiser an eyewitness, David Royale, described this horrific moment:

> The ss *Clan Ferguson* was steaming along – a fine-looking ship of around 12,000 tons, at approximately fourteen knots – following in our wake. I saw three Junkers Ju88s diving from astern but could not bring my gun to bear because of the training stops. In any case our after guns had opened up. They hit the leading aeroplane but not before he had let go his bombs, scoring direct hits. It was a sight I shall never forget (and Douglas Harding of GBN said, '… there will be men after this war with eyes that have seen too much'), one minute there was this fine vessel, the next a huge atomic-like explosion and she had gone, disappeared with just a blueish ring of flame on the water and a mushroom of smoke and flame thousands of feet into the sky. The other two Ju88s were caught in the blast and never reappeared, but that was a poor price to pay. Huge chunks of blasted ship splashed into the sea close to me, I thought some of the stern of *Charybdis* must have been struck. Actually only one of our crew was wounded by this rain of debris.

Watchers aboard the nearby *Waimarama* had seen firstly the *Empire Hope* struck by aerial missiles on their starboard beam, and then off their starboard bow the *Clan Ferguson* was likewise hit. Small wonder then they felt that enough was enough. An eyewitness recorded later:

> We hauled out of line after this. I saw a terrific burst of flame, half a mile high, shoot up into the air. I cannot imagine how any of her crew escaped but soon after we heard shouts in the water. We could not risk the ship going too near the flames and were obliged to proceed. I did not see any escort standing by her so do not think that there could have been any survivors from her. We continued at full speed keeping inside territorial waters to avoid mines laid outside. For a long time

the *Clan Ferguson* could be seen burning furiously and we saw several ships silhouetted by the light from her.

Despite the violence of the explosion many of her crew did in fact survive. Her Second Officer, Mr A. H. Black, gives a graphic description of those moments.

I could see the flames coming up from the engine-room skylight and the ship's side. The hatch covers were blown off No 4 hold and two landing craft stowed on top were also blown off. Of the ship's four lifeboats, No 3 boat was destroyed and all the others except No 1 boat caught fire. Three rafts were got away. There was a violent explosion in No 5 hold and the ship appeared to sink about seven minutes after being hit. The oil blazed on the water for 48 hours and petrol cans kept floating to the surface and catching fire, as did the oil, causing thick black smoke. In all 64 men got away and were eventually equally divided on the four rafts which drifted apart.[1]

A very gallant act was performed by Midshipman Allison, on his first voyage. Reaching a small raft, he pushed it along in front of him and helped several badly burnt men aboard. These he later transferred to a larger raft. Their blazing vessel drifted away leaving them alone save for the fading sounds of battle.

The *Wairangi* (Captain Richard Gordon) had lost control in what her master described later as 'the general confusion', and proceeded at her best speed alone. She too was attacked from the starboard by a Heinkel torpedo-bomber. The ship was swung hard to starboard and the two torpedoes missed astern. Soon afterwards she had to alter course to avoid the two blazing merchantmen.

The convoy was now in considerable disarray. The destroyer *Ledbury* sighted six ships on varying courses, mainly heading north-west. Lieutenant Hill at once swung his little destroyer round after them to herd them back on their correct course. The nearest ship proved to be the *Melbourne Star*, and she was overhauled and

---

[1] Even as late as 1959 she is recorded in some accounts as having been lost with all hands.

told to steer course 120 degrees, which she was in fact already about to do. One by one the other ships were overtaken and told to steer 120 degrees and that the Admiral was proceeding down the coast at slow speed waiting for them.

The *Dorset* (Captain Tuckett) had carried out several emergency turns to avoid air attacks and while under helm to avoid a damaged vessel had met the *Port Chalmers*. Captain Tuckett reported:

> Knowing the Convoy Commodore to be aboard I asked him for a course and speed. He told me he was returning to Gibraltar. I fell in astern but five minutes later, realising I did not wish to return, reversed course. *Melbourne Star* was in company and she also turned. We left the *Port Chalmers* steaming towards Gibraltar but she must have changed her mind later.

The liaison officer aboard the *Melbourne Star* stated that during the air raid and the bombing of two ships the vessel was 'headed off' and forced to turn round to port. The captain signalled the *Port Chalmers* for orders and received the reply 'Turn back'. Although the state of affairs at this time was in his opinion chaotic, the captain's view, from the time of the disaster, was a determination that the only thing to do was to head for Malta, and all the officers on the bridge were in agreement. The ship was on the point of turning round as soon as they had gained clear water when a destroyer came up and signalled 'Course 120 degrees' and they complied.

> To avoid mines seen dropping ahead, course was altered to starboard [the *Santa Elisa* (Captain T. Thompson) reported]. A destroyer hailed us and ordered us to steer 120 degrees. We joined up with two other stragglers but lost contact with all other ships.

Commodore Venables later recalled how this confusion came about:

> We were astern of the *Cairo* when she was hit. Our engines were put to full astern, and after getting clear we then proceeded to follow the convoy south. The burning ships

made visibility like daylight and after sighting a submarine to port I decided to try and save the ship by leaving the convoy from the rear. The ship proceeded at full speed to the westward. Two other ships were informed of my intentions and turned 16 points to follow me, they were not seen again, presumably because a destroyer found them and ordered them to rejoin the convoy. Another destroyer overtook me and gave instructions to proceed to Malta – which was my intention as soon as circumstances appeared favourable. Course was made towards the coast and then eastward.

This second destroyer was the *Bramham* who was overtaking the convoy astern. Her charge, the damaged *Deucalion*, had also fallen victim to the Luftwaffe many miles astern. At 7.46 pm two Junkers 88s had flown low over the Tunisian coastal hills, the dark background making them difficult to spot. The destroyer engaged them and they flew off after dropping a stick of bombs, two of which exploded 30 feet astern of the freighter, while another went off some 20 feet from her port bow.

After battling through this attack the *Deucalion* had reached a position some five miles from the Cani Rocks but she was destined to get no further towards her goal. Two Heinkels found both ships here at 9.15. They approached from the land side and by coasting in with their engines cut off out of the gloom they caught the two ships completely by surprise, no guns opening fire until it was too late. The first plane missed but the second, courageously gliding in at a height of only 50 feet, launched his torpedoes at a range of some 75 yards and both hit the steamer on the starboard quarter. No 6 hold, with its cargo of aviation spirit, at once exploded. She was plainly doomed and Captain Brown gave the order to abandon ship.

One of the naval gunners was trapped under a fallen life-raft badly wounded and unable to move. Although the ship threatened to explode beneath them at any moment, two of the midshipmen, J. Gregson and P. Bracewell, ran to his aid. Clearing away the debris they got the man clear, lowered him over the side and swam to the *Bramham* with him. This very brave action earned Gregson the Albert Medal, and later the George Cross, the highest civilian award for gallantry.

All the surviving crew were taken aboard the destroyer by which time the *Deucalion*'s decks were awash. Not wishing to attract the unwelcome attentions of Vichy patrols Lieutenant Baines hastened her end with a couple of depth-charges, the time being now 9.30 pm. The young destroyer skipper then swung the bows of his ship round to the east and hurried on to overtake the convoy.

The *Deucalion* was still blazing as they left but a big explosion not long afterwards probably marked the final end of this gallant vessel. To the east, the remainder of the convoy pressed on. The *Ohio* was finding it very difficult to hold course astern of *Ledbury* for the stern light of the destroyer was not visible from the tanker's after steering position and all directions concerning changes in course had to be passed via the one remaining intercom from the bridge amidships. Meantime the captain of the *Kenya*, sill unaware of the precise fate of Rear-Admiral Burrough, had signalled the convoy that he was assuming command. Burrough, on receipt of this signal, took *Ashanti* up through the shattered convoy to make contact with the head of the column. This now consisted of the three TSDS ships leading the two surviving cruisers, *Kenya* and *Manchester*, which Captain Russell had deployed as column leaders, while the *Pathfinder* and *Penn* were overtaking from astern after carrying out their rescue duties. Only a few merchantmen had managed to keep up with this squadron.

The *Glenorchy* had formed up with the *Almeria Lykes* astern the warship group during the air attack when *Kenya* had signalled for 13 knots and led off southward. But the other vessels were mainly out of touch; *Melbourne Star*'s captain confirms in his report the comment by the Naval liaison officer that the convoy was 'all scrummed up' when the air attack took place and after the ship had resumed her correct course she had found that she could see no escorts. Captain Macfarlane therefore hailed the *Santa Elisa*'s skipper and said: 'I'm going on to Malta, will you follow?' From the American freighter's bridge Captain Thompson had replied: 'Yes.'

Short and to the point! These two vessels were later joined by a third.

On his way up to the head of the column Rear-Admiral Burrough had had another narrow escape when, as related earlier,

Ashanti was attacked by a lone torpedo-bomber, the missile passing alongside the starboard bow of the destroyer, missing her by the smallest of margins. This was a fortunate let-off.

Perhaps not without some excuse, many of the merchantmen had thought themselves left to their own devices during the attack. The *Rochester Castle* had been straddled by two heavy bombs. Two frames in the engine-room were fractured and she started leaking. Fumes and cordite were drawn in by the engine-room fans, which almost made the machinery spaces uninhabitable. Despite this she battled on. She was some 400 yards astern of *Clan Ferguson* when that vessel was hit, but her own gunners were able to keep the enemy at a distance after that. Indeed *Rochester Castle*'s armament would have made many a destroyer captain envious. Apart from the usual useless 4.7-inch low-angle gun stuck aft, she had a 40-mm Bofors, no less than six Oerlikons, four light machine guns, four FAMs and a rocket gun firing 3-inch shells.

Her barrage defence, then, was impressive[1] and she was able to hold her general course towards Cape Bon. One of her engineers described the Skerki Channel as they entered it: the horizon was a mass of fire on water with destroyers standing by to pick up survivors.

The *Santa Elisa* had also been near-missed during the air raid. She was straddled by four bombs, which forced her to reduce speed. Among her complement was an Armed Guard party of United States Navy gunners under Ensign Gerhart Suppinger, and they very enthusiastically blazed away at everything that crossed their sights? By the time the air raid had died away Captain Thompson and his

[1] In fact none of the freighters of the convoy could be described as sitting ducks, as a list of some of the merchant ships' armaments makes clear:

Ohio. One 5-inch gun, one 3-inch, one 40-mm, six 20-mm. *Dorset*. One 4-inch, one 40-mm, six 20-mm, two depth charges.

Clan Ferguson. One 4-inch, two 40-mm, eight 20-mm.

Deucalion. One 4.7-inch, two 40-mm, six 20-mm, four depth charges.

Port Chalmers. One 4-inch, two 40-mm, six 20-mm.

Wairangi. One 6-inch, one 40-mm, six 20-mm, three depth charges.

Empire Hope. One 4.7-inch, one 40-mm, six 20-min, four depth charges.

Glenorchy. One 4-inch, two 40-mm, six 20-mm, three depth charges.

In addition all had numerous mountings of PAC rockets and FAM launchers, plus smaller weapons. Thus, although sometimes caught on their own, each ship, with a service team of gunners, could give some account of herself.

men found themselves out of touch with their convoy companions.

Commander Gibbs eventually contacted several of these vessels and formed them into single line ahead and set them at their best speed in an endeavour to close the gap between them and the warship group ahead.

The German airmen claimed to have sunk ten steamers and to have hit a cruiser in this attack. In truth they had only sunk three ships and damaged another seriously – still a good result in return for the loss of only one Junkers Ju88. They also reported the presence of a carrier, a small one, which was thought might be the *Unicorn*, with the convoy. Exactly why they made this assumption is unknown and anyway it was very soon discounted by German Air Intelligence.

As the leading group of the convoy approached the narrow neck of the channel they crossed the path of yet another Italian submarine. This was the *Alagi* (Tenente di Vascello Sergio Puccini). She had entered her patrol zone at 4 am that morning and ever since nine o'clock had heard the sounds of battle steadily drawing nearer to her. Two of her forward torpedo tubes were causing trouble and were not ready for use but towards evening they were repaired and she moved south to intercept. At eight o'clock Puccini made out a column of smoke through his periscope and closed towards it. This was probably the blazing *Ohio* but before Puccini could get near enough to his target the German bombers arrived and he had to sit back and witness their attack.

He recorded that the convoy took violent avoiding action and steered south. At 8.20 pm he claimed to have seen a destroyer struck by a bomb. He continued to observe, manoeuvring the *Alagi* to match the alterations in course of the bulk of the convoy. He could distinguish a cruiser of the 'Southampton' type–the *Manchester* in fact – leading the force, which seemed to be reforming at a range of 8–10,000 metres. Then the air attacks resumed again.

As he watched and waited he saw two steamers set on fire and a destroyer closing to help them. A stick of bombs fell close to these ships and another destroyer appeared to be hit on the stern and turned away. He also noted a heavily damaged cruiser close by – presumably either *Nigeria* or *Cairo*. The leading steamer was forced to slow down while the surviving vessels regrouped.

Now the force was approaching his position. Puccini fired a four-torpedo salvo at a range of 1,500–2,000 metres at the nearest big ship, the *Kenya*. Even as he fired his submarine was spotted both by *Port Chalmers* and by a vigilant lookout on the *Kenya*'s bridge and her helm was put hard over. The latter action probably saved the cruiser for the four torpedoes would almost certainly have torn her apart.

There had been no radar sighting from any of the other escorts. The *Kenya*'s violent avoiding action was almost a success. Three of Puccini's shots missed, two passing astern while another ran under the bridge without striking.

The fourth hit the ship near the stem and forefoot, and caused some damage between the keel and lower deck forward of, and including, No 6 bulkhead, which was destroyed. Severe damage from the keel to the upper deck extended aft as far as No 11 bulkhead. She had been moving at fourteen knots when struck and flooding occurred in all her for'ard compartments up to the waterline and her echo-sounding equipment was put out of action by the shock of the explosion.

It was now 9.12 and events were occurring with startling rapidity. The convoy itself was in unknown chaos and confusion.

Kenya, despite her damage, was able to maintain the convoy speed and soon rejoined *Manchester* ahead, where they were eventually joined by *Ashanti* and, a little later, by *Pathfinder*. Commander Gibbs reported to Rear-Admiral Burrough that the main group of merchant ships was some way astern and without protection. Rear-Admiral Burrough therefore sent the *Pathfinder* back to round them up.

The *Alagi* escaped without further trouble and Puccini was able to report hitting a cruiser and a merchant ship, but no freighter was hit at this time. At 10.13 pm the *Alagi* surfaced and transmitted a sighting report. 'On the horizon from 180 degrees around to 240 degrees we could see a continuous line of ships on fire at a distance of between 5–6,000 metres, Puccini recorded.

Isolated groups of ships kept going. The *Wairangi* had contacted the *Almeria Lykes* which took station astern and this little procession became three in number when the *Wairangi*'s sister-ship, the *Waimarama*, sighted them. At 10.20 she slipped in between them and in single line ahead they pressed on.

The *Ohio*, too, was making good progress. There was a slight panic when they approached the burning hulk of *Clan Ferguson*. Many of the tanker's compartments were open to the sea, which was ablaze with burning oil-fuel, but the *Ledbury* steered them well clear of the spreading pool of fire. Lit up as she was by this the *Ohio* had a lucky escape. It was at 11.48 pm, shortly after the tanker had passed by, that the submarine *Bronzo* (Tenente di Vascello Cesare Buldrini) sighted the drifting *Clan Ferguson* and sent her to the bottom with a torpedo which blew her bows off. A little earlier and the *Ohio*'s spectacular story would have had a premature end.

In this extended 'formation', the convoy rounded Cape Bon at 11.54 where the E-boat squadrons waited.

II

The formation now consisted of the leading warship group following the minesweeper destroyers. Only a few of the merchant vessels had kept up with this group, the *Glenorchy*, *Almeria Lykes* and *Wairangi*. Most of the other merchant vessels were strung out behind this group with only the *Pathfinder* as escort; these included the *Melbourne Star*, *Waimarama*, *Santa Elisa*, *Dorset* and *Rochester Castle*; astern of these were the *Ohio* and *Ledbury*, and still further astern lay *Port Chalmers* and *Penn*; *Brisbane Star* was picking her own route close in to the Tunisian coast. When the E-boats first made contact it was with the main warship force, which gave the merchantmen a short respite.

Half an hour after midnight these leading warships picked up the blips of small craft on their radar-screens and, as they did so, the E-boats[1] started their engines and fired the torpedoes at the leading vessels. A heavy fire with all guns was laid down to port by the convoy's escort and the ships turned to port to comb the

[1] The term 'E-boat' is used throughout the book to denote motor-torpedo craft of both the Italian and German navies, in order to distinguish them from British MTBs and so on.

torpedo tracks. These attacks were made by the boats of the Italian 18th Squadron, one of which, *Mas.556* (Tenente di Vascello Luigi Sala), claimed a hit. As they turned away they laid smoke to cover their withdrawal.

Soon they were skimming in again and a continuous running battle developed which lasted until past the Kelibia Light. Although the sea seemed to be covered by the tracks of numerous torpedoes, none struck home during the first series of attacks. Likewise the E-boats escaped without loss; although VHF transmissions between them were picked up by the *Ashanti*, which suggested they were receiving damage, none were in fact ever sunk by gunfire from convoy or escort.

They did, however, find these targets at the head of the convoy too well able to defend themselves for their liking and they slid back along the line where they soon found the isolated bodies of freighters plodding along.

The first German boat to deliver an attack was the *S.59* (Oberleutnant zur See Albert Muller) operating independently some five miles north-north-east of Cape Bon. He reported an attack in position 37°14'N, 11°06'E and claimed to have hit a 15,000-GRT tanker with two torpedoes and set her on fire. It is not certain which vessel he attacked but no ship was hit at the time claimed in this area.

Some two minutes later, south of Kelibia itself, the Italian boats *Ms. 16* (Capitano di Corvetta Giogio Manuti) and *Ms. 22* (Sottotenente di Vascello Franco Mezzadra) sighted the convoy close to Ras Mustafa. The *Ms. 16* made an attack at 1.04 firing her starboard torpedo at a cruiser at 800 metres' range, but due to a fault in the stabilising gear of the torpedo, it porpoised after launch and ran wide.

A further embarrassment to the convoy and escort was provided by the navigation lights off Cape Bon and Kelibia. Tunisia being neutral, these powerful beams were working as in peacetime, shining with a pitiless glare on British and Axis ships alike. The master of the *Almeria Lykes* reported that the revolving beam at Cape Bon was sufficiently powerful to illuminate and silhouette any ship passing within ten miles of the shore.

Rocky Royale aboard *Charybdis* was among many thousand Allied seamen who cursed these evil Vichy-French beacons that only aided the Axis attackers.

> The Kelibia light was to cost us dear. It was the lighthouse on the North African coast at the Narrows. It revolved steadily casting a huge shaft of light far out to sea and illuminating the ships of our force and the convoy alike to the enemy gaze. It made *Manchester* and other ships easy targets. As *Charybdis* entered the Narrows our Gunnery Officer, John Rusher (what a skilful gunner he was), asked our Skipper for permission to open fire on it. He saw the danger, but our Skipper had to say no-it was an International Light. No doubt the enemy would have thought differently. It was here then that we expected, quite correctly as it turned out, the E-boat attacks. We could actually hear the roaring of their engines, and, if I say it myself, our barrage of fire must have been awesome because radar showed them wheeling away en masse. This also meant, of course, that we had to turn towards them to comb their torpedoes which had obviously been launched beforehand. I would add here that this was another occasion when we were glad to have the 4.5-inch guns and not the 5.25-inch, because our rate of fire was so superior at close range.

At 1.07 the *Ms. 16* had worked round to another favourable firing position and she fired her port torpedo against another cruiser target. The *Ms. 22* also fired her torpedoes at the same ship. Tense seconds later the stern of the ship was lit up by vivid red-orange flame and flash. Their victim was the only undamaged cruiser of the escort, the *Manchester* (Captain H. Drew, DSC).

The two Italian boats were undetected until they suddenly emerged less than a hundred yards to starboard and very bravely drove in even closer before firing their torpedoes.[1] The British vessel turned sharply to meet them, firing full salvoes from her two

---

[1] An explanation for the surprise they achieved may lie in the fact that 'Pedestal' was passing the wreck of the *Havock*, which had run aground some months before and was clearly visible at 1 am. It is therefore probable that the two E-boats were hidden behind this wreck as the convoy approached them.

forward triple 6-inch turrets as she did so, but miraculously the two frail speeding boats were unscathed. The torpedo crashed home on the racing cruiser abreast the after engine-room on the starboard side, killing instantly an officer and twelve ratings. The jubilant E-boats later reported that they had blown her stern off.

The cruiser had up to then been giving as good as she had got in repelling E-boat attacks, as Bill Stroud told me:

'A' and 'B' turrets were the attacking guns and had been firing rapid salvoes to split them up as they came at us time and time again. Then two of them came from nowhere down our starboard side. On being illuminated by our own ships and heavily engaged they promptly fired their torpedoes at point-blank range and retreated into darkness at full speed. Until then we had come through unscathed despite near misses from both bombs and torpedoes.

G. V. Towell later remembered:

I was just trying to get a bit of shuteye when the ship gave one almighty lurch, and I could hear a deadly crunching sound, and that filthy smell of cordite. She listed badly to starboard, but stayed there, thank God.

One of the Royal Marine guns crews at the time was Ernest Hodgson. He was actually the lookout on the *Manchester*'s starboard gun deck.

I actually saw the two torpedo tracks coming at our starboard side and I reported this to the bridge, receiving the reply that they had spotted them also. I knew it was already too late to avoid them and just stood there helpless, knowing that there was absolutely nothing I could do in the few second left and no place I could go. Almost immediately there was an enormous bang and brilliant flashes and flame in the darkness and I was thrown off balance by the concussion. Both torpedoes hit us on our starboard side and the ship listed at once.

Watching the missiles streaking towards you out of the night was bad enough, below decks the bedlam of the previous day's fighting was worse, especially after the earlier torpedoings. Leading Stoker Albert Slater recalled:

> The first explosion plunged the engine-room into darkness and the second flung me from the platform on which I was standing. Only an uprush of water prevented me breaking my back in a fall to the engine-room floor. Then rising water carried me up towards the ceiling. I gave up all hope, waiting for the moment when the water should finally fill the entire engine-room. But suddenly the water ceased rising only a few feet from the ceiling. Then steam spread in a scalding cloud.

Despite this Slater struggled to the hatch and was dragged through to safety.

Bill Stroud again:

> The ship was now stopped, engine-room and boiler-rooms were flooded or on fire and the men on watch were helping fight the flames and rescue the engine-room survivors. All lights and power had failed but my turret was still operational by percussion firing until the training seized up and we were taking on a heavy list.

'Mac' McDonald dictated to me a graphic account of these moments which included this confirmation of the above.

> The first thing that happened was that all the lights went out. Fortunately there was no panic. Volunteers were called for to get the engine-room's crew out. Then we were all mustered on the upper deck. Captain Drew then told us as near as I can remember, 'She will do 2 to 2½ knots, she can answer the helm, sometimes.'

The engine-room and after boiler-room, oil fuel tanks and 4-inch ammunition magazines flooded at once. Two dynamos were put out of action and all lighting failed. Only the port outer shaft was in operation and the stricken vessel turned in a slow circle before coming to a halt. She was immobilised with a twelve-degree list to starboard, but after emergency power was supplied this was gradually reduced to about five degrees by counter-flooding.

Once more the sudden enemy success unnerved the merchantmen. *Wairangi* and *Almeria Lykes* had become separated earlier but the latter had independently made contact with the warship group and fallen in astern of the *Manchester*, the American vessel finding herself leading the British *Glenorchy*.

When the *Manchester* was hit [Mr Skelling of the *Glenorchy* recalled] we both followed her round thinking she was taking avoiding action. She must have warned the *Almeria Lykes* [that she had been hit], and she suddenly went hard to port across our bows. We rang down for full astern and avoided a collision.

Aboard the American ship the captain turned to the British liaison officer and said: 'Let's get to hell out of this!' Lieutenant-Commander Mitchell agreed. The *Almeria Lykes* moved out a mile to seaward; the *Glenorchy* on the other hand pressed on along her original course looking for the *Kenya*.

Astern of these two was the *Waimarama* and she also nearly ran full tilt into the *Manchester*. Her helm was put hard to port and they missed her by yards. It was an hour before they again sighted an escort.

Melbourne Star had earlier sighted the *Pathfinder* and had asked Commander Gibbs if he could follow him. Receiving an affirmative Captain Macfarlane had formed his little group of three vessels astern of the destroyer. At 1.40, close in to the Tunisian coast, four miles off Kelibia and in front of a minefield, *Pathfinder* – busily shepherding her little flock along – came across the damaged *Manchester*. As the destroyer turned in towards the cruiser the *Melbourne Star* led round to follow but the destroyer flashed to her to carry on and the three merchant ships, again on their own, continued off south of the minefields.

The two warship captains then held a shouted conversation, bridge to bridge. Captain Drew of *Manchester* felt hopeful that he might be able to effect sufficient repairs to make a break back to Gibraltar on his own. It was clear to Commander Gibbs that he could not leave the merchantmen completely unprotected in the middle of such a hornets' nest and that he must leave the damaged cruiser to cope as best she could. After embarking 158 of the *Manchester*'s crew, who were surplus to fighting requirements of the ship, he wished Captain Drew good luck and hurried on after the convoy.

A short time later he passed the *Melbourne Star* again, but Captain Macfarlane reported that, despite her best speed, his vessel could not keep up with the destroyer; the freighter gradually dropped astern. *Melbourne Star* herself had already outpaced her two other companions so once again they found themselves alone.

> Great activity was noticed up ahead [Captain Macfarlane wrote], gun flashes, coloured tracers, red, gold and pale green. My ship was herself giving a wonderful firework display from her exhaust, which could not be stopped.

Her cargo included 1,350 tons of high-octane spirit, 700 tons of kerosene and 1,450 tons of high explosive shell, plus heavy oil, which was no sinecure in the midst of this bedlam. Luckily no prowling E-boat spotted her.

Not so fortunate was the *Rochester Castle*. At 1.13 she sighted an E-boat, probably the *Ms.26*, which certainly attacked a steamer at this time. Before the helm could be put over the Italian vessel had fired a torpedo which hit the ship above the bilge keel in No 3 hold, blowing open a hole some twenty-five by eighteen. The hold flooded at once and the explosion wrecked two of the lifeboats. Despite this hit, coupled with earlier damage, *Rochester Castle* was able to continue at thirteen knots although well down by the head, a wonderful achievement by Captain Wren and his crew.

This attack was witnessed by the *Dorset* (Captain Jack Collier Tuckett). An E-boat crossed her bows from port to starboard and the merchant ship attempted to ram it. The E-boat slid across *Dorset*'s forefoot unharmed and ignoring Captain Tuckett's ship completely moved off into the night. A few minutes later they heard the sound of a torpedo striking home on a less fortunate companion. The slaughter continued. At 1.50 the leading group of warships was a little south of Kelibia when the *Ms.31* (Tenente di Vascello Antonio Calvani) found them. The *Glenorchy* was in a relatively safe position, having reformed close-astern of the main warship group, where she found that she was again following the *Almeria Lykes*. The American vessel after moving out from the formation had held a conference in which the captain had suggested making a bee-line for Malta at the ship's top speed as the best way of saving her from annihilation. Lieutenant-Commander Mitchell had strongly advised against this and soon afterwards, having apparently 'cut the corner', they had the good fortune to sight one of the minesweeping destroyers once more.

Earlier the *Glenorchy* had fought a brief engagement with an E-boat and claimed to have seen her blow up. This we now know to be a mistake but several Axis boats were damaged and *Glenorchy*'s opponent may well have been one of these. The *Ms.26* and *Ms.31* both returned to make further attacks at this time and it seems likely that it was the latter of these two boats which, just before 2 am, caught *Glenorchy* illuminated in the glare of a searchlight and hit her on the port side with two torpedoes. Calvani let fly two torpedoes from *Ms.31* at 700 metres' range and although heavily fired on by a destroyer, escaped unharmed.

Glenorchy's engine-room flooded and all the port lifeboats were destroyed. The ship listed heavily to port as the two starboard lifeboats were swung out. An eyewitness stated that there was some panic, several rafts were heaved over the side and some of her gunners jumped for it. Her cargo included aviation fuel so it was unwise to tarry. Captain Leslie ordered 'Abandon Ship' while Third Mate Mr R. M. Simon, threw overboard the secret documents and ship's books in a weighted bag. He then went round the ship as she settled making sure all the crew were safely away as well as the passengers. All 124 were accounted for and Captain Leslie told Simon to go.

He boarded a boat commanded by Second Mate Skelling but Captain Leslie himself refused to go. Despite considerable pleading he remained adamant. As the boat pushed away the First Mate, Mr Hanney, hailed them from one of the rafts and asked if everyone was safely away. On learning that Captain Leslie was still aboard he borrowed two oars from the boat and set off back to the ship declaring that they were not going to leave the captain. On his way back he picked up three men who had dived overboard but after rescuing them he again set off for the ship but was lost to sight.

At 2 am the head of the convoy was sighted by the *Ms.26* (Sottotenente di Vascello Bencini) some seven miles south of Kelibia. She was herself at once illuminated by star shells and by the light of these she identified a steamer and a destroyer. She immediately came under heavy and accurate fire from both and she twisted violently through the convoy in order to avoid this fire, turning up on to the formation's starboard side and replying with her own machine-guns. Bencini later reported that he could plainly hear the bullets splattering across the steamer's hull. Some 50 metres off the merchant ship's port bow he sighted a cruiser which he took to be of the '*Arethusa*' class and the *Ms.26* fired both torpedoes at this vessel at 2.20 am and claimed both as hits. This was not in fact the case.

On firing her torpedoes the Italian boat was once more subjected to star-shell illumination and surrounded by shell splashes from a destroyer and also her cruiser target. She weaved away towards the Tunisian coast dropping depth charges to confuse the destroyer, who pursued her until she reached the safety of the minefields, whereupon the destroyer gave up the chase.

This destroyer was the *Pathfinder*, which, in the words of Rear-Admiral Burrough, 'was always in the right place at the right time'. Her action is worth recording:

> Our engine's room telegraph clanged the order for full speed and our helm was put over to ram. At the same moment we caught the E-boat squarely in the beam of our big 44-inch searchlight, and every gun that would bear, 4-inch, pom-poms and Oerlikons, opened a rapid fire. Enveloped in shell splashes, the E-boat shot ahead and swung round laying a smoke screen.
>
> She disappeared behind the smoke, and we followed her through it, finding the screen was of brief duration. Once again the searchlight caught and held her and all the guns opened up; and once again she disappeared in a large

cloud of smoke. I do not know if we hit her or not, because we had already sighted signalling from another E-boat lying in the path of the convoy, and we swung round to head off this new menace.

Also at this time *Ms.25* (Tenente di Vascello Le Pera) and *Ms.23* (Sottotenente di Vascello Patrone) were attracted by Bencini's firework display, but were met by a fully alerted defence. *Ms.23* was unable to attack at all and although *Ms.25* fired at long range against a cruiser target she had no more fortune than her sister.

Tenente di Vascello Calvani now reappeared on the scene in *Ms.31* and shadowed the convoy south, sending out continuous reports by wireless of its movements. By 3.15 am she had reached the limits of her operational area and turned back north, meeting soon afterwards the other two boats of her squadron. They had a short conference and decided to return back north to finish off any stragglers they might find. At 5.15 *Ms.31* came upon her earlier victim, the *Glenorchy*, and some rafts from the *Clan Ferguson*.

There was a brief lull in the fighting as the surviving British ships steamed on. At 2.20 *Kenya* had altered course away from the Tunisian coast on a new bearing to take them to the south of Pantelleria and a quarter of an hour later she had the *Santa Elisa* in sight on her port quarter. Well astern the *Bramham* had made contact with the *Port Chalmers* around 0045 and while they were talking the *Penn* joined from the north after completing her rescue duties. They had all received W/T transmissions about the E-boat attacks and Lieutenant-Commander Swain decided to lead the freighter well clear of the suspected enemy concentrations by cutting through the minefields. In this manner, with *Penn* ahead and *Bramham* astern, the *Port Chalmers* came safely through the danger area and made up some of the time lost earlier.

Aboard the *Manchester* strenuous effects were being made to get the ship moving again but by 2.45 am it was clear that she could not be got under way. Captain Drew had been through all this before when *Manchester* had been disabled in a similar manner the previous year. On that occasion he had managed to get his ship back to Gibraltar. This time he had no such good fortune.

Despite all their efforts the ship remained immobile. The crew took to the carley floats and boats and the scuttling charges were fired, but the cruiser did not finally sink until some hours later, around 5.50 am, when she finally went down in about twenty fathoms. Some thirteen officers and 308 men, including those taken off by Commander Gibbs, were rescued, but the bulk of the crew were interned by the French. The Flight Commander of *Manchester*'s seaplane flight of Walrus amphibians, 'Chicko' Roberts, was one of these last:

> It was a long six-mile struggle to the Tunisian coast [he recalls] where we were taken prisoner by the Vichy French. My own first night ashore with a few men was spent in the local morgue. All that I can remember of that is that it had white tiles, was cold, that we were all delighted to be alive and that sleep was all we needed.

Meantime, at about 2.50 am the *Charybdis*, *Eskimo* and *Somali* had linked up with the escorts, steering through the convoy and joining the damaged *Kenya* and her destroyers. During the night *Ashanti* had reported sighting several loose horned mines and it seemed likely that the minesweeping destroyers had cut them. The *Icarus* (Lieutenant-Commander C. D. Maud, DSC) had almost certainly done so, noting earlier in the night a slight explosion, thought to be a mine, in the wake of her starboard paravane, which four minutes later was followed by a large explosion.

On the other hand the captain of the *Fury*, Lieutenant-Commander C. H. Campbell, was of the opinion that his vessel had cut no mines. Perturbed by the enforced inactivity of his ship in the face of the E-boat assault, he later wrote that he had been engaged in several anti-E-boat operations off the East Coast earlier in the war and that in his opinion the three TSDS ships would have been more gainfully employed in the protection of the convoy by fighting these boats. The risk of mining of the ships could have been accepted as the lesser danger.

Whatever the accuracy or correctness of his suggestion, it seems clearly in his favour that to a large extent these ships were wasted, as before dawn both sweeps belonging to *Fury* and *Icarus* had been carried away, while *Intrepid* only retained her starboard sweep.

Soon after 3 am the convoy was located by another wave of E-boats and the attacks started all over again.

At this time *Kenya* had both *Santa Elisa* and *Wairangi* in view close astern and at 3.10 two boats of the Italian 20th Squadron, Mas.552 (Sottotenente di Vascello Perasso) and *Mas.554* (Sottotenente di Vascello Calcagno) made attacks on this group. *Kenya* spotted the *Mas.552* as she approached and hotly engaged her with her close range armament. As she did so either she or her sister boat, both of which fired at the same time, torpedoed the *Wairangi*. Captain Gordon described the situation as it happened:

In position 36°35'N, 11°22'E, we sighted an E-boat some five hundred yards off the port side and also a torpedo track which struck the ship between No 3 tank and the coffer-dam on the forepart of the deep oil tank. There was an explosion, but not a very loud one, and there was no flash, but a large column of water. The ship took on a slight list to port, the engine room and No 3 hold filled rapidly. The engines were stopped and emergency lighting came on. It was found that No 4 boat was missing.

The pumps proved unable to cope with the inrush of the water but her gunners continued to fight back with all her weapons as further enemy units engaged her. At 3.40 the *Mas.554* made an attack on what he later described as an 8,000-ton ship and claimed to have sunk her. A SOS from the *Wairangi* was picked up half an hour later which the Italians took as a confirmation of this claim, but they had not yet finished off the *Wairangi*.

The *Almeria Lykes* was also hit at this time. She was zigzagging at thirteen knots on a course approximately 120 degrees true with the *Somali* in sight ahead, astern of one of the TSDS ships. According to the Action Summary there were 21 lookouts at their action stations, and they had been on duty for four days, sleeping and eating when possible, at their stations. The weather was clear, sea choppy, slight wind, no moonlight and visibility was recorded as poor.

She was brought under torpedo attack by two enemy boats, possibly the German *S.30* (Oberleutnant zur See Weber) and *S.36*

(Oberleutnant zur See Brauns), and they scored one hit near No 1 hold on the port side. *Almeria Lykes* had a cargo consisting of ammunition in all holds surrounded by 9,700 tons of general cargo and military equipment. No 1 hold contained bombs, but despite this there was only the single explosion of the torpedo and not an appalling chain reaction like that which had torn asunder the *Clan Ferguson* earlier. The Germans claimed to have destroyed two steamers in this attack, which took place in 36°40', 11°35'E.

The explosion split the ship at the line of the forepeak bulkhead; but the resulting submergence of the ship prevented any estimation of the full extent of the damage. One dynamo went out at once and the engines stopped about five minutes later.

Some considerable confusion broke out among her crew and they prepared to get away as soon as possible. Captain William Henderson therefore ordered 'Abandon Ship'. Thus it was that the ship was left afloat, but unmanned. While evacuating the vessel they were illuminated by star shell, and what were thought to have been three Vichy-French destroyers of the 'Simoun' class were sighted astern. They made no attempt at rescue and soon moved away.[1] While Lieutenant-Commander Mitchell and Captain Henderson went round the ship to check that everyone was clear, the rest of the crew pulled away in the boats to an escort vessel. She promptly told them that their ship was still afloat and that they should therefore go back; that was the last seen of the escort! By 4.30 am everyone was clear of the vessel, which was still afloat.

[1] Other vessels reported sighting 'three-funnelled French destroyers' during the night, several claiming to have been illuminated by them. In a letter to Mr Jim David, made available to the author, M. Jean Meirat, the French Naval Historian, stated that he was in command of the 7th Destroyer Division on the night in question and that all its three ships, the *Tramontane*, *Tornade* and *Typhon*, were in harbour at Bizerta all night. There was, however, a small French convoy off Sfax at the time escorted by a torpedo boat and a sloop. 'All day we heard the roaring of the battle of the British convoy passing not far from our shores,' he adds, 'but the two French escorts only took the normal precaution of preparing their AA weapons in case the Axis aircraft attacked them by mistake.'

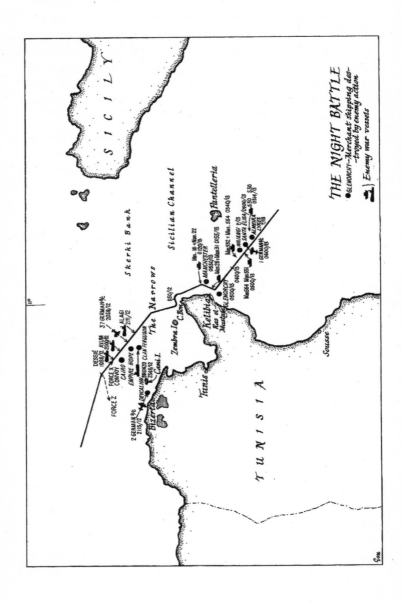

THE NIGHT BATTLE

● GLENORCHY—Merchant shipping destroyed by enemy action

⌐ Enemy war vessels

SICILY

Sicilian Channel

Skerki Bank

The Narrows

Pantelleria

Mn. 16 • Mn. 22 0120/13
MANCHESTER 0550/13
0550/13
Mas.552 • Mas.554 0340/13
WAIMARAMA 1/13
SANTA ELISA/0900/13 0530/13
Mas.26/Mas.31 0155/13 0400/13
0500/13 ALMERIA 034/13
Mas.564 Mas.551 LYKES 1/13
0500/13
1 GERMAN% 0600/13

37 GERMAN% 2058/12
ALAGI 2111/12
DESSIÉ 1958/12 • 2009/12 XVIM
FORCE X CONVOY
CAIRO
EMPIRE HOPE
• DEUCALION BRONZE CLAN FERGUSON
• 2568/12
Casa I.
FORCE Z
2 GERMAN% 2115/12

1050/12 C.Bon
Zembra I.
Kelibia
Ras el Mseed GLENORCHY 0500/13

Tunis
Bizerta
Sousse

TUNISIA

11°

At 4.48 the other American vessel the *Santa Elisa* was the next to go. She was well armed with 20-mm Oerlikon guns and these were very ably handled by her Armed Guard party. They exchanged vicious fire with the first attacker, the Italian *Mas.557* (Guarda-Marina Cafiero Battista) as she sliced past spraying the decks with machine-gun fire. The E-boats' shots narrowly missed Captain Thompson on the bridge and killed four of her Army gunners at their posts, one being shot through the throat. In return they hit the Italian boat and she sheered away; her torpedo missed, although she claimed a hit.

Another E-boat, *Mas.564* (Tenente di Vascello Iafrate), then attacked and scored a torpedo hit at point-blank range which struck the *Santa Elisa* abreast No 1 hold on the starboard side. Her cargo included aviation fuel and this ignited in a roaring explosion, which knocked several of her crew overboard. The ship was soon blazing from end to end, but her ship's company were able to launch three of the lifeboats and save themselves. All 28 got clear, although five were badly burnt.

Another ship had gone, but the night battle was almost over, the first traces of dawn were appearing in the eastern sky. At 5.08 the *Mas.553* (Tenente di Vascello Paolizza) made a run-in and fired at a merchant ship. He claimed to have hit a tanker and may have scored another hit on the *Santa Elisa*, but no other vessel was struck at this time. This marked the final assault by the Axis torpedo craft.

The German's boats claimed in all to have hit a steamer of 15,000 tons and set it ablaze; torpedoed a tanker of 10,000 tons and another of 12,000 tons; torpedoed one steamer of 8,000 tons and probably also another steamer. The Italians also made somewhat exaggerated claims, but the confusion of night fighting at high speed, when several boats might fire at the same target at the same time, made accurate recognition impossible and it is still impossible to assess precise claims. For the Italians Bragadin makes the following claim: 'These exceptional results, achieved despite the lack of the radar and asdic equipment with which the enemy units were equipped, demonstrates the valour and ability of the Italian crews.'

This summing-up is fair comment, for never before had so many merchant ships been lost in a single action throughout the entire war in the Mediterranean. Although the Axis E-boats and aircraft can claim the lion's share of these mercantile sinkings, it is surely to Tenente di Vascello Ferrini of the submarine *Axum* to which the chief laurels for the Axis night victory should be awarded. The successes of both the other two arms, aircraft and E-boat, owe much to the absolute disruption caused by his devastating submarine attack on the previous evening.

III

We have seen the ships – too many ships – hit, sunk and abandoned, but for their crews often their escape from a blazing vessel was just the prelude. It is to the scattered group of survivors, some badly wounded, others unscathed, that we must now turn.

Clan Ferguson's survivors were huddled on their rafts throughout the night. Each group had become separated from the others and, quite naturally, each one felt that his raft was the only one to survive the holocaust of the evening. Thus it was with great jubilation that the arrival of dawn brought all the rafts into view of each other. It also revealed land, in the hostile form of Zembra Island, but no effort was made to reach it. The boats were well provisioned and they felt sure that the escorts would be back to make a search for them before the day was out.

The sun rose higher in the heavens, but no help appeared. Then, towards noon, men on Second Officer Black's raft sighted what they took to be a corvette on the horizon. With great haste they ran up their red sail to attract attention, but to their intense disappointment it proved to be a submarine which steered towards them. It finally stopped some thirty yards away from the nearest raft and any hopes they might have had that it was British were soon dashed.

It was the *Bronzo* and Tenente di Vascello Buldrini hailed them from the conning tower and asked them in Italian if there were any wounded. Some reports have stated that on ascertaining that they were British the submarine made no further contact and, to their profound relief, moved off again. In fact Buldrini was not so callous as they made for he had actually repeated his question in English. On receiving no reply he radioed their position so that they could be rescued.

Captain Cossar recalled that there were two lookouts on the submarine's bridge who kept a vigilant watch throughout the whole episode, but that the submarine carried no pendant number, only a cartoon of Pinnochio painted on the conning-tower. After reporting their position to the Italian air-sea rescue headquarters in Sicily, the *Bronzo* moved off, passing through the large area of floating wreckage and debris from the sunken ships and soon vanished from sight.

Two hours later a big German Dornier floatplane appeared from the north-east and, after circling the British seamen, alighted on the water close by. 37 survivors were then taken aboard. Included among these were those of her crew who had been badly burned in the explosion and were by now in a very pitiful condition. The German Red Cross men treated these with the greatest care and kindness. One of the airmen told them that they would return for the remainder later and the big plane taxied over the waves, lifted off and droned away.

Another two hours passed, with the rafts drifting steadily towards the Tunisian coast. The wind grew fresher and started kicking the sea up into a choppy swell. Then the Dornier returned, but, instead of landing, it circled them maddeningly for a long period. The pilot seemed unable to decide whether or not to risk a second landing as the rafts were by now in French waters and the water surface, covered by all manner of flotsam, was breaking up in an unpleasant manner.

Eventually he flew away and left them. They continued to drift, the current taking them further down the coast, and by this time the rafts had become separated again. At about 7 pm another Axis aircraft spotted them. This was a small Italian floatplane with prominent Red Cross markings and she alighted beside two of the rafts. She managed to get seven men aboard but then, dangerously overladen, she was forced to take off. She soon disappeared to the north. This left two rafts, one under Captain Cossar and the other under Second Officer A. H. Black. It was now a case of who got them first, the Axis or Vichy.

The captain's raft was now much closer to land and they thought they could see a village on the coast. They steered their clumsy craft as best they could towards it but before they were half-way it was seen to be not a village at all but a stranded destroyer on the coast which they took to be Italian, but was in all probability the *Havock*. They were now barely a mile from Cape Bon and were under observation from ashore. Hopes were high that they would soon be ashore but these were dashed when a creaming bow wave was sighted out to sea. An Italian E-boat came up alongside one of the rafts and took aboard three officers.

The Vichy French now took a hand. According to the American Consul in Tunis, the sight of the Italians picking up British officers inside her territorial waters caused a 'nasty incident'. Their release was demanded by the French Admiral Durrien who, it is stated, sent gendarmes aboard the Italian vessel and took them off 'which infuriated the Italian Admiral Salza'.

The party from the captain's raft got ashore on the Tunisian coast about noon. They were found by two Italians who took them to their farm and gave them food, wine and cigarettes. Eventually Captain Cossar and his men were taken to Bonfichia Internment Camp and then later transferred to Le Kef. Here they met Black's party and were fortunate in finding a Vichy officer who was pro-British. 'Lieutenant Morelle of the Spahi Regiment,' Captain Cossar recalls, 'did everything he could for us; he was very pro-British and made himself very unpopular with the French authorities.'

While aboard the E-boat it had been revealed that the ship had been sunk around 9 pm on the 12th. This led the Italian Naval authorities to claim that the *Clan Ferguson* had been sunk by the *Alagi* in her attack. This is not very likely for most records show that she was in fact struck at 9.02 during the German air raid while the *Alagi* did not fire until ten minutes later; if we allow for some discrepancies on both sides the options remain open. In both the Luftwaffe and the Italians still stick to their respective claims. The Official British Naval Historian, Captain S. W. Roskill, RN, settles for the Luftwaffe and careful examination of the records seems to support this view.

On the 13th E-boats had picked up nine men from the *Glenorchy* including First Mate Hanney whom they mistook for her captain. In fact Hanney had failed in his attempt to rescue his captain due to the appearance of the Italian craft. Another of the survivors' boats, under the command of Second Mate Skelling, evaded them and finally got ashore just south of Kelibia at 8 am the next morning. All 50 were safely landed while another group in Simon's boat also landed at about the same time on the 13th. While they were disembarking they saw the ship still afloat not far from the shore.

Eight volunteers where eventually found to return to the ship but as they were about to re-embark on the raft they saw her finally turn over and sink; two minutes later heavy explosions set the floating oil on fire.

All *Glenorchy*'s crew were taken to an internment camp near Sfax, eventually gaining release from this unwholesome place when the Allies landed in North Africa in November. Their story had a happy ending for on 2nd December they finally arrived back in the Clyde, whence they had set out so many months before, after a passage from North Africa aboard the liner *Orontes*.

The *Wairangi* was also left earlier, stopped and under attack. Her engineers tried desperately to restart the engines, but it was a losing battle. The Chief Engineer, Alexander Chalmers, tried repeatedly to nurse his engines back to life while at the same time trying to cope with the inrush of water, the pumps proving inadequate. The Axis attacks reached a dangerous pitch with, it seemed, ships firing away and being torpedoed all around them. Eventually Captain Gordon decided that the situation was hopeless and, as there was no hope of a tow, he did not feel justified in risking further the lives of his crew.

The vessel was still fairly stable and in view of the possibility of her remaining afloat after being abandoned and taken by the enemy next day as a prize, Captain Gordon decided to scuttle her. The charges were set and the crew who had taken to the boats pulled away and awaited results.

After some time the sounds of battle had receded and it became apparent that the ship was not sinking fast enough. A party of volunteers, led by Chalmers, then went back to the ship. They entered the flooded engine-rooms and, despite the obvious danger, broke the water-cooling pipe and opened several watertight doors. For this gallant act Chalmers was awarded the DSC. The party then returned to the boats and they all drifted in the vicinity of the ship until dawn. It was now a question of whether the Axis found them or the Royal Navy. Several aircraft were sighted and in fact the Germans and Italians were both flying reconnaissance sorties from before first light. Six of the Grosseto Heinkels were airborne at four o'clock on an armed reconnaissance and it was they who found the *Wairangi* at six o'clock on the 13th.

The crew were engaged in transferring some men from the rafts into the boats when the first plane swooped down. It launched two torpedoes at the ship but both missed. A little later another Heinkel carried out a similar attack and again both torpedoes missed the stationary target. This is inexplicable; the German crews had certainly proved their accuracy the previous evening, but perhaps two days' continuous sorties with only a small number of aircrew available were taking their toll in strain. The airmen subsequently reported sinking a freighter which led later assessors to think that they had assisted in the sinking of the *Waimarama*, but this was not so.

At about 8 am Captain Gordon sighted two destroyers investigating the *Wairangi* and he drew attention to himself with an Aldis lamp; some time later the *Eskimo* (Commander E. G. Le Geyt, DSC) who had been returning to search for the damaged *Manchester*, came up and took them aboard. Their ship was still afloat when the destroyer finally left the area with all the survivors aboard, although the poop was awash. In all 79 were rescued.

The two American ships had been hit quite close to each other, but their fates were very different. *Santa Elisa* caught fire quickly and her crew got away in the boats. They were sighted by the *Penn* and *Bramham* who were escorting the *Port Chalmers* and both destroyers stopped to pick them up. After taking the ship's company from the boats the *Penn* followed on after the Commodore's ship but *Bramham* circled the gutted wreck deciding whether to sink her or not.

The *Almeria Lykes'* story was more intricate. All 105 of her crew and gunners got safely away in three lifeboats, but by daybreak it was seen that the ship itself was still afloat and in a seaworthy condition; the *Wairangi* was also in sight, motionless in the distance. Captain Henderson therefore decided to call for volunteers to re-board her and continue the voyage to Malta with her desperately needed cargo.

The enemy aircraft were overhead taking photographs and as a result the majority of the crew refused vehemently to return to the vessel, on the grounds that any such action would at once invite retaliation from the aircraft in the form of bombing and strafing.

The crew had certainly had a hard two days, but their attitude left something to be desired. Captain Henderson had, earlier in the voyage, recommended that the Britons aboard should eat at separate tables in view of his crew's attitude, although there were no untoward incidents. The crewmen were not very enthusiastic sailors on the whole – despite, by British standards, astronomically high wages – and during the voyage had expressed a determination to demand more pay on reaching harbour as they were not getting proper food. It seems that they were upset at, among other things, not having four eggs for their breakfast!

Finally only the captain, the British liaison officer, the First Assistant Engineer, Mr H. Brown, a junior officer cadet – Henry Harris – and a purser – G. Webb – went back aboard to scuttle the vessel as they could not sail her alone. Captain Henderson himself set the charges, which duly exploded, destroying some bulkheads of No 3 hold and opened up the engines to the sea. Beyond this the charge seemed to have very little effect due, in Henderson's opinion, to the trapped air having no free vent.

The *Almeria Lykes* was still afloat when the destroyer *Somali* found them at 9.30 am. While the crew was being picked up Captain Henderson suggested to the destroyer's skipper, Commander E. N. V. Currey, DSC, that he should ensure the final destruction of the ship to prevent her falling into enemy hands; this Currey undertook to do, but in fact it was not successfully carried out. Like the *Wairangi*, she was still afloat when the two British destroyers left the area to continue their search for the damaged cruiser. Commander Le Geyt reported that he left them afloat as he thought there might still be a chance of getting them brought in to Malta later.

It should be emphasised that the conduct, both of Captain Henderson and the Armed Guard party of the US Navy and the Army gunners, was beyond reproach.

Captain Henderson particularly praised the Armed Guard party under the command of Ensign Simon P. Hirschbegg, USNR:

The gun crews behaved nobly. All were young lads with little experience but as long as there was anything to shoot at, they kept up the fire.

Mitchell is equally complimentary of Captain Henderson, whom he found an excellent commander and very co-operative. Willie Henderson from Galveston Texas, had previously served as a commissioned officer in both the United States and the Royal Navies and was a skipper in the highest traditions of both those services. It as unfortunate that some of his crew lacked his experience which would have steadied them.

It was not only the men of the American and Merchant Navies who had to undergo prolonged tension that night; far away to the west it had also been a long and wearisome ordeal for the men of two British destroyers.

We last saw the crippled *Foresight* with her fellow destroyer *Tartar* standing by in the midst of the great enemy air attack during the afternoon of the 12th. By 7.55 that evening Commander Tyrwhitt had managed to establish a tow alongside and was making headway to the west. All seemed to be going well when on the horizon they sighted the evil forms of five torpedo-bombers approaching them. While preparing to put up a barrage against these intruders the towing wire fouled *Tartar*'s propellers. They were saved from what could have been a very nasty situation, when the aircraft, after nosing around out of gun-range, turned north and disappeared. It was later thought that these aircraft might have been the Beaufighters of 248 Squadron from Malta searching for the convoy and Force X.

Shortly afterwards *Nigeria* and her escorting 'Hunts' came upon the scene. The *Bicester* was detached from the escort to find out what was happening. She closed them and saw that the towing wire had parted, but her captain, Lieutenant-Commander S. W. F. Bennets, decided reluctantly that he was needed far more by *Nigeria*, so after a short while he left them and proceeded to resume his screening duties.

Attempts at untangling the wire eventually succeeded but were interrupted by an attack by two Junkers Ju88s which dropped what appeared to be depth charges. Once they had gone, the *Foresight* was taken in tow astern. It had been decided that in view of the continued enemy presence, the risk of further alongside tow would be too great. The destroyers started again their painfully slow progress towards far-distant Gibraltar.

It was now dusk, but at 8.50 the dim shapes of fast surface forces were made out crossing eastward to the north of them. No British forces were known to be in the vicinity and Commander Tyrwhitt knew nothing of the whereabouts of the Italian cruiser squadron reported earlier. Without hesitation *Tartar* again slipped the tow and placed herself between *Foresight* and the probable enemy, gun crews closed up, torpedo tubes trained towards the unknown ships.

Long seconds passed before Commander Tyrwhitt made out their silhouettes as a 'Dido' class cruiser and two 'Tribals' from his own flotilla. Much relieved, he attempted, by repeated signalling, to attract the attention of this force to ask for assistance, but the hurrying squadron sped past without any acknowledgement and soon disappeared into the night.[1]

They were now isolated again deep in hostile waters. At first the flooding aboard *Foresight* appeared to have been halted but only seven knots was the maximum speed considered safe; any quicker and the wire would snap. As the night passed the little destroyer,

[1] They were of course the *Charybdis*, *Eskimo* and *Somali* speeding to reinforce Force X but Commander Tyrwhitt was unaware at that time of their mission.

veteran of many a hard-fought action in the Mediterranean, slowly settled aft despite all attempts by her damage control parties. At 5.15 am on the 13th the towing spring parted for the second time together with a preventor. Again they re-passed the tow, but the dawn found her with upper decks awash.

From 8.15 they were persistently shadowed by enemy planes, it was clearly only a matter of time before they whistled up the bombers and the *Foresight* was completely unable to manoeuvre. As if this was not enough, *Tartar* sighted a submarine periscope at 8.30. This was the *U-73*. After his successful attack on the *Eagle* and subsequent escape, Rosenbaum had steered after the convoy, listening to the reports of the Axis aircraft and hoping to find easy pickings among the many ships reported damaged or straggling.

He fired a spread of four torpedoes at the two destroyers and reported hearing one hit. He was not able to verify his claim – which in fact was unfounded – for on sighting his periscope the *Tartar* again loosed the tow and counter-attacked vigorously, liberally plastering the area with depth-charges.

After satisfying himself that the submarine had been driven away Commander Tyrwhitt reluctantly decided that the *Foresight* was now too much of a liability in such dangerous waters and that the risks for both ships and their companies was too great. He held a consultation with Lieutenant-Commander Fell, after receiving a signal from him, and they agreed that there was now little hope of saving the ship.

Her sister ship, the *Fearless*, had been damaged in a similar way in 1941 and she had also had to be sunk after efforts at towing. They considered this precedent and decided that they must now do likewise. After the remaining members of the crew who were still aboard had been embarked, the *Foresight* was finally given the *coup de grâce* with a torpedo from *Tartar* who had laboured so hard to save her. At 9.55 she sank in 218 degrees some thirteen miles from Galitia Island. Eight officers and 173 ratings were rescued from her total complement.

Laden with these survivors *Tartar* worked up to full speed for a lone dash back to Gibraltar.

Another warship of the Royal Navy enjoyed an uninterrupted passage through the Sicilian Channel during this period. The submarine *Otus* (Lieutenant-Commander J. W. Collett) was returning from Malta after running through a vital cargo of spares and petrol. Apart from the usual heart-in-mouth crossing through the minefields of *QBB.255* she was undetected and was clear of the danger zone by the 13th.

IV

At the same time as these adventures were taking place, one isolated British merchant captain was using all his skill, patience and even downright impudence to bring his ship safely through the many hazards of that deadly stretch of water.

Captain Riley, after parting from the *Pathfinder* earlier, had steered his ship *Brisbane Star* straight for the Tunisian coastline and once in the shallows he had followed the shore south past Kelibia. She had sighted a vessel lurking there and identified her as a French 'Leopard' class destroyer. Not being certain, she kept well clear and the unknown ship either failed to spot them or was too concerned with her own security and allowed them to pass. It has been suggested that this was the *Malocello*, but there is no account of her being present on the night of the 12th/13th. If it had been *Malocello*, it can surely be said that the Italian thereby missed a wonderful opportunity, for his job was to sink British ships using this route and whether he used his guns or his mines – which in fact scored no success at all – the end result was what counted. It seems most likely in fact that it was one of the French boats reported by other ships.

Captain Riley did not stop to argue the point, but pushed on at his best speed of eight knots; daybreak found him crossing the Gulf of Hammamet.

The *Ohio* was also making good progress. Supreme efforts were necessary to hold the damaged vessel on her course. Her deck was split across the centre almost to amidships and with every yaw of her helm the buckled metal tore and groaned, threatening to allow the heavy ship to break in half. It was necessary to keep a continuous five degrees on the starboard helm to compensate for the pull caused by the great rent in her side. By 3 am the tanker had managed to attain a speed of thirteen knots and by dawn she had almost caught up with the remaining ships of the convoy.

Melbourne Star had steered well to the south and eventually caught up with the leading destroyers. She found, however, to use Captain Macfarlane's words, that they were nobody's baby. Every time he steered to take up position astern of one of the destroyers the escort would zigzag and pull away. At dawn he finally received permission to take station on one of the warships, but at this moment the *Ashanti* came up from the remainder of the convoy, which was revealed to be well astern of him, and formed alongside the *Melbourne Star*'s starboard side where she hailed Captain Macfarlane and ordered him to turn round and join the others. It turned out that the big freighter was following close astern a minesweeping destroyer which had lost its sweeps!

Captain Macfarlane was not aware of his precarious position-his vessel drew far more water than the destroyer so she could not be relied on to detonate the mines for him-and having found a comfortable position close to an escort, was loath to abandon it. He shouted back to *Ashanti* that he was quite happy where he was. Back came the stern rebuke: 'I am the Admiral.'

Melbourne Star turned silently and rejoined the convoy, taking station astern of the *Waimarama*.

Thus it was that only half the convoy survived the night, fully aware that daybreak would bring no relief, only the bombers and, for all they knew, Italian cruiser and destroyer squadrons as well. Aboard the depleted numbers of the escorting warships, haggard and exhausted men stood ready to repel what would be the enemy's decisive attacks. Very few of them in the know gave themselves much of a chance. Operation 'Pedestal' appeared to be destined for the same fate as 'Harpoon', but on a much larger scale.

Against everything that the Axis could send against them there seemed little that the remaining British ships could do except go down fighting.

Chapter Six

Naked Under Heaven

I

IN fact the dawn of the 13th brought no sudden appearance of the fighting tops of the Italian squadrons over the northern horizon. The previous evening the ships of Admiral da Zara's cruiser divisions had concentrated about a hundred miles north of Ustica and had changed course to bring the convoy to battle south of Pantelleria at first light. The junction of the various Axis formations on the 12th had been reported to Headquarters at Malta, but though this was clear confirmation of the enemy's intention to attack, it was felt that there was no need for undue alarm; the covering ships of the escort were at this time at full strength and the convoy was itself intact.

It was a startling change that faced HQ at Malta when they received news of the heavy casualties suffered by both convoy and escort from submarine and air attacks. The situation was completely changed and Air Vice-Marshal Park and Vice-Admiral Leatham were at once forced to put in hand the quickest and more immediate counter moves in their power.

This was no easy task. The air striking strength of Malta consisted only of fifteen torpedo-bombers of the RAF and these had been at continuous stand-by for two days, but they could not take off to attack until dawn – by which time it would clearly be too late. The only other aircraft capable of hitting at the enemy fleet were the two Fleet Air Arm Albacores at Hal Far and an assortment of reconnaissance aircraft of dubious capability and performance. The two old biplanes were at once sent off on their own.

A Wellington VIII, 'O for Orange', was despatched at last light to take over shadowing from the Baltimore of Pilot Officer Munroe and at 11.05 pm she reported making contact with the Italian ships steering south at twenty knots, 35 miles west-north-west of Ustica. Air Vice-Marshal Park ordered her to illuminate the Axis fleet and make plain language sighting reports every half hour in order to convey to the enemy that a striking force of considerable size and power was on its way. This she did, but it had no effect on the Italian units. Another Wellington VIII, 'Z for Zebra', was also told to make plain language reports and to attack with bombs. This was done, but again had little effect. The two Albacores had been despatched to make their attacks, but would not be able to reach the scene for some time.

It was with considerable relief, then, that at 0 156 on the 13th, one of the shadowing aircraft reported that the enemy had turned north-east, *away* from the convoy. Park continued to sent out deceptive messages in case this was just a feint by the enemy and at 3.10 am 'O for Orange' reported that the Italian ships were still maintaining the course 060 degrees towards Palermo at 20 knots. Another aircraft, 'Y for Yorker', took up the story. She broadcast an 'Illuminate and attack' call to nonexistent Liberators at 3.45 am. Vice-Admiral Leatham had meantime recalled the already airborne Albacores and signalled the two British submarines on patrol to the north of Sicily: 'Enemy cruisers coming your way.'

What brought about this sudden and, to the British, providential abandonment of the Italian plan – a plan which held the highest promise of achieving the complete annihilation of the convoy? The Official British Naval Historian seems in no doubt that it was the RAF, which was responsible:

> The RAF in Malta conducted a skilful and convincing bluff to deceive them [the Italians] into the belief that strong air striking forces were on the way to deal with them. No enemy surface ships actually ventured south of Sicily.

He offers no other reason for the withdrawal of the Italian cruiser divisions at the last moment. Churchill's account in *The Second World War*, came closer to the truth:

> It should have been within the enemy's power, as it was clearly in his interest, to destroy this convoy utterly. Two Italian cruiser squadrons sailed to intercept it on the morning of the 13th south of Pantelleria when it was already heavily damaged and dispersed. They needed strong air

support to enable them to operate so close to Malta, and here the efforts of Admiral Vian's earlier action in March against the Italian Navy bore fruit. Unwilling again to co-operate with the Italian Fleet, the German air force insisted on attacking alone. A heated controversy arose at Headquarters and a German Admiral records that an appeal was made to Mussolini, on whose intervention the cruisers were withdrawn before they got to the Sicilian Narrows.

The Admiral referred to here was Vice-Admiral Weichold and in his version of the dispute he recalls that he and the Italian Naval authorities made repeated efforts at General Kesselring's headquarters to ensure that the cruisers had air cover. 'This provoked a heated discussion among the staffs of the various services,' Weichold recorded, 'in the course of which the representatives of the two navies found themselves alone against all the other chiefs.'

It is recorded in the German Naval Staff War Diary for 12th August, clearly spelled out with a view to future recriminations, that

The question of whether the Italians can send out two cruiser squadrons depends on whether the available fighter protection will be assigned to the Naval forces or the Air Force bomber planes. The Duce will probably decide in favour of the Air Force.

The Admiral, German Naval Command, Italy, has done everything in his power to support the planned fleet action. The Admiral feels it will mean missing a big chance of annihilating the largest convoy undertaken so far in the Mediterranean after the heavy enemy forces, superior in numbers and arms, have withdrawn.

Mussolini soon resolved the dilemma in his own fashion. The German Naval Diary recorded on the 13th:

As had been expected, the Duce decided against the participation of the fleet in this operation. The Italian cruiser force was ordered to return to port.

In fact Supermarina had issued the orders for the withdrawal to Admiral da Zara around midnight; therefore, although the RAF's skilful deceptions may have reinforced this decision, the die was already cast before they had begun to take action. 'In this fashion,' wrote Admiral Weichold later, 'a splendid opportunity for a crushing victory by the Italian ships was thrown away, even as they were already at sea and heading for the battle area.'

In Weichold's opinion, Kesselring and his subordinates had a 'bigoted opinion' about air results and this had a bad effect on operation decisions.

Kesselring himself has recorded that he had little sympathy for the Italian Navy:

> The Italian navy [he wrote in his Memoirs] was regarded as a *pièce de résistance* and was therefore used sparingly – an attitude which caused special internal difficulties. A further trouble lay in its being stationed in different harbours; to assemble it cost time and wasted fuel. Finally, one or other battleship was either not ready to put to sea, or was not fuelled, or was in dock. On top of this there were the extraordinary technical deficiencies which deservedly earned the Italian navy the nickname 'Fine-weather Fleet'. Its doubtful seaworthiness called for increased air protection and that, with the limited strength of the Axis air forces in the Mediterranean, imposed ridiculous demands on the German Luftwaffe, whose hands were already full protecting convoys; the German airmen, who flew 75–90 per cent of all sorties, had consequently to be bled white.

The Italian air force took the line that it was the fear of the diversionary force discovered in the Eastern Mediterranean which caused Supermarina to abandon their original intentions and switch the cruisers to the Eastern basin to reinforce the 8th Cruiser Division at Navarino. Indeed there could have been a grave threat here to the Italians had Vian come further west with a repetition of the 'Vigorous' convoy, for the Axis had nothing in reserve to sail against it and a convoy from the east would have stood a very good chance of getting through to Malta.

Whatever the reason, the abandonment of the surface sortie not only meant the lifting of the gravest threat to 'Pedestal' but also the loss of several thousand tons of much needed oil fuel to the Axis by their high speed steaming, and, also, to a further, more disastrous, consequence.

On the abandonment of the operation, the 3rd Cruiser Division set course for Naples while the 7th, with the *Muzio Attendolo*, returned to Messina. In the path of this second group were stationed two British submarines, the *Safari* (Commander Ben Bryant, DSC) to the north-west of Palermo and the *Unbroken* (Lieutenant A. C. Mars) west of Messina itself, south of the Aeolian islands. The cruisers by-passed *Safari*'s position at 3 am steering due east, straight it would seem into Mars' lap, but *Unbroken* was not on her station off Cape Milazzo, but 30 miles to the north.

Unbroken had taken up her patrol position on the morning of the 10th, two miles north of the Milazzo lighthouse, which is some eighteen miles from Messina. It was a notoriously dangerous spot, being the favourite lurking ground for our submarines; the Italians, being well aware of the fact, conducted vigorous anti-submarine sweeps over it every time one of their squadrons left harbour. It was while *Unbroken* was studying the area that the Italians made such a sweep and apparently contacted her. Harried and depth-charged throughout the day, the British boat was driven north and Mars decided to find himself a new patrol area well clear of his original position. He reasoned that the enemy would hardly despatch their cruisers through that zone knowing an enemy boat to be present and decided that the most appropriate area for an interception would be roughly half-way between Stromboli and Salina, and by dawn on the 11th he had reached his new beat. Throughout the next two days he cruised undisturbed, trusting fervently in his intuition.

It was 3.15 when he received the report from the Captain Submarines, at Malta, Captain Simpson, that the enemy were steering towards his original position and should be there about 7.30 am. Mars now had to decide whether to steer back at his best speed, in which case he would be in the right position if the enemy was re-routed slightly northward of where he had been depth-charged, or to take his chance and stay where he was. He chose the latter course and at 7.25 was rewarded with the sight of four cruisers in line ahead steaming straight towards him. He also counted eight destroyers and two seaplanes guarding them, making his attack an extremely difficult one.

He manoeuvred to take up his firing position, and finally selected the nearest heavy cruiser as his main target, with one of the light cruisers slightly overlapping her in case he missed. Only three of the destroyers were on his side of the formation but they were steering courses destined to take them very close. He gritted his teeth and continued his approach. The speed of the Italian squadron was estimated at 25 knots and his four bow torpedoes were set at 14 and 16 feet depths.

Tension rose as first one and then the other destroyer churned past the British submarine's position. The third destroyer was so close that Mars recalled a momentary glimpse of a 'scruffy sailor smoking a 'bine as he leaned against a depth-charge thrower'.

Finally the last escort roared past and, as the sights came on, Mars fired a full four-torpedo salvo.

Immediately after firing he took *Unbroken* down to 80 feet on a south-westerly course at nine knots. Two minutes fifteen seconds later came the mighty crash of a torpedo hitting home followed fifteen seconds later by a second.

The first hit was scored on the heavy cruiser *Bolzano* (Capitano di Vascello Mario Mezzadra), and it penetrated her oil tank. There was only a single casualty, but the resulting fire quickly spread and threatened to ignite the ship's magazines. To prevent this the section was flooded and the cruiser was finally run ashore on the island of Panarea at 1.30 pm. She was not finally refloated until two days later when she was taken to Naples for repair.

The second torpedo struck the light cruiser *Muzio Attendolo* (Capitano di Vascello Mario Schiavuta) for'ard, blowing off the entire bow section of the ship for a length of 60 feet. In spite of this she succeeded in reaching Messina under her own power at 6.45 pm that same evening. Neither vessel was completely repaired before the end of the war and both were finally destroyed in dock.

For 45 minutes the Italian destroyers hunted the *Unbroken*; Mars counted 105 depth charges, most of them very close. Fortunately they were set to explode at a shallow depth and as the British submarine was running at 120 feet by this time, this probably saved her. By 9.30 the enemy vessels had given up the chase and *Unbroken*, with no torpedoes left, was able to steal away from the scene of the action. She finally returned to Malta on 18th August. Mars was subsequently decorated for his success – a fitting reward for playing his hunches.

This disaster was the final action in the part played by the ill-starred Admiral da Zara and his powerful surface force. All the planning and high-speed steaming had availed them nothing more than yet another humiliation. The two ships of the 7th Division arrived at Naples at 11 am, while the *Gorizia* and *Trieste*, escorted by the destroyer *Camicia Nera* entered Messina at 11.45.

In the words of Admiral Weichold, 'a more useless waste of fighting power cannot be imagined'. Meanwhile Ciano was busy recording in his Diary:

> All attention is concentrated on the battle in the Mediterranean. It would seem that things are developing rather well for us, although the loss of *Bolzano* and the damage suffered by the *Attendolo* were a high price to pay. Mussolini is moderately satisfied with the results, *because the guns of the Navy were not engaged in the battle*.[1]

II

However Mussolini felt about it, the withdrawal of the Italian cruisers was a profound relief to all the British authorities, and it must have seemed a miracle to Rear-Admiral Burrough. He had earlier ordered all the available escorts to form up with the leading group in readiness to fight a defensive action against the expected surface attack but the force available to him at first light on the 13th was hardly impressive. Other than the three minesweeping

[1] Author's italics.

destroyers, he could only muster one damaged 6-inch cruiser, the *Kenya*, and the *Charybdis* with her puny 4.5-inch guns as heavy ships. He had the three big 'Tribals' and the *Pathfinder* as his only Fleet destroyers. His other warships were somewhat scattered.

The *Bramham* was standing by the abandoned *Santa Elisa*; *Penn* was coming up from astern with *Port Chalmers*; while the *Ledbury* and *Ohio* were some five miles astern of the main body. This now consisted of the *Melbourne Star*, *Waimarama* and *Rochester Castle*. Rear-Admiral Burrough had received no firm news of the fate of the *Manchester* and on learning that the Italians had abandoned their intentions to intercept with their surface forces he despatched the *Eskimo* and *Somali* to search for her.

Meanwhile Captain Tuckett on the *Dorset* had taken a course to the north of the main route and dawn found him on his own in very dangerous waters. He considered his position and as he had no idea of the fate of the rest of the convoy, he decided to make a run for Malta at his best speed. He was over 100 miles from his goal but he realised that his chances were slim and decided that his only hope lay in fighter support. He therefore radioed his position to Malta and asked for air cover. His message was picked up ashore but they assumed it to be a request from the *Brisbane Star* which was the only vessel Malta knew to be steering an independent course.

That Captain Tuckett was correct in his assumptions there was no doubt. Unencumbered as they felt themselves to be by the need to protect the Italian cruiser force, the men of the Luftwaffe were confident that they could now ensure the final destruction of the convoy on their own. From before dawn they had been flying reconnaissance sorties and were soon in touch with all the various groups of British ships. Their first success was the elimination of the *Santa Elisa*, which was struck by bombs from a single Junkers Ju88 at six o'clock, in what Lieutenant Baines described as a 'deliberate' attack. The ship caught fire and was rent by severe explosions, which were visible from the convoy. *Bramham* steered to overtake the *Penn* once it was clear that nothing more could be done for her.

The convoy itself was brought under attack by twelve Ju88s who found it just after 8 am some 30 miles south-south-east of

Pantelleria. The RAF had flown off Beaufighters to give them assistance, but once again the lack of effective fighter-control meant that they at first failed to find the convoy so the early German attacks had only to penetrate the thin barrage of the escorts.

Without fighter direction ships there was little the escort could do to guide the RAF planes to their targets.

My Flag Lieutenant [Rear-Admiral Burrough recalls] had been working frantically all night to try and fix up a home-made set in the hope that we could talk to our fighters when they arrived, and at one time he seemed successful.

Communication with Spitfires on VHF was of course impossible but we had asked Vice-Admiral Malta to arrange for Beaufighters to work on 5570 KCs(HF). SOO worked a board for the Air Plot and Flags alongside him on the bridge of the *Ashanti* started doing his stuff. His face was a study, as he proceeded to call *Bacon-Apples* for the best part of an hour, listening intently all the while. Sometimes his face would light up with expectation, only to be quickly followed by a look of disappointment. Suddenly his face was wreathed in smiles and he commenced a conversation, which was quite unintelligible to me, and was punctuated by glances at a Beaufighter in the sky and frequent looks at the plot. What he was in fact trying to do was give the Beaufighter a course to steer to intercept the enemy; but the Beaufighter didn't appear to be obeying his instructions. After more guarded conversation in code, poor Flags assumed an expression of despair and flung down the receiver. He had just discovered that he wasn't talking to the Beaufighter at all, but to the cruiser *Charybdis*.

By this time the remains of the convoy was formed in single line ahead, *Rochester Castle* leading, followed by *Waimarama*, *Melbourne Star* and *Ohio*. *Port Chalmers* had still not caught up. The Junkers attacked in shallow dives from between 6,000 and 2,000 feet. The majority made a dead set at the *Ohio* and she was surrounded with bomb bursts and towering walls of spray, but the escorts managed to break up the dives of all her assailants with the

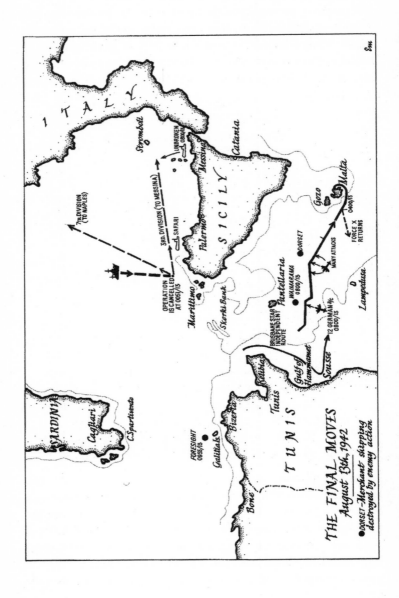

THE FINAL MOVES
August 13th, 1942

●DORSET—Merchant shipping
destroyed by enemy action

result that she came unscathed through this assault.

Three bombers turned their attentions to the *Waimarama*, the first missing wildly as the flak exploded around the nose of the aircraft. *Waimarama* was steaming at 13.5 knots, but was unable to avoid the next attack. Two bombers screamed down on her, the first releasing a five-bomb stick which was extremely accurate, four of them scoring direct hits; no cargo ship could survive such punishment. All four bombs hit close together about the bridge, which disappeared as the vessel blew up with an enormous explosion, a huge ball of flame being followed by a gigantic column of smoke through which her masts could be seen collapsing inwards into the heart of the furnace like matchsticks.

The *Waimarama* was carrying a deck cargo of petrol stowed in tins which at once ignited in a searing blast which swept the mutilated vessel from bow to stern and spread in a roaring sheet of flame as the ship disintegrated. In seconds she listed to starboard, righted herself and went down leaving only a huge area of flaming sea and a dense oily cloud of smoke. The captain of the *Charybdis* reported that the second Junkers, caught in this mighty blast, itself disintegrated in mid-air.

It seemed impossible for anyone aboard to survive such a holocaust, and indeed her casualties were severe. All the officers, including her Captain, R. S. Pearce, were lost save one, her Third Wireless Operator, Mr J. Jackson.

His escape was truly miraculous as he was standing on the bridge when the bomb hit. He was immediately enveloped in flames, and ran through the bridge deckhouse and down to the boat deck. For brief seconds he stood amidst the flaming desolation, then seeing men shouting and splashing in the water alongside he jumped overboard to join them. He could not swim and remembered very little after hitting the water. He owed his life to Cadet F. W. Treves; this young boy, only seventeen, was on his first trip to sea but he acted like a veteran and rescued several of his shipmates. He was awarded the British Empire Medal and Lloyd's War Medal for his gallantry and bravery.

In all thirty-three of the ship's company were rescued, due in no small measure to Roger Hill of the *Ledbury*. Ignoring the sea of fire the young lieutenant edged his small destroyer as near as he could to the spot where the ship had gone down and lowered the boats. They could hear the screams and cries of the trapped men caught by the flames and they were forced to leave those furthest from the inferno until later. The courage of these survivors was fantastic, many of them shouting encouragement as the destroyer, with scrambling nets rigged, moved past them into the blazing sea.

While the ship's boats moved around the edge of this area of carnage the *Ledbury* plunged into the heart of the fire four times to reach men trapped in pockets of flame-free sea. From Force X it appeared that she must surely be lost, but she re-emerged each time only to plunge back in again. On the last attempt great bravery was shown by Steward Reginald Sida who volunteered to go over the side with a rope to attach it to a man trapped on a burning raft, knowing full well that at any time the destroyer might have to back out and leave him to his fate.

So intense were the flames and so great was the explosion which sank the *Waimarama* that 36 of the crew of the *Melbourne Star*, which was following close astern of the ill-fated vessel, abandoned ship thinking that their own vessel was ablaze. Indeed it was a miracle that she was not, for there had been no time for her to avoid the searing flames or the burning sea. Although Captain Macfarlane ordered the helm hard to port, his ship was showered with falling debris after the explosion, steel plates five feet long and other jagged hunks of metal cascaded aboard while a 6-inch shell crashed into the roof of the captain's cabin.

As the ship passed through the grave of her companion the fierce heat threatened to ignite her own cargo, the paint blistered and the lifeboats caught fire. Captain Macfarlane ordered all hands to muster for'ard in readiness to leave the ship and in the chaos of the moment many took to the water. One of her kerosene tanks ignited, but in seconds she was through the worst of it. Most of those who had jumped found themselves in a worse situation, but fortunately the indefatigable *Ledbury* was on hand to rescue them.

The *Ohio*, also, only just managed to avoid the flames, Captain

Mason swinging her around to port just in time. Even so the flames threatened to engulf his ship.

In all 87 of *Waimarama*'s company were lost in that shattering explosion.

Over the horizon Captain Tuckett of the *Dorset* sighted the flak bursts in the sky and heard the roar of the explosion. It appeared that the convoy was hard pressed, but he had no hesitation in steering towards the battle; any protection and company he felt better than none. Soon after, his ship was sighted to the north by the convoy and told to join.

The ships did not have long to recover from this deadly blow, for the Axis had waves of aircraft in the air to deliver the knockout punch. The Royal Air Force was also fully stretched and despite the crippling lack of direction did magnificent work in the latter part of the day. 248 Squadron provided sorties of four Beaufighters to escort the convoy from dawn to within 100 miles of Malta but these failed to locate the ships. The short-range Spitfires were to take over fighter cover at 70–80 miles. The long-range Spitfires were supposed to be operating at extreme endurance distances of 120 miles, but they were seen over the ships 170 miles out so determined were they to do all in their power to get the ships through.

The fighter cover was organized by Wing Commander T. D. Miller, while the Command Navigator, Squadron Leader Addington, was almost permanently on duty throughout the last stage of the operation. Thanks to their efforts many of the incoming raids were intercepted and broken up, but as long as the ships were so close to Sicily it was inevitable that many of the numerous bomber strikes would get through to the convoy. For the already weary gunners of the escorts it seemed that the brilliant blue sky was never clear of vicious, gull-winged, black-crossed attackers.

As the day wore on, one assault merged with another, one raid followed another, and still the bombers came. In all 26 Ju88s took part in the first raids between 8.10 and 8.42 but not all of them found the convoy. On their return to base they claimed incorrectly to have sunk one cruiser, and four steamers. Only one plane was lost. The next attack was mounted by the Stukas of 102 Gruppo, sixteen of which left Sicily at 9 am escorted by Macchi 202s and were sent in to attack seven ships escorted by cruisers and destroyers which had been reported in the area. After a short flight over the sea eight located the convoy and in the engagement with British fighters the Macchis claimed to have shot down one Hurricane and one Spitfire. One Italian fighter was lost.

Once again the dive-bombers found the *Ohio* irresistible bait. *Ashanti*'s skipper later remembered the scene:

> *Ohio* had caught up and I stationed my destroyer close on her beam. Before we had left Scapa I had got the depot ship *Tyne* to cram into *Ashanti* as many Oerlikon guns as humanly possible, including one right aft among the depth charges. Experience in the Arctic had shown this gun to be the best answer to Stukas; their dives were very steep giving the gunners a 'no deflection' shot. Sure enough they made a beeline for the *Ohio* and we nailed more than one of them.

Rear-Admiral Burrough described this attack as of a most determined nature. Once more the sky was rent with lines of tracer, bursting shells and plunging bombers. The Ju87s deployed in their usual manner, coming in steeply from several angles, timing their dives so that the ships always had several aircraft to shoot at, thus reducing the effect of the barrage. Despite the intensity of the attack the tanker again came through but she was near-missed by one 500-pound bomb which exploded fine off her bow, flooding her fore-peak tanks and twisting and buckling several of her bow plates. The tanker shuddered, shook herself free of the towering splash and kept coming, but her battered hull and strained engines could obviously not take much more of this type of punishment. One Stuka, hit in her dive by the combined fire of the *Ohio* and the *Ashanti*, was torn apart. Another was hit fair and square by 20-mm shells but they failed to stop her. At full throttle she thundered hard into the tanker's side after bouncing off the sea and crashed with a scream of tearing metal on to the tanker's poop. Flames and smoke drifted over the *Ohio*, but she was still under control. Her single low-angled gun was twisted out of alignment by the concussion and hung uselessly at a drunken angle.

The Malta Spitfires got in a brief attack against the bombers and claimed to have destroyed one, but an error by the gunners of the *Dorset* caused the loss of one of the British fighters, which was shot down in flames with the loss of the pilot.

Again the Luftwaffe came boring in, this time a further twenty Ju88s attacked from ahead. It was another dangerous assault with near misses churning up the sea around the freighters and once again the *Ohio* suffered. A bomber was heavily hit by gunfire, belly-flopped across the sea fifty feet from the tanker and slithered into *Ohio* in a shower of flames. Luckily the plane had already dropped her bombs but this additional shock, coupled with further explosions near by, blew out the boiler fires. All the engine-room lights went out and the ship went on to the emergency lighting; she stopped dead in the water, while the rest of the convoy surged on ahead.

At 11.20 came another Italian attempt, a force of twelve Sm79s escorted by fourteen Mc202s being sighted ahead. While their escorts clashed with the Spitfires in wild dogfights overhead the torpedo-bombers deployed to commence their attack. One of them dropped his torpedo at extreme range but the others seemed determined to press in closer and might have proven dangerous. At this juncture *Pathfinder* again took a hand:

> One can get very tired of being attacked by aeroplanes [her captain recorded later]; we had to alter course to avoid the torpedoes; and so we decided to do the attacking ourselves. We increased speed to thirty knots and turned straight out to seaward to meet the Sm79s.
>
> The torpedo-bombers were flying at masthead height and we steered for the middle of their formation. We opened fire as soon as we came within range, engaging on both sides of the ship at once with every gun we had. The noise was tremendous and I personally remember it as the most exhilarating and enjoyable moment of the war. The nearest Sm79 was almost within biscuit toss, and the whole formation was surrounded by shell bursts and streams of tracer bullets,

through which they dived, twisted and climbed, dropping their torpedoes in almost all directions except the convoy. One Sm79 caught fire, and we could but hope that the others were as full of holes as they scattered and steered back towards Sicily. The attack broken up, we turned under full rudder to rejoin the convoy, with the comfortable feeling of a stone-waller who had given way to human nature and hit a boundary.

Pathfinder's vigorous and spirited action had thrown the Italian pilots completely out of their stride and most of their torpedoes missed the ships well clear. Only one was accurate and this became entangled by its fin in the starboard paravane of the *Port Chalmers*' minesweeping gear. This left Captain Pinkey in an unenviable position with the live torpedo tied close to his side and threatening to swing in and detonate against her thin plates at any moment.

Somewhat at a loss at this unexpected situation Captain Pinkey flashed the nearest escorts for advice. Commander Gibbs suggested that he should cut the paravane wire and swing the helm hard over. In the end the clump chain for'ard was unshackled and let go and the derrick was then let go. Their dangerous companion then sank quickly as the *Port Chalmers* drew clear. Some minutes later it exploded on the bottom – in about 400 fathoms – and although the ship was well clear Captain Pinkey described the uplift of the explosion as tremendous.

During an earlier dive-bombing attack the *Dorset* had come to grief. She was struck aft by a heavy bomb, which penetrated No 4 hold. The engine-room was flooded and a large fire was started in the hold, which was next to the one, which contained the high-octane. All the electric pumps failed due to the lack of current and there was no option but to abandon ship. It had been intended to use the scuttling charges to finish her off, but due to a misunderstanding they were left in the flooded part of the ship when the crew came up on deck. Like many of her companions before her *Dorset* was thus left ablaze but afloat.

Aboard the *Dorset*, which had endured so much so successfully hitherto, the end when it did come came with cruel suddenness and heartbreaking finality. Apprentice Desmond Dickens recalled how:

At 0945 there came a very heavy air attack indeed, by Stukas. They circled round for a minute or so and then decided to attack *Dorset* and *Ohio*, which were easier to attack than the other ships. Six went to deal with *Dorset* and three others to *Ohio*. Down they came lower and lower – we gave them all we had, but still they came, screeching louder and louder; then they let go their bombs – one could even see them coming straight for us. Amidst the awful whine and din I prayed harder than ever before and God heard those prayers for not one of the bombs hit the ship directly. Three went on either side and the ship was lifted right out of the water six times. 'Please God,' gasped the man at the wheel …

As soon as this terrific bombardment was over a brief inspection of *Dorset*'s engine-room was made, but it was found useless to do anything. Water was pouring in from a gaping hole on the starboard side, and the generators were completely wrecked. No 4 hatch was ablaze in the lower hold so the order to 'Abandon Ship' was given. We had done all we could, but they had got us at last. The boats were lowered and it is fortunate that all the crew were picked up by HM destroyer *Bramham*.

Rochester Castle had been damaged again by near misses in the first heavy attack at 8 am but this had not reduced her speed. At ten o'clock she was severely shaken by three bombs which exploded under her bows, lifting the ship out of the water and dislocating her engines. Fires were started which soon began to spread and this necessitated the flooding of a magazine. Her engines were restarted after ten minutes but it took far longer to bring the blaze under control; it was then found that this had damaged her steering mechanism.

By the time her steering was fixed she was laden with over four thousand tons of water which made keeping her on course a nightmare, but Captain Wren and his crew succeeded magnificently despite the fact that her freeboard was reduced to less then six feet.

The destroyers *Penn* and *Ledbury* were sent back to find *Ohio* while *Bramham* picked up the crew of the *Dorset*. The convoy, now reduced once more to a mere three ships, was by this time under the cover of the short-range Spitfires and despite persistent attempts by the enemy, they kept the bombers at a distance. By 2.30 the Malta Escort Force made contact to reinforce the convoy escort. For the *Port Chalmers*, *Rochester Castle* and *Melbourne Star* the worst of their ordeal was now over. At 4 pm these survivors had Malta in sight and the warships of Force X – including the *Pathfinder*, which with the *Penn* was originally intended to join the Mediterranean fleet at Port Said – hauled round to the west. By 6.25 the three merchantmen slowly steamed into the still, calm water of Valletta harbour, welcomed by cheering crowds of Maltese and bands playing at the harbour entrance. Three ships out of fourteen, but without the vital oil tanker, even this achievement would be valueless.

III

Three ships out of fourteen, but to the west there remained a further three ships of the convoy still afloat. All attention was now to be focused on the efforts to get these vessels *Ohio*, *Dorset* and *Brisbane Star* in. The last, *Brisbane Star*, was the only one still entirely on her own. She was down by the head with ten feet of water in No 1 hold, but still capable of eight knots. Captain Riley knew that they would need more than their fair share of luck to get through to Malta unprotected during the daylight hours of the 13th. Indeed almost as soon as the dawn brought the sun up over the Gulf of Hammamet they were sighted by one of the early morning search planes, an Sm79 from Sicily.

There was nothing Captain Riley could do except trust to the fates. Technically, being in territorial waters, neither the ship nor the plane had the right to open fire, unless they were attacked. It was therefore a matter of bluff as to who was panicked into letting fly first. In order to provoke the freighter the Italian pilot circled the *Brisbane Star*, carefully noting her armaments and the gaping hole in her bow. It was obvious she was one of the convoy, but the pilot, being an Italian, was very strict in observing international law. He therefore made a series of dummy runs as if to launch his torpedoes, in the hope of provoking the gunners, but in this he was unsuccessful. Three times he banked and came in frighteningly at masthead height, but to no avail.

After the third attempt the pilot ruefully realised that he was going to get no change from Captain Riley and, after a brief period noting her course and speed, he flew off to the north. Captain Riley noted in his report that the pilot was a gentleman and observed the rules of war, but the Naval liaison officer, after the Italian had flown away, only awaited the arrival of a Teutonic gentleman to finish the job. It was doubted whether the Luftwaffe would be as fussy about rules as their Italian counterparts – but in the event no other aircraft followed.

They were now crossing the Gulf close to the shore and not surprisingly they were soon challenged by the prickly Vichy authorities. At ten o'clock the signal station at Hammamet started signalling frantically at them. There followed a somewhat absurd exchange of signals:

Hammamet: You should hoist your signal letters.
Brisbane Star: Please excuse me.
Hammamet: You should anchor.
Brisbane Star: My anchors are fouled. I cannot anchor.
Hammamet: You appear to be dragging your bow and stern anchors.
Brisbane Star: I have no stern anchor.
Hammamet: Do you require salvage?
Brisbane Star: No.
Hammamet: It is not safe to go too fast.

Somewhat tired of this corny cross-talk act, Captain Riley had been cautiously edging his bows round towards the open sea and in reply to this final piece of advice he hoisted a jumble of flags to keep the French authorities guessing and steamed away. The French remained silent as he disappeared.

Thankful as he was to have escaped from the Vichy French with a mere exchange of signals and useless information, Captain Riley soon found himself facing another problem. On leaving the safety of the coastal waters he laid himself open to further enemy assault and after a few hours' further steaming he spotted what he took to be an enemy submarine keeping pace with him just outside territorial waters, obviously waiting for them to make the break for Malta.

It is not certain which submarine this was; only the *Asteria* was stationed to the south of Sicily, but she made no sighting report. All the British submarines were on their patrol line to the north-east and they had been ordered to dive soon after 6 am when it was confirmed that they would not be needed. It may have been French, but to whichever nationality it belonged, it shadowed the *Brisbane Star* patiently for the next hour or so. As if this complication was not sufficient, the Vichy French made an official reappearance.

It was nearly five o'clock and *Brisbane Star* was well south of her desired position and the submarine was still with her. A small French patrol boat stood out from Monastir Bay and signalled Captain Riley to stop. Signalling unintelligible messages back to him the British freighter altered course and attempted to shake him off. After half an hour the French captain finally got tired of the chase and, losing patience, fired a warning shot which landed ten yards off *Brisbane Star*'s bow. Captain Riley had no alternative but to heave to and once he had done so his ship was boarded by two Vichy French officers.

They were the essence of correctness and formality, but insisted that the British vessel should follow them back to Tunisia and be interned for the rest of the war. Captain Riley was equal to the occasion; he invited them both down to his cabin for a drink. Here he plied them liberally with both whisky and charm – and his Irish blarney evidently cut through even Vichy ice for within that time he managed to persuade them not to proceed with their plans. Not only did they allow him to proceed, they also took off one of the hands who had been badly injured by the torpedo explosion and wished the *Brisbane Star* '*Bon Voyage*'.

Captain Riley was subsequently awarded the OBE and his citation included a tribute to his 'initiative, tact, clear-thinking and determination'; it cannot be disputed that he well earned this praise.

The mollified Frenchmen steamed back to port, leaving Riley the task of losing the submarine. The coming of dusk greatly eased his problem and among the shoals and sandbars he finally satisfied himself that he had shaken her off. At nightfall on the 13th, after a very eventful day, *Brisbane Star* nosed her crumpled bows towards Malta and commenced the last leg of her dash to safety.

IV

The burning *Dorset* was less lucky. Her crew rescued by the *Bramham*, she lay disabled and helpless under the shadow of the enemy air bases and throughout the rest of the afternoon was prey to repeated attempts by the Luftwaffe to finish her off.

Despite her immobilisation, she showed no immediate signs of going down and after a while Captain Tuckett persuaded Lieutenant Baines to allow him to re-board his vessel with a view to getting her in to Malta after all. Accompanied by the Naval liaison officer, the Chief Officer and the Engineering Officer, Captain Tuckett was put aboard to make an examination to see if there really was any chance of *Bramham* attempting a tow. The heat was intense and it soon became apparent that the fires had a very good hold on her and the idea was dropped as being impracticable. It was now late afternoon and the enemy planes had been active all day in their vicinity, the main brunt of their attentions falling on the *Ohio*.

A small group of Ju88s lifted off from their airfield at 5.47 pm and soon afterwards they located the *Dorset* and selected her as their target. Despite the fact that she was stationary they only scored one hit, a large bomb bursting on her foredeck which rekindled the blaze with renewed intensity. Her fate was now sealed and she began to settle well down by the stern. At 7 pm she was hit yet again and went down rapidly.

Seen through the eyes of the young apprentice Desmond Dickens, the end of this fine vessel was indeed tragic. He was to record:

> To go alongside either ship now was suicidal, for aircraft were always in the vicinity; so we were going to wait until darkness came, and then try and tow the two ships (*Dorset* and *Ohio*) in. As time went on, however, *Dorset* was hit again by bombs and was seen to be settling by the stern; by

1800 the 4-inch gun deck astern was awash, and by 1930 there was no hope. Gradually that majestic-looking ship went lower and lower, and by 1955 *Dorset* was no more – what a pathetic sight that was – that great ship which had done so much to keep this England of ours full of food.

She went down with colours flying, the Red Duster had done its best.

The *Bramham* steered to join the little group around the *Ohio*, fighting off an extremely heavy air attack by ten dive-bombers as she did so. Although now beginning to be worried by fuel shortages, Lieutenant Baines was forced to go at full speed to avoid being hit and, at 25 knots and amid a shower of bombs, *Bramham* joined the *Penn*. Vice-Admiral Leatham at Malta later felt that had the tug *Jaunty* accompanied the convoy right through as originally planned the *Dorset* might have been got in; he was obviously unaware of the tug's speed defect.

V

After picking up the survivors of the *Almeria Lykes* and the *Wairangi*, the two 'Tribal' class destroyers continued on towards the Tunisian coast in search of *Manchester*. Eventually they came upon floating debris and sighted several carley rafts full of survivors from the cruiser. They rescued all those they could find and while doing so they could see several hundred more being formed up in columns ashore by Vichy troops and marched away to prison camps. Powerless to intervene they extended their search for further survivors still afloat. They were aided in this errand of mercy by an Italian Red Cross plane which dropped a life raft near some of the '*Manchester*s' who were without aid.

The subsequent treatment handed out by the Vichy authorities to the '*Manchester*s' who got ashore was not a very edifying story.

We were incarcerated in a Beau Geste type fort in this large Saharan oasis [one survivor recalled]. *Manchester*'s survivors were by no means the only inmates of this camp [*Havock*'s crew and some Fleet Air Arm pilots were also present]. Food was minimal, dysentery was rife and perhaps the major difference between this camp and many others was that we did not get Red Cross food parcels in the same way as those who were prisoners of the Germans and Italians. This was Laghouat Camp, Algiers. I well remember that my wife tried to send me a parcel of clothing as nights were very cold in the desert and I only had one pair of shorts and a shirt. She was advised by the International Red Cross that she could send me a parcel, but that it was most unlikely that it would ever reach me intact.

In fact I did get the parcel, but on arrival it. contained several folded newspapers in Arabic script and two packets of Algerian dates. We were released after the Allied landing in North Africa and my stay in this camp was limited to three months, by which time I, a large six feet, fifteen stoner, weighed eight and a half stone!

Having satisfied himself that they had found all the remainder Commander Le Geyt then shaped course back to Gibraltar. The fact that the *Manchester* had been scuttled and the survivors picked up had still not reached Rear-Admiral Burrough and fearful that she might still need assistance he ordered the *Ledbury* to go back and aid the search.

On the way back she was taken under attack by two Italian torpedo-bombers. Like all the other men of Force X the crew of the *Ledbury* were by this time completely exhausted, but this threat found them responding with as much determination as ever. Lieutenant Hill thought that the enemy planes were old and slow and he felt he had every chance of scoring a valuable morale-boosting victory. He ordered the 4-inch guns to cease-fire in order to lure the torpedo-bombers in close; he wanted to make certain of their destruction.

As the leading aircraft approached to within Oerlikon range all the guns engaged it and quickly scored numerous hits, which caused it to crash burning into the sea. While they were occupied with the first aircraft, the second had time to launch his torpedoes at the destroyer and attempted to get clear, but before he could do so the short-range weapons switched targets. Raked through and through the second Italian bomber was also destroyed, a heartening sight to the weary sailors. His missiles, which ran very close, were avoided.

Soon after this incident the *Ledbury* made landfall opposite Hammamet and started a diligent search for the missing cruiser. For two hours they followed the coastline but of course found no trace of their erstwhile companion. The signal station at Hammamet indignantly protesting about this procession of British ships up and down their shores challenged her, asking her to show her signal letters, Lieutenant Hill replied with Italian recognition flags and the Vichy seemed satisfied by this.

Several of the men they had rescued from the burning sea that morning had since died of their wounds aboard and they were buried during the afternoon, the canvas-covered bodies slipping over the side weighed down with 4-inch armour-piercing shells. After some considerable time without any luck in their quest, a signal was received from the RAF at Malta informing them that an enemy cruiser and two destroyers had been sighted off Zembra. This turned out later to have been a false sighting but at the time the receipt of it convinced Lieutenant Hill that he would be unable to continue the search. He set course to the east to find the *Ohio* once more.

The tanker had been left, stopped and with a five degree list. Desperate work in the engine-room had now resulted – within half an hour – in getting her under way once again at sixteen knots, but the respite was only a brief one. She was brought under fresh air attack and another succession of near misses shattered the electrical fuel pumps and tore the main switch from the bulkhead. Once more all lights were extinguished and the tanker slowed to a standstill.

Chief Engineer Wyld reported to Captain Mason the extent of the damage: he was asked to make a full inspection, but this only confirmed the fact that *Ohio*'s engines were finished; oil in the water meant that nothing more could be done for the crippled ship short of a tow, and there was no tug.

Lieutenant-Commander Swain of the *Penn* decided to attempt this task himself. A party under Second Officer McKilligan went forward on to the debris-littered fo'c'sle of the tanker to clear an area to take the line and *Penn* passed over a ten-inch manila. While doing so they were bombed and strafed by a lone Ju88, which scored near misses and further aggravated the tanker's position.

The towline was secured and *Penn*, a mere 1, 540-tonner, her 40,000 SHP engines straining as the 30,000 tons deadweight of the tanker took effect, attempted to move the *Ohio*. The tanker was now drawing some thirty-seven feet and the huge rent in her hull counteracted the tow and turned her steadily to port. Gradually, as the strain increased, she pulled away until the destroyer was pulling at ninety degrees angle and the wind, far from assisting, was gently drifting the lifeless hulk backwards.

Penn tried again to bring the tanker's head round, but with the same result – merely moving her in a slow, sluggish circle. Another attack developed and *Penn* in order to manoeuvre to meet it went hard ahead and parted the towline with a crack. Despite the fire from the two ships, one bomber planted his bombs close alongside the tanker where they exploded amidships under her keel. Already torn and stretched, this explosion opened the rent still further and it was plain that she was fated very soon to split asunder.

As the attack died away Captain Mason hailed the *Penn* and informed Lieutenant-Commander Swain that her only hope was to have two ships with towlines head and astern, one to act as a rudder; this was not possible, however, for *Penn* was the only escort now present.

There seemed no alternative but to abandon the tanker. At 2.15 the tired crew of *Ohio* were taken aboard the destroyer where they soon fell asleep, for, like their skipper, most of them had been at action stations now for three days, during which their ship had been a constant attraction for every form of attack. The *Penn* circled the drifting vessel awaiting reinforcements, but nobody aboard the escort expected her to stay afloat long enough for another attempt to be made.

The Axis continued to mount attack after attack, although the weight they directed against the lone tanker was nullified by the effects of the Royal Air Force. Between 3.57 and 7 pm, 26 Ju88s and seven Heinkel 111 s were sent out in small groups and at 5.02 the Italians sent out five of 102 Gruppo's Stukas powerfully escorted by no less than 24 Mc202 fighters, in an attempt to bulldoze their way through the protecting fighter defences.

The Royal Air Force maintained a standing patrol of sixteen Spitfires at all times over the *Ohio*, which was a formidable barrier. In the ensuing fighting the RAF pilots claimed to have despatched three of the Mc202s and several of the Ju87s. One of the Beaufighters was forced to ditch not far from Pantelleria, but the crew escaped. It was feared that they would be almost certainly picked up by the enemy but Wing Commander Satchell volunteered to attempt a rescue in a captured Italian Cant 506B floatplane. Despite a long search he failed to find the airmen, but four of 248's fighters spotted their dinghy. Unfortunately they were unable to raise Satchell on the radio and the Beaufighter crew were eventually picked up by an Italian Dornier. Other Beaufighters overhead were ordered to leave the rescuer alone and she flew to Sicily with them.

Meantime, at 5.40, the minesweeper *Rye* (Lieutenant J. A. Pearson, DSC, RNR) of the Malta Escort Force, joined the *Penn* in company with the motor-launches *Ml.121* and *Ml.168*, both of which were despatched from the main body of the force because they lacked minesweeps.

Lieutenant-Commander Swain had a conference with Pearson and they decided to do the best they could with this small force to get the *Ohio* moving again, although their task seemed hopeless. Somewhat refreshed by their short rest, the bulk of the tanker's crew volunteered to go back aboard her again with a Naval party from the destroyer to assist in the new attempt. The ship was now drawing no less than 38 feet with her list slowly increasing and her bows dipping ever lower, but undaunted they set to work.

At 5.45 pm the tow was once more made fast from *Penn* and she moved slowly ahead again. It was to no avail; just a repetition of their earlier efforts, with the deadweight of the tanker turning her to port and overrunning the tow. It was clear that no further progress would be made with the rudder thus jammed so a party went below to clear it. Within half an hour they had cast off the emergency steering gear and rigged a hand steering gear by attaching cables to the chains and revving them through the relieving tackles. This enabled Captain Mason to report to Swain that they had fixed the rudder to give them about five degrees to starboard which it was hoped would counteract her port swing.

The destroyer took the strain and the *Ohio*, with a quick shudder, began to move. Carefully Swain increased his speed until they were moving at five knots, the tanker, however, still yawed and edged, dragging the *Penn* back into her again. After a short time they were force to stop and Swain and Pearson had another get-together. By passing 500 fathoms of her sweep wire into the destroyer, the *Rye* was to act as a stabiliser. This was accomplished at 6.35 and both naval vessels went ahead together. This time success crowned their efforts and at four or five knots the tanker began to make slow progress.

It was at this crucial time that the German bombers put in another unwelcome appearance; four Ju88s appeared ahead, having been missed by the Spitfire patrol. They commenced their dives and, knowing that their chances of avoiding being hit were small, Captain Mason ordered all his men who were below decks, topside. The four bombers broke formation, circled the ships picking their easiest approach and then made independent attacks from astern where the amount of barrage fire was at its lowest density.

Moving sluggishly there was nothing the tanker could do but sit and wait for it; soon one heavy bomb erupted hard astern of her, once more knocking out her rudder. Another bomber scored a direct hit, the bomb bursting on the tanker's boiler tops after crushing through the fore-end of the boat deck and starting a fire there. It also blew a ventilator on to one of the Bofors guns, trapping one of its crew beneath the wreckage.

The crew ran to pull him clear, but Gunner Brown had severe internal injuries and died later aboard one of the warships. Captain Mason's assessment of the damage revealed that the engine-room was completely wrecked and the rudder was useless. Moreover in moving to meet the attack *Penn* had once more been forced to cast off the tow. Miraculously the ship still held together by her keel but the strain was now intolerable and under renewed attacks the two motor launches came alongside her to take off all hands. Both *Penn* and *Rye* were near-missed in these raids, but escaped serious damage. One of the motor launches, *Ml.168*, was badly shaken and developed engine defects. Swain sent her back to Malta.

They were now right back at square one and Captain Mason was completely exhausted. While he slept aboard *Penn* Lieutenant-Commander Swain and Lieutenant-Commander Pearson had another talk. During the air raid, as related earlier, the group had been joined by the *Bramham* laden with survivors from the *Dorset* and she took up an anti-submarine patrol round the group as a party under the command of *Penn*'s executive officer, Lieutenant G. G. Marten, went back on board *Ohio* to make ready for yet another towing effort.

This time *Rye* was allocated the towing position ahead using the chain cable while *Penn* ran in astern of the tanker and made fast. In this position it was hoped she would stop the *Ohio* swinging, even without a rudder. It was 10.25 pm before the tow recommenced and this time good progress was made, initially at some four knots. Captain (as he now is) Pearson kindly made his log of events available to the author and in those terse statements much is revealed by reading between the semi-formal lines. The commanding officer of the *Rye* recorded these desperate hours thus:

1700 Sighted *Ohio*.

1730 Being engaged by enemy aircraft.

1740 Torpedo bombing attack.

1745 Joined *Ohio* and *Penn* in latitude 36 degrees, 00 minutes North, Longitude 12 degrees 59 minutes East. *Penn* re-connects her tow and resumes towing.

1815 Rye's sweepwires made fast to *Penn* and *Ohio*, veered to 500 fathoms. *Rye* commenced towing.

1845 A succession of bombing attacks, estimated sixteen aircraft. Four bombs fall twenty yards off to port and four twenty yards ahead. *Rye* disappeared from sight but emerged unscathed.

2042 Penn slips her and *Rye*'s tow ropes owing to heavy

bombing attack.

2052 Last attack of evening driven off by *Penn*. On heaving in sweepwires they were found to be badly twisted and knotted. 250 fathoms from each wire had to be cut off. Two 3_-inch flexible steel wire ropes were added to each wire to make up loss.

2200 *Rye* went alongside *Ohio*. A party of seamen under Leading Seaman Rowland Prior were put aboard *Ohio* to connect towropes.

2230 Commenced towing. *Penn* then passes a line from her bow to *Ohio*'s stern and steers *Ohio* acting as a stern tug. Ships making about four knots.

Through the dark Mediterranean night the little collection of ships moved forward at this agonisingly slow speed.

VI

From the Axis viewpoint, the fading of daylight on the 13th virtually brought to an end their interest in the surviving ships of the convoy proper. They now set to inflict as much damage as possible on the returning warships of Force X. This provided a much-needed respite for the group around the crippled tanker and was another major error on the part of the enemy Air Staffs.

On the 13th the Germans reported that no final results of the offensive operations had been received, but that contact was being maintained up to a point close to the southern coast of the island. At 2 pm no more than four or five merchant vessels, and four to six light escort vessels, were reported in the convoy then some twenty miles west of Malta.

In the evening the German Air Staff received reports of three cruisers and four destroyers proceeding westward north-west of Malta, which they correctly gauged as 'probably the escort forces detached from what was left of the convoy, which in the meantime had entered Valletta'. Their report also added that 'since it is pretty certain that 21 merchant vessels left the Straits of Gibraltar in an easterly direction, and that no more than five or six may be assumed to have reached the harbour of Valletta, the fact that an extraordinary success has been achieved is beyond doubt'.

This constant over-estimation of the numbers of the freighters in the convoy and the many inaccurate reports by the airmen of claimed sinkings was to lead to wild propaganda from the Axis during the days following. Meanwhile the Germans sent the two undamaged boats of the 3rd E-boat Flotilla back into the area between Cape Bon and Cape Blanc to search for damaged or returning vessels.

Supermarina also felt that, following the heavy air attacks and reports of successes by the returning pilots, easy pickings would be available to the remaining submarines. Therefore at seven that evening the Italian submarine command, Maricomsom, signalled all available boats already in Tunisian waters: 'Surface and proceed at once concentrating greatest maximum strength to search for damaged enemy units.'

The ships of Force X were meantime steering through the evening of the 13th for position R, some twelve miles to the south of Linosa, led by the *Intrepid* with her one remaining sweep. *Kenya* with her damaged bow had been able to maintain the fifteen knots of the convoy on the outward passage, but it was not known what speed she was capable of in the crash back. Eventually she worked up to a magnificent twenty-eight knots, at which speed, she threw up an enormous bow wave from her shattered stem, but it was evident that her ship's company had done wonders in shoring up her bulkheads for she held this speed without difficulty. Just after midnight they passed Cape Bon and turned west and almost at once they came upon the E-boats lying in ambush for them.[1] Searchlights caught one and she was immediately engaged with full salvos from *Kenya*. Making heavy clouds of smoke she turned away. This boat was the *Mas.556* (Tenente di Vascello Sala) who had moments earlier sighted three vessels, which he took to be two torpedo boats and a light cruiser.

He was illuminated and brought under heavy fire, but he managed to launch two torpedoes at 500 metres' range against the biggest unit,

[1] The squadron was deployed in single line ahead for the night passage in the order *Intrepid, Ashanti, Kenya, Charybdis, Pathfinder, Icarus* and *Fury*.

at 0145, and he then disengaged swiftly, dropping depth-charges as he did so. The Italian boat was undamaged by the heavy fire and Sala reported hearing both his torpedoes striking home, though this was not actually the case. Once safely clear he broadcast a sighting report and this was picked up by the nearest Italian unit, the submarine *Granito* (Tenente di Vascello Leo Sposito).

At 3.40 *Granito* surfaced and assumed an intercepting course of 160 degrees and an hour later was rewarded with the sight of dim shapes moving swiftly towards her. She was close to the Fratelli Rocks and there was little time for her to manoeuvre before the leading vessels of Force X were on top of her.

The two nearest ships were 4,000 metres away with another behind them and all appeared to be zigzagging at speed. With the range closing fast the Italian boat got off two snap shots with his bow tubes. The leading British ships were now almost upon the surfaced submarine and the *Granito*'s skipper had to turn violently to avoid being run down. As he did so he got off another two torpedoes, the second of which was at a vessel he identified as a cruiser of the 'London' class.[1]

The two shots in fact only just missed the *Ashanti*; the *Kenya*, next astern, sighted the U-boat and attempted to ram her. As she swept past and turned, so did the *Granito* in a much tighter circle and the cruiser missed. While turning Sposito fired a further two torpedoes from his stern tubes, he then executed a rapid dive and escaped unscathed. His hydrophones picked up the sounds of his missiles hitting a target only 60 seconds after launch, which led him to think that he had sunk either the heavy cruiser or perhaps a battleship. Once more the Italians were mistaken and all the torpedoes were avoided. Force X cleared the straits by dawn and at daybreak were south-south-east of Galitia Island, and here, soon afterwards, the Luftwaffe rediscovered them. From 7.30 am

[1] Her target was in fact the *Kenya*. The *London* was an 8-inch cruiser of the 'County' class which had been rebuilt in the early years of the war and strongly resembled the more modern but smaller 'Colony' class ships to which *Kenya* belonged. Sposito had only a fleeting glance at his target so the mistake is understandable.

Normally there would have been no error for the 'County' class ships were three-funnelled, slab-sided and quite unlike anything else in any navy.

onwards the Germans mounted a round-the-clock offensive against the small group as they hurried westward.

The first strike was delivered by seventeen Ju88s, which had left their bases at dawn. They arrived over the British squadron in three groups and made their attacks between 7.30 and 9.11. The five destroyers were spread out ahead of the two cruisers and the *Kenya* managed to further increase her speed to 26 knots during the day. Obviously damaged as she was and being the largest ship in the force, she made a very alluring target and was usually singled out for the bulk of the attacks.

The first batch of these, by three, six and eight Ju88s respectively, caused no damage or loss to either side, but as the day wore on the Axis airmen increased their efforts, both in size and in intensity. From 1000 to 1300 attacks were almost incessant and included dive-bombing, high-level bombing, torpedo bombing and the dropping of mines or circling torpedoes by low-flying aircraft. This latter was evidently an attempt on the part of the enemy to slow down the force and keep it within range of the airfields. Between 10.30 and 10.50 a particularly severe attack developed by Luftwaffe formations comprising nine Ju88s and thirteen Ju87s, later joined by fifteen Italian S84s, high-level bombing, from Sicily. Fortunately the Italian squadron arrived slightly later than the others, but even so it was a most severe synchronised assault and most of the ships were shaken by near misses. Anti-aircraft ammunition was being used up at a high rate in beating off the Stuka attacks with barrage fire and some concern was felt that ships might run short.

It was during this raid that one Stuka succeeded in scoring a hit on the *Kenya*, a 500-pound bomb hitting her for'ard and glancing off her side armour just below the upper deck on the port side. It exploded underwater close alongside and severe shock was felt within the ship but no mechanical failures resulted. Only minor damage was caused to some electrical equipment and the echo sounder was once more put out of action. A small fire broke out in the boiler-room which resulted in some loss of speed for a short period, but within twenty minutes she had again worked up from 16 knots to 25. Three men were killed by a premature 4-inch shell burst.

The German pilots on return to their aerodromes assessed their results as hits on both cruisers, but the *Charybdis* was actually untouched. The Italian high-level attacks were avoided by violent alterations of course and zigzagging and caused no damage.

At midday eight Sm79 torpedo-bombers from Sardinia put in an appearance, but heavy barrage fire broke up their formation before they got close enough for accuracy and, although the airmen again claimed a torpedo hit on a cruiser, all their missiles were avoided. The same lack of result was obtained by a second force of Sm79s from Sicily, they also claiming a hit on a ubiquitous cruiser. A further four torpedo-bombers approached the force at 1.25 but again barrage fire drove them away and one was forced to crash-land in Tunisia.

Out ahead of the cruisers, the destroyer *Pathfinder* sighted three Br20 bombers, low on the horizon ahead, and as they watched they saw them dropping black parachutes. Suspecting further aerial minelaying similar to that encountered the previous day Rear-Admiral Burrough took his ships in a wide sweep clear of the area. Some time later distant underwater explosions were heard from the ships, which seemed to confirm their diagnosis, but no account of such an attack is contained in Italian records.

This proved to be the final contact they had with the Axis air forces, but in this they were lucky. Another strong striking force had been mounted by the Luftwaffe, every fit aircraft being ordered into the air. In all 37 Ju88s, and five He 111s lifted off from their airfields in Sicily at 1 pm for a final all-out assault. Fortunately for the British squadron, heavy cloud began forming and visibility rapidly deteriorated. The questing bombers roamed to and fro across the ships' previous route but the diversion to avoid the parachute mines had taken the ships some miles to the north. Fascinated, Force X watched the aircraft searching for them, plotting the bombers' baffled movements on the ships' radar screens, but the force escaped detection and the Luftwaffe returned empty-handed to their bases in the evening.

Meanwhile Vice-Admiral Syfret had been cruising with the *Nelson*, *Victorious*, *Phoebe*, *Sirius* and destroyers to the north of Algiers since the previous night.

> During D.5 I was uncertain of the position of Force X [wrote Syfret] and how it was faring, though from intercepted signals it was clear that they were being subjected to air

attacks to the west of Galitia Island. With the object of being near at hand if support was required Force Z cruised to the northward of Algiers until about 1500/D.5 when I was relieved to receive a signal from Rear-Admiral, Commanding 10th Cruiser Squadron, giving me his noon position, course and speed as 37°21'N, 06°27'E, 272 degrees, twenty knots. Course of Force Z was then set to make contact.

The two squadrons met, after an Albacore had made contact at 6 pm, and the combined force withdrew to Gibraltar, arriving at 6 pm the following day. The tanker group, Force R, had been cruising to the western end of the basin but when it was realised that they would not be required by Force X they too were sent back to Gibraltar.

Ashanti was badly in need of a refit and her supply of fresh water was very low [Rear-Admiral Burrough recalled]. For four days I had not shaved nor changed my clothes which were still covered with black oil from the torpedoed *Nigeria*; but on the afternoon of the 14th, escorted by my Coxswain, I descended, wrapped in a towel, to the upper deck and took a salt-water shower in full view of an interested ship's company.

Arriving at Gibraltar I found orders from the Admiralty awaiting me telling me to haul down my Flag and fly home at once to plan another operation.

By this time all the other naval forces had arrived back at the Rock. The *Nigeria*, eleven foot down by the head, and escorted by *Bicester*, *Derwent* and *Wilton*, had only been subjected to one ineffective attack by three torpedo-bombers on the 13th, which they had little trouble in avoiding. All the enemy submarines lying in wait for the returning ships had been avoided, although one made an attack on *Nigeria*'s force south of Alboran on the 14th.

Tartar had joined this group and all five arrived back in the early hours of the 13th. Also safely in were the *Eskimo* and *Somali*, laden with *Manchester*'s survivors. Their passage had been uneventful save for a machine-gun attack by a lone Ju88 at 5.05 on the 13th. While these scattered forces were making their various ways back to Gibraltar plans were being completed for a final postscript to the operation.

This was a final sortie by *Furious* to fly off further Spitfires to Malta. Needless to say the Italian Intelligence knew of this foray before it took place and on the night of the 17th/18th they sailed several submarines to intercepting positions. The *Profido* left Messina, the *Ascianghi*, *Alagi* and *Asteria* from Trapani, the *Avorio* from Cagliari and the *Platino* from Maddalena. The *Brin* and *Wolframo*, which were returning to their bases, were re-routed to the area north of Bizerta. Evidently the Italians half-expected another convoy operation, but once *Furious* had completed her mission on the 17th and turned back, all these boats were recalled on the 19th.

VII

We must now retrace our steps to the night of the 13th where far to the east a long and hard struggle had been going on around the crippled *Ohio* in a series of desperate attempts to get the vital tanker into Malta.

At midnight on the 13th/14th the *Ohio* was still slowly under way through the combined efforts of the *Penn* and *Rye*. They had been making slow but steady speed at four knots and there were hopes that at last the end was in sight. The *Rye* in the towing position at one o'clock attempted a slight increase in speed and the result was fatal; the tanker yawed badly to port, snapping the towline. Captain Pearson recorded events thus:

> Both 3-inch wires parted. *Penn* and *Bramham* proceed alongside *Ohio*, one each side and attempted to tow her. *Rye* made a 10-inch manila fast and towed from ahead.

Lieutenant-Commander Swain now decided to adopt the suggestion from Lieutenant Baines of the *Ledbury*, that an alongside tow might do the trick. Accordingly the *Penn* was carefully brought alongside the *Ohio* and made fast. At 1.10 the destroyer gingerly went slow ahead, but despite this the tanker refused to move. Swain rang down for increased power; closing his mind to the grinding together of the ships' plates and the damage this was doing to the frail hull of his destroyer, he made another effort, but it met with little success. However, it was now obvious that one destroyer on her own did not have the ability to do the job and that any further attempts to try it this way would result in seriously disabling the *Penn*. The attempt was therefore stopped.

There was nothing for it but to cast off once more and await daylight before trying a further effort. For the next three hours the *Penn* and *Rye* circled the *Ohio* which lay awkwardly and low in the water, her decks twisting and groaning with every movement of the sea.

This brief respite enabled the dog-tired crews on all the ships to catch a few more hours' rest and by the first half-light of dawn on the 14th they were ready to renew the battle. Once more the *Penn* went alongside and made fast. And yet again, at 4 am, as they commenced moving, the *Ohio* yawed wildly and the tow parted. Next the *Rye* tried to take both ships in tow using a ten-inch manila aboard the tanker, and a sweep wire attached to *Penn*'s cable. At 5.05 this resulted in another failure for once more the *Ohio* took control, her massive deadweight swinging irresistibly away and parting both wires. It seemed impossible.

At 7.15 they were rejoined by the *Bramham* returning from her fruitless search for the *Manchester*. The *Rye* now passed three hundred yards of sweep wire into *Ohio* while *Bramham* made fast astern of the tanker, in order to act as a steering tug while the *Penn* remained clear. They got under way as before but the *Bramham* still could not prevent the stubborn tanker swinging away and eight o'clock saw the hawsers parted once more. It was heartbreaking, but now the minesweeper *Speedy* and three motor launches arrived from Malta and Commander Jerome, as Senior Officer, took over salvage attempts. Captain Mason went back on board to make an inspection of his shattered ship and was soon reporting to Jerome: 'I think that with luck we'll last twelve hours and that should be enough for you to get us to Malta.'

At 10.50 there took place the final air attack against the crippled tanker: five Ju87s of the Italian 102 Gruppo escorted by twenty Mc202s made an attempt to finish her off. Fortunately the RAF had been maintaining their strong air umbrella over the ships; as well as several Beaufighters, there were always sixteen Spitfires from 229 and 249 Squadrons overhead. They briskly engaged the Italian fighters, but were unable to prevent one Stuka landing yet another bomb close alongside the tanker.

This bomb, of an estimated 1,000 pounds, burst hard in the *Ohio*'s wake, flinging her forward with its concussion, twisting her screws out of alignment and holing her stern. Already dangerously low in the water this new inrush of water made her position critical. The RAF destroyed one Stuka and one of the Mc202s without loss to themselves, and thereafter parried other raids, but these were few, nor were they launched in heavy force. Even so it would seem that this final blow would be sufficient.

That even this last blow failed says much for the American shipyard, which built *Ohio* and reflects the soundness of the design of the big ship. Captain Mason made a further report to Jerome: although he fully recognised that there was a strong possibility of her breaking in half at any time, in his opinion, an effort should still be made to tow in the for'ard half if this happened; this section, as he pointed out, contained 75% of her oil fuel cargo.

As the enemy bombers droned away the naval escorts sprang into new life. The *Bramham* was carefully brought alongside the tanker's port side and made fast. Volunteers, including survivors from the *Waimarama*, *Melbourne Star* and *Santa Elisa*, as well as naval ratings, were put aboard to man her remaining weapons and assist in the new towing arrangements. Lieutenant-Commander Swain then edged the *Penn* up on the tanker's starboard side and also made fast.

Another party armed with portable pumps from the destroyer to replace those destroyed on the *Ohio* also went on board to increase her buoyancy and pump out her engine-rooms. With a destroyer on either side and the *Ledbury* secured astern to act as a rudder the *Rye* positioned herself for towing. Around the mass of ships the minesweepers *Speedy*, *Hebe* and *Hythe* formed a protective circle.

First attempts were held up because *Ledbury*'s wire hawser threatened to foul the tanker's twisted screws, but this was avoided by the destroyer going ahead slowly on one engine while the wire was inched clear. Exhaustion among all the men of the little flotilla was beginning to tell with more and more alarming effects. There was nothing strange in this, for all had been at full alert for more than three days and two nights, under constant attacks from above and below the surface. Many had been worn out before the day started and now the added strain was beginning to reach unmanageable proportions. The only wonder was that those, like Captain Mason, who had endured so much, should have kept going for so long, and that others, like Lieutenant-Commander Swain and the captains of the *Bramham* and *Ledbury*, continued to direct their exhausted crews with clarity and vigour. It was inevitable that under such conditions all the crews from skippers down to the humblest AB found small problems aggravated and minor errors increased as worn-out minds and tired bodies struggled to cope with an ever-worsening position.

Soon after the tow had commenced it became apparent that the *Ohio*, as stubborn as ever, was not responding as she should and that the *Ledbury* was slowly but surely being dragged round with her. Finally the destroyer ended up alongside the *Penn* and attempting to rectify the drift resulted in the *Rye* losing the towing wire altogether. The group came to another halt.

Commander Jerome now organised a further effort and with both destroyers going slow ahead on either side of the tanker she finally began to move ahead on a straight course. They worked up to five knots before Captain Mason warned that his ship would not hold together with any further increase. At this snail's pace they continued towards Malta, but with every tortuous mile the level of the water in the flooded engine-rooms of the tanker increased. At noon yet another setback was suffered when one of the *Bramham*'s wires parted under the increasing strain. Under the direction of her First Lieutenant, the Marquess of Milford Haven, OBE, the tow was cast off and a new wire secured and the wearisome journey was resumed.

Meantime Supermarina had signalled the submarine *Asteria* (Tenente di Vascello Pasquale Beltrame) whose function it was to pick off such stragglers:

At thirty-five miles, 205 degrees from Gozo lighthouse, proceeding towards Malta, a tanker under tow. Search and attack with utmost resolution.

However, the *Asteria* had been attacked herself and slightly damaged by British aircraft and she made no sighting at all.

Under the scorching Mediterranean sun the British flotilla pressed on and by late afternoon the distant coastline of Malta came slowly into sight, the southern shores of the low-lying island gradually becoming plainer as they crawled towards it. Their goal was in sight, but still there was no certainty that the *Ohio* would make it. The waters around the island and especially in the long approach to the main harbour, were thick with mines and the only channel swept and kept clear was long and involved several abrupt changes of course. In her present condition it seemed very unlikely that *Ohio* could be manoeuvred through it.

As they approached the entrance to the channel off Delimara Point the destroyers began the complicated process of turning 30,000 tons of steel into the gap in the minefields. As they turned tenderly to port the towing wires, unable to take this extra demand on them, once more parted with a sharp crack. Close by the dangerous waters the whole complicated process of re-securing the tow began again.

They had been joined by this time by more ships, the ancient tug *Robust* and the STU *Supply*. The King's Harbour Master was aboard the tug and he now took charge of the arrangements. The *Robust* was secured to the tanker and, belching smoke, tried to move her but the tanker contemptuously resisted the efforts of the old veteran and began to pull the tug into the side of the *Penn*. Attempts at unshipping the towing wire failed and she crashed hard into the destroyer, holing her above the waterline. This round lost, the *Robust* was sent back to Malta while the destroyers resumed their duties once again.

Soon the tanker was under way into the swept channel, but anxiety was far from over as dusk settled over the group. While they were edging slowly up the channel, watchers on the radar plots were disturbed to see the blip of a small unit, apparently tailing them. It was thought that this must be an enemy submarine.

The Coastal Defence Batteries under the command of Colonel C. J. White went to full alert. Searchlights probed the area to the south of the swept channel and the escorts' gun crews also stood to.

Had there been a submarine there at that moment she could have hardly have failed to sink the *Ohio*, almost motionless as she was, the lights flickering over her and silhouetting her against the dark night. Anxious signals from the destroyer captains to the Army authorities put a stop to this dangerous illumination.

There was some confusion when the *Hebe* opened fire on an object thought to be a submarine's conning-tower and only an emergency order prevented the 9.2-inch heavy batteries ashore from blasting her out of the water, because they mistook this for an enemy attack. Further confusion arose when many other contacts, as if of fast-moving surface craft, were picked up on the radar screens approaching from the north-east. Taking no chances the shore batteries laid down a strong barrage in the path of these and after a time they disappeared. None of their E-boats were reported by the Axis to be off Malta at this time, but whatever the cause of the blips the British were convinced that the gunners had foiled a strong attempt by the Italians to sink the *Ohio* in the swept channel. And as to submarines, *Asteria* was the only enemy boat anywhere near and she, forced to submerge by earlier aircraft attacks, reported nothing of interest during her patrol.

As the night progressed more ships put out from Valletta to render aid including the three tugs *Carbine*, *Coronation* and *Robust* which left harbour at 2.30 pm. Help was needed still, for as the towing formation approached Zonkor Point it was necessary for the tanker to execute another different turn. Cautiously the *Penn* and *Bramham* nursed her round; then, with the turn half-made, the *Ohio* began yet again to make her incurable drift, edging herself and the two helpless destroyers into the minefield.

The *Ledbury* came alongside and passed her six-inch wire into the tanker and tried to pull the three ships round again. Two of the motor launches also assisted by pushing as hard as they could against the destroyer's bows. It was an agonising battle with little movement either way; for a time it was touch and go whether or not the whole group would end up in the minefield, so close to their goal.

At 6 pm the situation was remedied by the arrival of the Malta tugs and one of these made fast ahead and one astern; with the two destroyers still lashed on either side of the tanker as splints, the

Ohio was again proceeding up the channel towards the harbour entrance. By eight o'clock they had passed through the entrance to a fabulous welcome. The ancient battlements were lined with cheering throngs of Maltese and a band was playing with gusto to accompany them on their way. Even so the last mile was never-ending, with her decks awash and her torn and rent hull protesting at every movement there was still a grave fear that even at this eleventh hour the *Ohio* might sink and block the channel.

Penn had now been cast off and the *Bramham* remained alone to hold the ship together for the final few hundred yards to her berth. Slowly the gallant *Ohio* crawled towards the wreck of another tanker, the *Plumleaf*, which lay with its upperworks just above the water. *Bramham* now cast off and a naval auxiliary, the *Boxol* took over. As she slid into her place and was secured the dockyard men swarmed aboard her with pumps and pipes to unload her vital cargo before she settled. The *Boxol* also began embarking the precious fuel into her own tanks. It was a race against time for as the oil fuel was pumped out of her fore tanks her heavy after part continued to sink and threatened to break her in half. In addition it was now fully light and the risk of a sneak bombing attack could not be ruled out.

Strangely enough, as if admitting defeat, the Regia Aeronautica and the Luftwaffe made no attempts to disrupt the unloading of the ships once they had reached harbour. Already the *Rochester Castle*, *Melbourne Star* and *Port Chalmers* had completed discharging and the gallant *Brisbane Star*, which had reached safety the previous day under an umbrella of Spitfires, was similarly almost empty.

The last gallons of precious fuel were hardly pumped clear of the *Ohio*'s tanks before the tanker, her task accomplished, at last, settled finally on the bottom of Valletta Harbour. This marked the end of Operation 'Pedestal'.

Chapter Seven

The Tilting of the Scales

I

THE axis made no air attacks on Valletta harbour while the ships were unloading, although elaborate and detailed plans had been made to complete this task swiftly just in case. Codenamed Operation 'Ceres', it entailed the mobilising of all the dockyard workers and the greater bulk of the off-duty servicemen of the garrison. The plans had been laid with the view of unloading far more than five ships, but from those which finally arrived at Malta some 32,000 tons of general cargo was obtained. This was much less than had been hoped for, but it still meant that the island was given breathing space of two further vital months.

As vital as the stores, provisions and ammunition, was *Ohio*'s cargo of oil fuel, without which all the defensive and offensive capability of the garrison would have soon come to a standstill. Worthily the master of the tanker, the gallant Captain Mason who just would not accept defeat, was awarded the George Cross for his superb contribution in bringing in his ship despite her impossible condition. Other masters and crew also received just awards for the determination and courage they had shown. Indeed the bravery of these non-combatants in the face of the heaviest scale of attack ever mounted against a force of merchant ships at sea was remarkable.

A survivor from *Ohio* jotted down the traumatic events of those last hours later when he had recovered from his exhaustion:

On Thursday afternoon we were once again left on our own with the destroyer *Penn* circling round us at about 200 yard radius. Another merchant ship, *Dorset*, had been abandoned after being hit and was about six miles from us. At 1 pm the *Penn* attempted to take us in tow, but our rudder was hard over and could not be moved which caused us to go round in a circle. It was then decided to abandon ship and come back during dark when some additional escorts would arrive. The *Penn* took all hands on board and continued to circle the tanker. We had three raids during the afternoon, three planes being destroyed by fighters from Malta. No bombs hit the ship.

At 5.0 we were put back on board, two destroyers taking us in tow at 6.0, then a swarm of Junkers 88s came over, one bomb going down the engine-room. I saw the bombs coming and managed to run clear. On looking up saw a huge column of water falling on us from a near miss also a large ventilator, again I had to run for cover. The vent dropped in the Bofors gun nest, seriously injuring one of the crew. Again we abandoned ship.

I went below and collected my personal belongings – Doreen's photo, bible, prayer book and anything else lying around. On going on the boat deck the boats had been lowered and the injured soldier left in gunpit. I carried him down and got him into a boat. I then went to my boat station; my boat had cast off leaving the skipper and myself. A motor launch came alongside and took us off picking up others from a boat. Others were picked up by the destroyer and a motor launch. The destroyers *Penn* and *Bramham* then tied alongside one either side and took the tanker in tow. We then had another air attack, which was driven off, the planes finishing off the *Dorset*. We eventually arrived at Malta at 8.0 am Sat morning the quays lined with cheering people and the army band playing. It was a real thrill and almost made the trip feel worthwhile. The old tanker was placed in a berth and then rested on the dock bottom her back broken but practically all her cargo intact.

The survivors on the destroyers made a good job of clearing the ship whilst alongside everything movable or of any value having been taken. I lost all my kit even my bedclothes had gone!

Since being in Malta have been living in an air-raid shelter in the dock, along with about 80 naval ratings, survivors off different ships. Am longing for the day when I shall be told to muster for embarkation. The food is very meagre. 32 are victualled in my mess, we get 9 loaves, 1 lb butter, ½lb tea, 2lb sugar and bully beef to last 24 hrs. Everyone is perpetually hungry and like a lot of wolves.

*

It remained only to count the cost. The First Sea Lord, Admiral of the Fleet Sir A. Dudley Pound, in a letter to Admiral Cunningham summed up 'Pedestal': 'We paid a heavy price but personally I think we got out of it lightly considering the risks we had to run and the tremendous concentration of everything ... which we had to face.'

The price was indeed heavy. Of the fourteen proud ships, which had left the Clyde such a brief time before, nine were sunk and two of the others were so badly damaged that they barely remained afloat. The other three were all suffering from damage in varying degrees; indeed the *Ohio* was destined never to sail again. Some time after *Ohio* had completed discharging, she was towed away to a quiet backwater of Valletta harbour were she finally broke in half. Used as a storehouse and a barracks, she was finally towed out of Valletta in September 1946 and sunk by gunfire. The other merchantmen did not finally reach their home ports again until the spring of 1943. Britain could ill-afford the loss of so much modern fast tonnage; throughout the whole war it was lack of such ships which was one of the most persistent headaches that the armed forces and the Government had to face. As the war progressed, with amphibious operations ever growing in size and scale, so even more acute did the problem become.

Nor could the Royal Navy lightly brush aside the casualties they had received. The 'Pedestal' operation had proved by far the most costly of all the Mediterranean convoys and this at a time when every ship was worth its weight in gold. The loss of the *Eagle*, *Manchester*, *Cairo* and *Foresight* were grievous blows in themselves, but in addition the Navy had the *Indomitable*, *Nigeria*, *Kenya*, *Ithuriel*, *Wolverine* and *Penn* all put out of action for a considerable period of time.

And these were only the mere losses in material; the casualties among the merchant seamen and the Royal Navy personnel were equally severe – Churchill mentions a figure of 350 officers and men, which although found to be on the high side, was accurate enough to indicate that 'Pedestal' cost the lives of far more men than even the disastrous PQ17 convoy which had been slaughtered the previous month.[1]

In addition to the ships and their crews the Fleet Air Arm had lost thirteen aircraft in combat as well as the sixteen Sea Hurricanes which went down with the *Eagle*. The Royal Air Force had lost five planes, one Beaufighter and four Spitfires. From the time the convoy had come within range of Malta-based aircraft until the remaining ships reached harbour – that is during 32 hours of daylight, the RAF flew 414 fighter sorties, 292 by short-range Spitfires, 97 by long-range Spitfires and 25 by Beaufighters.

It is small wonder then, when comparing their own casualties with the heavy British losses, that the Italians jubilantly claimed a major victory. They had lost only the submarines *Cobalto* and *Dagabur*, and had another, the *Giada*, badly damaged. Their heaviest casualties were the two cruisers hit by the *Unbroken*, but they could reasonably claim that these vessels were only damaged, not sunk.

In fact the picture was somewhat different, for whereas all the Royal Navy's vessels were subsequently, and surprisingly quickly, repaired and continued to give good service in many subsequent campaigns, neither of the Italian cruisers ever again put to sea as fighting ships. The 8-inch cruiser *Bolzano* was taken to Spezia to be repaired but this was proceeded with only very slowly and with the Italian surrender the Germans seized her. They were no more successful in making her operational and she was finally sunk in harbour there by British 'human torpedoes' in June 1944.

Muzio Attendolo was equally rendered impotent and was finally finished off at Naples during a series of heavy air raids on that port

[1] Apart from the *Eagle*, *Indomitable*, *Cairo* and *Foresight* the Naval casualties were: *Rodney* – four wounded; *Victorious* – four officers and two men killed, one officer and one man wounded; *Nigeria* – four officers and 48 men killed, two wounded; *Kenya* – three men killed, one wounded; *Charybdis* – one man wounded; *Eskimo* – one wounded; *Bicester* – three wounded; *Wishart* – one missing.

by American bombers on the night of 2nd December 1942. None the less it must be admitted the *Battle of Mid-August*, as the Italians named this operation, was a victory in the material sense for the Axis, and especially for the light units of the Italian Navy. They had never shone as a major sea power and in all the major fleet actions in which they had been engaged they had come off the worse no matter what the odds. But their small battle units had always, right from the Great War, been of a different calibre indeed. The Italian Navy can be justly proud of the record of their midget torpedoes, *Mas*-boats and other small units, whose achievements included badly-damaging the battleships *Queen Elizabeth* and *Valiant* in Alexandria harbour, and the heavy cruiser *York* in Suda Bay, Crete, as well as the major part they played in the destruction of 'Pedestal'.

The Italian press was certainly in no doubt as to whom victory belonged and their radio bulletins were equally certain. On the 13th for example they were claiming many successes and as the operation proceeded the list of sinkings grew more impressive. On the 13th they broadcast:

Our submarines, *Mas* and motor boats, squadrons of bombers, dive and torpedo-bombers with many fighters in masses took turns in attacking with torpedoes and bombs hitting numerous units of the convoy in spite of violent fire and the reactions of the enemy fighters.

In the battle the following results were achieved against the convoy:

By our Naval forces: one cruiser and three steamers.

By our Air forces: one cruiser, one destroyer and three steamers.

By the German forces: the aircraft carrier *Eagle* and four steamers.

Many steamers and naval vessels were hit and damaged and thirty-two enemy planes destroyed. Thirteen of our planes failed to return.

In the Bulletin number 809 the following day they were even more enthusiastic:

In the Mediterranean further attacks against the enemy vessels which survived yesterday's attacks have resulted in more successes.

Submarines and small torpedo units sank one cruiser, one destroyer and three steamers; torpedo-bombers and bombers sank four steamers and hit with a torpedo a battleship. German air force units sank four steamers. The ship hit on the 11th by the submarine *Uarsciek* and which returned to Gibraltar is the *Furious*. Among the cruisers sunk is the *Manchester*.

Finally on the 15th Bulletin number 810 read:

During the day operations continued against the enemy aero-naval forces now dispersed. A *Mas* torpedoed a destroyer at close range, formations of dive-bombers sank a large warship, torpedo-bombers torpedoed a cruiser while another group hit a battleship. Our fighters have shot down four Spitfires.

Exaggeration is common in wartime, and was especially common on both sides where the claims of aircrew for the sinking of warships were concerned. This is understandable; seen from a bomber at a great height or through heavy flak, at speed and in the few seconds available, a near miss and a direct hit are easily confused. Time and time again throughout the war both Axis and Allied airmen alike repeated their claims to have sunk enemy warships only to find, as an American historian has recorded, these "sunken enemy units" turning up in the next battle unmarked.

Aircrew of all the major combatants were not, as a rule, trained in attacking warship targets. Although most of them were capable of flying missions against huge motionless targets like Hamburg, Dresden or Tokyo, such targets were easy to locate, did not take avoiding action and were still there to be checked the next day. Only select units, like LG. 1 on the German side, were trained in anti-ship tactics. In fact the British were no more accurate in their claims and counter-claims during this action. The figure of thirty-nine Axis bombers shot down by the Fleet Air Arm, although long known to be inaccurate, has been repeated time and time again in histories, presumably as a result of Winston Churchill's congratulatory telegram made at the time of the battle and *before* all the facts had come to light.[1] This was the accepted figure at the time, but the British Official Historian has recorded that 'our claims were in excess of actual achievements'. Despite this, the higher figure is frequently quoted. It was also thought that '… at least one and possibly two' E-boats had been destroyed, but it is now known that none were in fact sunk. The Germans admitted at the time that their units met with very strong resistance, 'they could not wait to watch the ships sink', which perhaps explains some of the unsubstantiated British claims of sinkings.

Since then the Italians have published a series of excellent books which deal in great detail with all their wartime operations. The Air Force History written by Generale Giuseppe Santoro is quite objective in dealing with the action and in its summing-up, in strict contrast to the claims made at the time by the Regia Aeronautica. Santoro attributes the failure of many of the Italian air force attacks to the experimental nature of some of them, and also claims that luck played a substantial part. To justify this latter he cites the hits on *Victorious*, the loss of the radio-controlled plane or flying bomb, and the *Port Chalmers* accidentally catching an aerial torpedo in her paravanes as examples of how the near certainty of sinking or heavy damage can be avoided by chance.

This may certainly be true of the incidents he quotes, but in every campaign or battle there is an element of luck, and it was not merely a surfeit of good fortune which enabled the convoy to come through the heavy air raids of the 12th almost unscathed. What defeated the Axis airmen was a combination of brilliant work by the Fleet Air Arm, the heaviest anti-aircraft barrage put up by a British Naval force

---

[1] Prime Minister to Fleet Lord and First Sea Lord, 17th August 1942:

Please convey my compliments to Admirals Syfret, Burrough and Lyster and all officers and men engaged in the magnificent crash-through of supplies to Malta, which cannot fail to have an important influence on the immediate future of the war in the Mediterranean.

Papers here report thirteen enemy aircraft shot down but this was only by the Maltaforce, and I have seen no mention of the thirty-nine additional shot down by the carrier's fighters which puts a very different complexion on the air fighting.

up to that time and the steadiness of courage of the merchant seamen in obeying complicated manoeuvring orders in the face of the enemy.

Santoro concludes that the failure of the Italians to use their cruiser squadrons against the remnants of the convoy at dawn of the 13th meant that 'the British Navy obtained a strategic success', and that the arrival of the five steamers at Valletta, especially the damaged oil tanker, 'was a notable contribution to their victory'.

With regard to the Luftwaffe the British Air Historical Section states: 'The effect of the serviceability and strength of the Luftwaffe in the Mediterranean of Operation 'Pedestal' must not be overlooked, as it had a direct impact on Rommel's offensive at Alam Halfa, which was originally planned for the 26th August.' J. Richard Smith of *Group 66* adds: 'It is interesting to note that the serviceability figures for both units (KGr.606 and KGr.806) given on 20th August are very low, about half of the available strength.'

The actual Luftwaffe casualties were itemised in carefully detailed lists, but these were made up over a long period and not all losses were recorded on the day they took place. Many of the aircraft lost over the sea had 'unknown' listed as to their exact cause of loss or fate. Nor are the available records at the Bundesarchiv complete. From sources that are available however some losses can be itemised. For example, on 10th August the loss of two aircraft, both Ju88A-4 bombers, was logged over the convoy during the dusk attack. These two were 1572 of KGr.806 operating from Catania and piloted by Lieutenant Pietsch, and 140066 of the 9th Staffeln, KG77 piloted by Helmet Streubal. The following day another Junkers Ju88A-4, piloted by Arno Kopishchel, from KGr.806 was recorded as lost with its entire crew. As the air fighting reached a crescendo on 12th August so the losses increased dramatically. I/LG.1 losing three aircraft that day, 140105 piloted by Hauptmann Werner Luben; 0074 piloted by Walter Bastian and 5600 piloted by Werner Vogt, while its sister unit. II/LG. 1, also lost three Ju88s, 2203, piloted by Oberleutnant Helmut Gerlich, 140090 piloted by Leutnant Hans Hedrich and 140197 piloted by Siegfried Fieiler. The loss of six aircraft from this highly trained, specialist anti-shipping unit was a heavy blow.

The 9 Staffel of KG54 was led by Oberleutnant Wolfgang Schultz from Catania in the attacks which sank the *Waimarama* and from this attack only Schultz himself, his aircraft barely flyable so full of holes was it, and two other crews managed to return.

Again, despite post-war claims to the effect that in just one incident, the crippling of *Indomitable*, '... the Sea Hurricane division which had just taken off destroyed five of the Ju87s after the attack ...', in truth, only two Stukas from StG3 were actually destroyed throughout the whole operation!

If the Axis records are incomplete there is no doubt that Allied claims were vastly and wildly exaggerated. And of course Stukas were always reported as being German. In fact the Italian Stukas fared worse with regard to losses as they attacked very gallantly despite the loss of most of their escorting fighters before the attacks commenced, as Generale B. A. Antonio Cumbat told the author:

I lost both my two wingmen, Cremonesi and Casavola and their gunners. I didn't get any witnesses of their loss or manner of it, I only knew that I had lost two very young and enthusiastic pilots from my small unit who died attacking the enemy bravely. Nine of us left Pantelleria, but only eight arrived at the rendezvous over the convoy because Tonelli was forced back with engine trouble. In spite of every effort by our fighter escort only four of us eventually landed back at Castelventrano, because Rizzi and Melotti, with their aircraft damaged, were diverted back to Pantelleria while Cremonesi and Casavola with their gunners didn't make it back because they were shot down by the anti-aircraft guns of the ships.

During the second attack early on the 13th, again nine of us took off. After an hour's flight, Garotti with his gunner De Rosa landed at Pantelleria with engine failures and two Stukas failed to return from the sortie, Raimondo with his gunner Tarabotti, and Savini with his gunner Patella. What happened to the latter pair is one of the most incredible stories of the war.

They had been hit by anti-aircraft gunfire from the convoy at the very moment they were pulling out of their attack dives, flak hitting their engine and water radiators. A bullet

242

entered the main cabin, cut through the fuel supply tap, and exploded in the dashboard. Savini had no choice but to ditch in the sea; their altitude was too low for them to bale out with parachutes. As a result of their impacting on the surface their Stuka plunged and capsized in the wave troughs ending up belly-up from an altitude of 20–30 metres. At that moment Patella succeeded in throwing out the life raft and immediately afterwards he was hurtled into the sea, together with Savini. The waves and strong current carried Patella far away. Luckily for him, as he could not swim, Savini fell close to the overturned Stuka and managed to cling to it. When the plane eventually sank, the heavy engine dragging it down nose-first, he moved up to the tail, and when that vanished beneath the waves he found himself by some miracle immediately adjacent to the life-raft Patella had thrown out. Thankfully he clambered aboard it. He was alone, Patella was nowhere to be seen, just a vast expanse of sea and sky.

Campari, with Guarino as his gunner, on another Ju87 had realised what had taken place and, after doing a few evasive turns in the midst of the furious flak barrage, they closed their compatriot and threw over their own life-raft for him. Patella saw it falling towards him and it landed fairly close, but he could not reach it! He was exhausted. Having unlaced his shoes, taken off his flying suit, and swallowed a considerable amount of sea water in the process, he lay on his back to rest, slipping rapidly into a state of unconsciousness.

After an hour, or maybe more, he came round again because he heard the sound of a Stuka engine overhead. Hardly daring to believe it, he looked up. It was Stringa, his squadron commander, who, having landed back at Castelvetrano with his aircraft resembling a sieve and with the machine-gun in his right wing dangling, had made them refuel a more airworthy Stuka and, without any fighter escort whatsoever, had taken off again to return, with his faithful gunner Boglione, to try and find any survivors from his unit.

Savini, on his life-raft, also saw the mercy Stuka and fired two flares to attract its attention, but in vain. Instead Patella saw them and succeeded therefore in tracing his companion. They were close, but still could not actually see each other due to the steepness of the waves. Patella called Savini who answered after a few minutes; and by means of hails and shouts Patella also managed to reach the life raft and climb aboard.

Thus, re-united again, they were carried by the current and the waves. A considerable period passed and by chance they saw the life raft which had been thrown out to them by Campari and Guarino. By rowing they tried to reach it, but it was useless because it was torn. There was nothing to be done but recover the oars and the emergency kits with the provisions, the Verey pistol and the signal flares.

Savini and Patella had been six or seven hours in their life raft trying to steer themselves, approximately, north-west towards where they thought Pantelleria lay, some 50 miles away. But instead the current was carrying them south-westward. Hours passed, the sun was setting when suddenly they heard a whistle, but saw nobody and anything nearby! The whistle was repeated and they finally got a glimpse of a head floating on waves, about 100 metres away. Rowing they got closer and shouted for the man to identify himself. Initially they got no reply, not surprisingly, because the survivor did not understand Italian, because he was the British Beaufighter navigator named McFarlane, who had parachuted from his own aircraft when his machine had been shot down in flames by Italian fighters earlier that day and his pilot, Jay, killed. He had been immersed in the water ever since in that general area until a weird fate brought all three shipwrecked airmen together!

Savini and Patella helped him aboard their raft. They found McFarlane had a wounded knee but nothing too serious. Thus the three mortal enemies lay exhausted in their life-raft, no longer trying to kill each other or fight, but going together towards a common destiny, carried by the impartial Mediterranean currents ...

The next day another sortie was made and Cumbat and his gunner were also forced to ditch. Happily all were ultimately rescued and survived after further incredible adventures of which this is only just the beginning. Unfortunately we do not have the space to relate the whole fantastic story, which later involved French and German airmen also, and a series of rescues and floatplane hijacks.

The Italian Naval History quotes Supermarina's final assessment of the battle. They felt that the importance of the convoy to the Allies was reflected in the strength of the escort and in the large tonnage of precious merchant vessels committed to it. Despite the heavy escort the small units of the Italian Navy, they felt, made an undisputable contribution to the defeat of the convoy by sinking two cruisers [sic] and four steamers and by damaging another four or five steamers and one destroyer.

The German Admiral in the theatre was more outspoken in his post-war summing up:

Units of the convoy which had broken through were effectively attacked off Cape Bon by the German/Italian air forces on the 13th [sic]. To the continental observer British losses seemed to represent a big victory for the Axis, and they were accordingly exploited for propaganda purposes.

But in reality the facts were quite different since in spite of these successes the Air Force had not been able to prevent the British forces, among which were five merchant vessels, from reaching Valletta. Thereby the enemy gained the strategic end of his operation in spite of what it may have cost him.

The British operation was not a defeat but a strategic failure of the first order by the Axis, the repercussions of which would one day be felt.

All of which was endorsed by the British authorities both at the time and since. Winston Churchill was especially pleased and for good reason; he had been having an exceedingly tough time explaining to Marshal Stalin why the Russia convoys had been suspended for the summer months following the PQ17 debacle, and at this time the loss of Tobruk was also weighing heavily upon him. Had 'Pedestal' not been the strategic success it was claimed to be, then Malta would have fallen within weeks and this would have been a blow which Britain, or more especially the War Cabinet, might not have been able to take quietly, after so many other defeats.

The reward justified the price exacted [Churchill recorded]. Revictualled and replenished with ammunition and vital stores, the strength of Malta revived. But submarines returned to the island and, with the striking forces of the Royal Air Force, regained their dominating position in the Central Mediterranean.

It was not quite like that. The 10th Submarine Flotilla had been operating in some strength prior to August and the strength of the Royal Air Force strike forces was not to reach a higher level until some weeks later.[1] Nevertheless had 'Pedestal' or more particularly the *Ohio*, not got through, the submarines would soon have had to withdraw. The only ships of the Royal Navy at Malta, other than the minesweeping force, were the *Penn*, *Ledbury* and *Bramham* but there was no question of these damaged ships remaining to form a surface strike force for long, although they were on stand-by for one such sortie, they only remained at Malta long enough to restore and replenish before returning to Gibraltar, where they arrived on 21st August.

The bravery of the majority of the men on both sides, the achievements of those in getting the convoy through and what they went through in doing so are unrivalled and need no embellishment. As in all battles there was another side which was suppressed. Nor was British reporting of the battle in any way objective.

[1] Due to the need to provide support for the build-up for the El Alamein offensive and to hold Rommel in check, tasks which had the first call on its resources, the Navy's surface striking force did not return to the island until November when Force K was re-formed with the cruisers *Dido* and *Euryalus*.

Cadet Waine aboard *Brisbane Star* gave me account of what took place and what was not allowed to be known then, or since:

My duties at action stations were to keep the signals and action with the liaison officer and R.N. signals team of three men on the bridge and act as captain's messenger. If necessary I was also to fire FAMs and pig trough rockets when the ship was under direct attack, having had special training in these weapons.

I helped compile the official report from the action log of the *Brisbane Star* and this report was suppressed. On our return to the UK in 1943 all members of crew had to sign the official secrets act and all material referring to the convoy was confiscated even down to the copies of *The Times of Malta*, including the famous preparation for surrender issue. A junior engineer, Parlour, attempted to smuggle through his personal diary of the action and was convicted and sentenced to ten years in prison.

The generally accepted story of the *Brisbane Star* has always been the bland account by Taffrail but the attempted mutiny and appeal to scuttle has always been suppressed as has the content of the wireless messages before the dash from Tunisia to Malta. There was an article printed in a Buenos Aires paper later during the voyage in which Captain Riley accused his crew of being cowards. The story is rather involved and all the parties indeed acted with integrity and I always felt that Captain Riley's judgement was harsh and unwarranted in the events which eventually led to the ship reaching Malta.

Captain Riley was awarded the DSO as were the other merchant captains of the surviving vessels apart from Captain Mason who was awarded the George Cross. The DSO awards were immediate and the first occasion on which they were awarded to Merchant Navy captains. Senior Officers on the merchant ships were awarded DSCs, again a first occasion. All the DEMS naval and army gunners were awarded medals and liaison signallers and NCO gunners were awarded DSMs. (This latter series of awards was opposed by Captain Riley as some men had abandoned their posts when the ship was torpedoed and dashed for the boats.)

David Royle relates the feelings of the *Charybdis* men themselves when they later viewed the resulting propaganda film with the sickly voice-over so typical of the fourth-rate British media cover of the time and since.

The commander had the film *Malta Convoy* run through for me in the men's recreation room. A terrifying picture. This ship was the only one that got through to Malta without casualties. Out of a convoy of fifteen [*sic*] merchant ships only five got into harbour and one of these was bombed and sunk when she got there. The photography was excellent but the commentary rather tiresome, too much of 'our brave sailor lads' stuff. God knows it's difficult to describe courage and gallantry but it must not be done with such unctuous clichés.

On the conduct of the operation itself, Vice-Admiral Syfret had this to say:

The losses suffered by Force F were regrettably heavy and the numbers of merchant ships which reached Malta disappointingly small. But I have no fault to find with the personnel of the fleet because better results were not achieved. On the contrary, Commanding Officers generally have praised the fine bearing and spirit shown by their ship's companies, many of whom were very young and to whom battle was a new experience. I am proud to associate myself with these tributes and, in particular, give credit to those whose duties kept them below decks during submarine and air and E-boat attacks. The task of Force X was always difficult and hazardous. Unhappily a serious disaster befell them almost at once and heavily tipped the scales in favour of the enemy. Nevertheless they continued undaunted and determined, and fighting their way through many and heavy attacks by U-boats and E-boats and aircraft, they delivered five of their charges to Malta and then fought their way back to Gibraltar. In doing this they showed a display of fortitude and determination of which all may be proud and in particular their courageous and resolute leader Rear-Admiral H. M. Burrough, CB, DSO. Tribute has been paid to the personnel of HM ships but both officers and men will desire to give first place to the conduct, courage and determination of the Masters, officers and men of the merchant ships. The steadfast manner in which these ships pressed on their way to Malta through all attacks, answering every manoeuvring order like a well-trained fleet unit, was a most inspiring sight. Many of these fine men and their ships were lost but the memory of their conduct will remain an inspiration to all who were privileged to sail with them.

No more fitting tribute could be paid to the men of the Mercantile Marine who in this, and in hundreds of other convoys throughout the whole of six years of unending warfare at sea, displayed those very same qualities which this nation accepts, without comment, as typical. Their reward after similar steadfastness at the Falklands, was the dole queue. Truly politicians have short memories.

II

Was it all worth the price as Churchill claimed? Accepting, as we must that Malta would have fallen without the convoy, then the answer must be yes. As early as 28th August the Joint Planning Staff were considering the effect on Malta's defence by the removal of one infantry battalion and one machine gun company for duty elsewhere, which gives a measure of how things had improved. No indications which could be interpreted as pointing to an enemy attempt to take Malta had been received since the previous May.

All the German and Italian parachute troops in the Mediterranean area were, in fact, either in Egypt or *en route* there. There was no accumulation of shipping in Italian or Sicilian harbours to denote a build-up for invasion and all the 300 German air transport aircraft (Ju52s) were fully extended flying in troops and supplies to Rommel's Panzer Armee poised ready to take Cairo and the Suez Canal.

Before any such move could be made the re-concentration of Axis forces would require at least a month it was thought but this was unlikely.

Meanwhile on the island Lord Gort was able to announce a very slight easing of the ration limitations. It was not much, food still remained meagre, but it was an indication that the grim deadline had not been reached and that the island could carry on in good heart and that things would get better. He added, 'Recently we have seen four merchant ships and an oiler reach Malta; this represents the largest number of ships which has arrived in the Grand Harbour since September of last year. No sight could have been more welcome to all of us than the arrival of the convoy after so many weeks of anxious waiting and we all know that this great achievement was accomplished thanks to the dauntless courage and determination of the Royal Navy and Merchant Navy ...'

Once the torpedo-bombers and submarines got back into their stride on his traffic routes, the Axis powers were forced to once more route their North African convoys by way of Greece and the Corinth Canal and Crete, an incredible detour, which added days to the journey. So overawed were they at Malta's capabilities that many ships sailed not once but three or four times from Italian ports only to be turned back each time when they spotted British reconnaissance aircraft. In August 35% of the total Axis supplies despatched failed to get through. In September, with the RAF averaging fifteen bomber sorties a week and with six or seven submarines on patrol, over 100,000 tons of Rommel's urgently needed supplies were sent to the seabed.

> The month of October [Captain Roskill records] marked a climax in the relentless pressure exerted by all arms, but especially by our submarines and aircraft, against the enemy's supply lines to Africa. Axis shipping losses rose steeply and it is now known that Rommel was thereby

deprived of precious fuel and supplies at a critical juncture.

Thus it was that when General Montgomery launched his crushing assault at El Alamein on 23rd of October, his opponent was already suffering gravely from this chronic shortage of supply and as the months of victory followed this situation worsened progressively. With the rapid advance on land came the corresponding easing of conditions at sea and in November the siege of Malta was finally lifted by a convoy from the east, Operation 'Stoneage', which was almost unopposed by the Axis.

"Malta was the rock on which our hopes in the Mediterranean foundered."

A statement, taken from the Official Italian NID reports on the war in the Mediterranean, is surely the vindication of all the men who died fighting through the 'Santa Marija' convoy, WS5.21, 'Pedestal'.

Appendix One

Merchant Ships of Convoy WS.5.21.

Convoy Commodore: Commodore A. G. Venables, R.N. (ret'd)

Almeria Lykes	Captain W. Henderson 7,773 tons. Lykes Brothers Steamship Co.
Brisbane Star	Captain F. N. Riley 12,791 tons. Blue Star Line.
Clan Ferguson	Captain A. R. Cossar 7,347 tons. Scottish Steamship Co.
Deucalion	Captain R. Brown 7,516 tons. Blue Funnel Line.
Empire Hope	Captain G. Williams 12,688 tons. Ministry of War Transport/Shaw Saville & Albion.
Dorset	Captain J. C. Tuckett 10,624 tons. Federal Steam Navigation Co. Ltd.
Glenorchy	Captain G. Leslie 8,982 tons. Glen Line Ltd.
Melbourne Star	Captain D. R. Macfarlane 12,806 tons. Blue Star Line.
Ohio	Captain D. Mason 9,514 tons. Ministry of War Transport/Texaco.
Port Chalmers	Captain H. G. Pinkey 8,535 tons. Port Line Ltd.
Rochester Castle	Captain R. Wren 7,795 tons. Union Castle Line.
Santa Elisa	Captain T. Thompson 8,379 tons. Grace Line.
Waimarama	Captain R. S. Pearce 12,843 tons. Shaw Saville & Albion.
Wairangi	Captain H. R. Gordon 12,400 tons. Shaw Saville & Albion.

Complied from Lloyd's Register of Shipping 1941–42; General Register of Shipping and Seamen, Cardiff; United States Maritime Commission, Washington, D.C.

Appendix Two

British Naval Forces

Codenames of Forces taking part:

Force *F*	The Force as a whole
Force P	Convoy and escort; U.K. – rendezvous
Force *M*	*Victorious*, *Argus* and escort; U.K. – rendezvous
Force *J*	*Eagle* and escort; Gibraltar – rendezvous
Force *K*	*Indomitable* and escort; Freetown – rendezvous
Force *G*	Carriers and escorts; after rendezvous for '*Berserk*'
Force *R*	Oilers and escort
Force *W*	*Abbeydale* and escort. For '*Berserk*'
Force *X*	Escort through to Malta. (Close Escort)
Force *Z*	Force F less Force X
Force *Y*	Convoy and escort. Malta-Gibraltar. 'Ascendant'

Composition of Forces

Force *Z*

Battleships:

Nelson	Flag S.O. Force *F*, Vice-Admiral Sir E. Neville Syfret, CB Captain H. B. Jacomb
Rodney	Captain J. W. Rivett-Carnac, DSC

Aircraft-Carriers:

Victorious	Flag R/Admiral A/C's, Home Fleet; Read-Admiral Sir A. L. St. A. Lyster, CB Captain H. C. Bovell
Indomitable	Captain T. H. Troubridge
Eagle	Captain L. D. Mackintosh, DSC
Furious	Captain T. O. Bulteel

Light Cruisers:

Phoebe	Captain C. P. Frend
Sirius	Captain P. W. B. Brooking
Charybdis	Captain G. A. W. Voelcker

Destroyers:

Laforey	Captain (D), 19th DF; Captain R. M. J. Hutton
Lightning	Commander H. G. Walters, DSC
Lookout	Lieutenant-Commander C. P. F. Brown
Quentin	Lieutenant-Commander A. H. P. Noble, DSC
Somali	Commander E. N. V. Currey, DSC
Eskimo	Commander E. G. Le Geyt, DSC
Tartar	Commander St. J. R. J. Tyrwhitt, DSC
Ithuriel	Lieutenant-Commander D. H. Maitland-Makgill-Crichton, DSC
Antelope	Lieutenant-Commander E. N. Sinclair
Wishart	Commander H. G. Scott
Vansittart	Lieutenant-Commander T. Johnston, DSC
Westcott	Commander I. H. Bockett-Pugh, DSO
Wrestler	Lieutenant R. W. B. Lacon, DSC
Zetland	Lieutenant J. V. Wilkenson
Wilton	Lieutenant A. P. Northey, DSC

Force *X*

Light Cruisers:

Nigeria	Rear-Admiral, 10th C. S.: Rear-Admiral H. M. Burrough, CB, DSO
	Captain S. H. Paton
Kenya	Captain A. S. Russell
Manchester	Captain H. Drew, DSC
Cairo	Acting-Captain C. C. Hardy, DSO

Destroyers:

Ashanti	Captain (D) 6th DF; Commander R. G. Onslow, DSO
Intrepid	Commander E. A. de W. Kitcat
Icarus	Lieutenant-Commander C. D. Maud, DSC
Foresight	Lieutenant-Commander R. A. Fell
Fury	Lieutenant-Commander C. H. Campbell, DSC
Pathfinder	Commander E. A. Gibbs, DSO
Penn	Lieutenant-Commander J. H. Swain

Derwent	Commander R. H. Wright, DSC
Bramham	Lieutenant E. F. Baines
Bicester	Lieutenant-Commander S. W. F. Bennets
Ledbury	Lieutenant-Commander R. P. Hill

Escorts for Force *Y*

Destroyer:

Matchless	Lieutenant-Commander J. Mowlam
Badsworth	Lieutenant G. T. S. Gray, DSC

Force *R*

Fleet Oilers:

Brown Ranger	Master D. B. C. Ralph
Dingledale	Master R. T. Duthie

Corvettes:

Jonquil	Lieutenant-Commander R. E. H. Partington, RD, RNR
Geranium	Temp-Lieutenant-Commander A. Foxall, RNR
Spirea	Lieutenant-Commander R. S. Miller, DSC, RD, RNR
Coltsfoot	Temp-Lieutenant Hon. W. K. Rous, RNVR
Salvonia	Temp-Lieutenant G. M. M. Robinson

Tug:

Jaunty	Lieutenant-Commander H. Osburn, OBE, RNR

Attached for *Berserk*

Aircraft Carrier:

Argus	Captain G. T. Philip, DSC

Force *W*

Fleet Oiler:

Abbeydale	Master A. Edwards

Corvettes:

Burdock	Lieutenant-Commander E. H. Lynes, RNR
Armeiria	Lieutenant M. Todd, RNR

Attached from Western Approaches for escort duties:

Keppel	Commander J. E. Broome

Malcolm	Commander A. B. Russell
Amazon	Lieutenant-Commander Lord Teynham
Venomous	Commander H. W. Falcon-Steward
Wolverine	Lieutenant-Commander P. W. Gretton, OBE, DSC
Vidette	Lieutenant-Commander E. N. Walmsley, DSC

Malta Escort Force:

17th Minesweeping Flotilla (S.O. Acting Commander A. E. Doran)

Speedy	Lieutenant-Commander A. E. Doran
Rye	Lieutenant J. A. Pearson, DSC, RNR
Hebe	Lieutenant-Commander G. Mowatt, RD, RNVR
Hythe	Lieutenant-Commander L. B. Miller

3rd Motor Launch Flotilla

ML.121	Lieutenant-Commander E. J. Strowlger, RNVR, (S.O.)
ML.126	
ML.134	
ML.135	
ML.168	
ML.459	
ML.462	

Submarines on Patrol

10th Submarine Flotilla (Malta)

S.O. Captain G. W. G. Simpson

Safari	Commander B. Bryant, DSC
Unbroken	Lieutenant A. C. G. Mars
Uproar	Lieutenant J. B. Kershaw, DSO
Ultimatum	Lieutenant P. R. Harrison, DSC
Unruffled	Lieutenant J. S. Stevens, DSO, DSC
Utmost	Lieutenant A. W. Langridge
United	Lieutenant T. E. Barlow
Una	Lieutenant D. S. R. Martin
P.222	Lieutenant-Commander A. J. Mackenzie

Appendix Three

The Fleet Air Arm
Victorious

16 Fulmars	809 Squadron (Lieutenant E. G. Savage)
	884 Squadron (Lieutenant N. G. Hallett)
5 Sea Hurricanes	885 Squadron (Lieutenant R. H. P. Carver)
12 Albacores	832 Squadron (Lt-Cdr. W. J. Lucas)

Indomitable

9 Martlets	806 Squadron (Lieutenant R. L. Johnston)
22 Sea Hurricanes	800 Squadron (Lt-Cdr J. M. Bruen)
	880 Squadron (Lt-Cdr F. E. U. Todd)
16 Albacores	827 and 831 Squadrons (Lt-Cdr D. K. Buchanan-Dunlop)

Eagle

16 Sea Hurricanes	801 Squadron (Lt-Cdr R. Brabner, MP, RNVR)
4 Sea Hurricanes	813 Squadron

Argus

6 Sea Hurricanes (As reserves)	804 Squadron (Captain A. E. Marsh, RM)

Furious

42 Spitfires, Mark VB	– For Malta
4 Albacores	823 Squadron (spares) Hal Far Airfield (Malta)
27 Albacores	828 Squadron (Lieutenant G. M. Haynes, RAN)
1 Swordfish	830 Squadron (Captain K. L. Ford, RM)

Appendix Four

The Royal Air Force

C-in-C Malta: Air Vice-Marshal Sir Keith Park

Fighters:

126 Squadron	Spitfires
185 Squadron	Spitfires
229 Squadron	Spitfires
249 Squadron	Spitfires
1435 Squadron Spitfires	
235 Squadron	Coastal Beaufighters
248 Squadron	Coastal Beaufighters
252 Squadron	Coastal Beaufighters
89 Squadron	Night Beaufighters

Torpedo Bombers:

39 Squadron	Beauforts
86 Squadron	Beauforts
217 Squadron	Beauforts

Night Bombers:

38 Squadron	Wellingtons
40 Squadron	Wellingtons
159 Squadron	Liberators

Day Bombers:

55 Squadron	Baltimores

Reconnaissance:

69 Squadron	Baltimores, Wellingtons and P.R.U. Spitfires

From Middle East Command:

203 Squadron	Marylands

Appendix Five

Axis Naval Forces

Italian:

Heavy Cruisers – 3rd Cruiser Division:

Gorizia	Flag of Ammiraglio di Divisione; Angelo Parona Capitano di Vascello Paolo Melodia
Bolzano	Capitano di Vascello Mario Mezzadra
Trieste	Capitano di Vascello Umberto Rouselle

Destroyers – Elements of 10th and 11th Divisions:

Aviera	Capitano di Vascello Gastone Minotti
Geniere	Capitano di Fregata Marco Notarbartolo
Camiciai Nera	Capitano di Fregata Adriano Foscari
Legionario	Capitano di Fregata Corrado Tagliamonte
Ascari	Capitano di Fregata Teodorico Capone
Corsaro	Capitano di Fregata Lionello Sagamoso
Grecale	Capitano di Fregata Luigi Gasparrini

Light Cruisers – 7th Cruiser Division:

Eugenio di Savoia	Flag of Ammiraglio di Divisione Alberto da Zara Capitano di Vascello Franco Zannoni
Muzio Attendolo	Capitano di Vascello Mario Schiavuta
Raimondo Montecuccoli	Capitano di Vascello Arturo Solari

Destroyers – Elements of 10th and 13th Divisions:

Maestrale	Capitano di Vascello Riccardo Pontremoli
Gioberti	Capitano di Fregata Vittorio Prato
Oriani	Capitano di Fregata Paole Pesci
Fuciliere	Capitano di Fregata Ujberto Del Grande

Minelaying Destroyer:

Malocello	Commandante Pierfrancesco Tona

Motor Torpedo Boats (*Ms* and *Mas*-boats):

2nd Squadron:

Ms.16	Capitano di Corvetta Giorgio Manuti
Ms.22	Sottotenente di Vascella Franco Mezzadra

Ms.23	Sottotenente di Vascello Giacomo Patrone
Ms.25	Tenente di Vascello Franco Le Pera
Ms.26	Sottotenente di Vascello Alberto Bencini
Ms.31	Tenente di Vascello Antonio Calvani 15th Squadron:
Mas.549	Tenente di Vascello Andrea Giuffra
Mas.543	Nocchiere 2cl.C.1.c.D. Leone Tirelli
Mas.548	Guardiamarina Miro Karis
Mas.563	Tenente di Vascello Gino Maveri 18th Squadron:
Mas.553	Tenente di Vascello Carlo Paolizza
Mas.556	Tenente di Vascello Luigi Sala
Mas.560	Nocchiere 2cl.C.I.c.D. Luigi Bolognesi
Mas.562	Guardiamarina Francesco Luciano 20th Squadron:
Mas.562	Sottotenente di Vascello Rolando Perasso
Mas.554	Sottotenente di Vascello Marco Galcagno
Mas.557	Guardiamarina Giovani Cafiero
Mas.564	Nocchiere 2cl.C.1.D. Giuseppe Iafrate Independent Operation:
Mas. 533	C.W.O. 2cl Luigi Riccardo
Submarines:	
Asteria	Tenente di Vascello Pasquale Beltrame
Ascianghi	Tenente di Vascello Rodolfo Bombig
Alagi	Tenente di Vascello Sergio Puccini
Avorio	Tenente di Vascello Mario Priggione
Axum	Tenente di Vascello Renato Ferrini
Bronzo	Tenente di Vascello Cesare Buldrini
Brin	Tenente di Vascello Luigi Andreotti
Cobalto	Tenente di Vascello Raffaello Amicarelli
Dessie	Tenente di Vascello Renato Scandolo
Dandolo	Tenente di Vascello Giovanni Febbraro
Dagabur	Tenente di Vascello Renato Pecori
Emo	Tenente di Vascello Giuseppe Franco
Giada	Tenente di Vascello Gaspare Cavallina
Granito	Tenente di Vascello Leo Sposito

Otaria	Tenente di Vascello Alberto Gorini
Uarsciek	Tenente di Vascello Gaetano Targia
Velella	Tenente di Vascello Giovanni Febbraro
Wolframio	Tenente di Vascello Giovanni Manunta

N. B. Tenente di Vascello Febbraro took over command of the *Velella* after handing over *Dandolo* to Capitano di Corvetta Alberto Campanella on 14th August.

German:

Motor Torpedo Boats (S-boats):

3rd Flotilla:	S.O. Kommandante Kemnade
S.30	Oberleutnant zur See Weber
S.36	Oberleutnant zur See Brauns
S.59	Oberleutnant zur See Albert Miiller
S.58	Oberleutnant zur See Wuppermann (Fuhrerboot)

Submarines:

U-73	Kapitänleutnant Helmut Rosenbaum
U-205	Kapitänleutnant Franz-Georg Rerchke
U-333	Kapitänleutnant Peter Erich Cremer. (Left La Pallice.for Med. 11th August and returned with engine trouble after air attack on 24th)

Appendix Six

Axis Air Strength
Italian: (1. – Sardinia)
Long Range Reconnaissance:

9 Cant. Z.1007b	28 *Stormo*

Medium Bombers:

24 S.84	32 *Stormo*

Torpedo Bombers:

30 Sm.79	130 *Gruppo*
12 Sm. 79	105 *Stormo* (254 & 255 *Squadriglie*)
10 S.85	130 *Gruppo*

Fighter Bombers:

9 Cr.42	160 *Gruppo*

Single Engined Fighters:

16 Cr.42	160 *Gruppo*
22 Mc.202	153 *Gruppo*
28 Re.2001	2 Gruppo and 362 *Squadriglia*
14 G.50	24 *Gruppo*
(2 – Sicily)	

Medium Bombers:

25 S.84, Sm.79, Br.20	Various Commands

Reconnaissance:

11 Sm.79, Cr.25	Various Commands

Torpedo Bombers:

15 Sm.79	132 *Stormo* (278 & 281 *Squadriglie*)
6 S.84	

Dive Bombers:

36 Ju.87-D	102 *Gruppo*

Single Engined Fighters:

27 Mc202	25 & 155 *Gruppi*
20 Cr.42	46 & 47 *Gruppi*

Plus the 'Special Attack Force', one Sm. 79, one Cant. Z.1007b, two Re. 2001.

German: (Serviceable aircraft only)

Long Range Reconnaissance:

2 Ju.88	*Gruppe Stab*	
122 Trapani		
7 Ju.88 and Bf.109	*1(F) 122*	Catania and Elmas
5 Ju.88	*2(F) 122*	Sicily

Medium Bombers:

2 Ju.88	*Stab KG 54*	Catania
20 Ju.88	*K.Gr.606*	Catania
21 Ju.88	*K.Gr.806*	Catania
3 Ju.88	*Stab. KG.77*	Comiso and Gerbini
13 Ju.88	*II/KG 77*	Comiso and Gerbini
15 ju.88	*III/KG 77*	Comiso and Gerbini
28 Ju.88-A4/Trop	*LG.I*	Gerbini

Dive Bombers:

26 Ju.87-D	*I/St. G.3*	Trapani

Twin Engine Fighters:

4 Bf.110 C-4	*8/ZG.26*	Transferred from Kastelli, Crete

Night Fighters:

12 Bf.100	*I/NG.2*	Sicily

Single Engined Fighters:

3 Bf.109G	*Stab JG53*	Sicily and Pantelleria
15 Bf.109G	*II/JG53*	
13 Bf.109F	*I/JG77*	Elmas, Sardinia

Torpedo Bombers:

6 He111-III-H6	*II/KG.26*	Gerbini
28 Ju.88	*I/KG.54.*	Gerbini and Pantelleria

Appendix Seven

These extracts from the Diary and cuttings of the DEMS gunner reflect succinctly the gallantry of all those who sailed or served aboard the merchant vessels of the 'Pedestal' convoy. They are included as a tribute to those very gallant men.

1: Pocket Diary for 1942

25 June	Draft to *Ohio*
27 June	Officially drafted to *Ohio*
20 July (Mon)	Arrived back in Glasgow (after leave which included *No Orchids for Miss Blandish*) at 1600
24 July (Fri)	4 S.G. (Seaman Gunners) joined ship
25 July (Sat)	Tugs on strike, held up
26 July (Sun)	Held up. Rutland House
27 July (Mon)	Beresford and Albert Bowling
28 July (Tues)	Left Bowling arrived Loch Long
29 July (Wed)	Loch Long taking cargo
30 July (Thurs	Taking cargo Loch Long
31 July (Fri)	At anchor, Tail 'o Bank. Sigs and W.T. joined
1 Aug (Sat)	At anchor Tail 'o Bank
2 Aug (Sun)	Left Tail 'o Bank 9 pm in convoy' destination unknown, looks like Malta
3 Aug (Mon)	Captain tells us we are going Malta. Strong escort, 14 ships in convoy.
4 Aug (Tues)	Sub warning. Depth charges dropped, *Nelson* and *Rodney* with us, 2 cruisers, 12 destroyers
5 Aug (Wed)	Sub and air warnings, nothing seen
6 Aug (Thur)	Depth charges dropped. AA practice firing. Weather hot
7 Aug (Fri)	Aircraft carrier joined convoy escort. Not feeling too good
8 Aug (Sat)	Feeling much better. 3 aircraft carriers joined convoy
9 Aug (Sun)	5th aircraft carrier joined convoy. Mock battle. Lighthouse in view 11 pm
10 Aug (Mon)	Passed through straits 2 am all quiet

11 Aug (Tues)	Aircraft carrier *Eagle* sunk by sub at 1.5. Slight air activity during afternoon.
12 Aug (Weds)	Torpedoed. Ship stopped 4 hrs. Bombed several ships sunk. E-boats during night. Several air attacks. *Deucalion* hit, *Indomitable* hit.
13 Aug (Thurs)	Air attack bombed. Engines out of commission. Towed by *Penn* abandoned ship. Went back. Bomb down engine room. Off again
14 Aug (Fri)	On *ML 121 Ohio* in tow, back broken. Air attacks.
15 Aug (Sat)	Landed at Malta 0800. Transferred to shelters. Living like rats. Very little food.

2: Page from notebook written in pencil, undated

SS *Ohio*, for Mr Miller

Rounds fired in action during voyage to Malta Aug 1942

20 mm Oerlikon	4330 (approx)
30 mm	263
3" HA	24

Fired in practice during same period

3"	3
20 mm	40
30 mm	20

3: Letters and Telegrams

Handwritten Note on lined paper by Mason

Malta s/s *Ohio*
18th Aug 1942

To whom it may concern,

I cannot speak too highly of the seven Royal Naval Gunners (DEMS ratings) under Gunlayer Pilling who accompanied the vessel on this voyage. Following torpedo attack they manned the guns, withstanding practically forty-eight hours of continuous bombing. I wish them every success in the future

Mason, Master.

Centre at Chancery of the Orders of Knighthood, St. James's Palace, S.W.1.

8th Sept. 1942

The KING has been graciously pleased to award the GEORGE CROSS to Capt. Dudley Mason, Master, s.s. '*Ohio*'

During the passage to Malta of an important convoy Capt. Mason's ship suffered most violent onslaught. She was a focus of attack throughout and was torpedoed early one night. Although gravely damaged, her engines were kept going and the Master made a magnificent passage by hand steering and without compass. The ship's gunners helped to bring down one of the attacking aircraft. The vessel was hit again before morning, but though she did not sink, her engine room was wrecked. She was then towed. The unwieldy condition of the vessel and persistent enemy attacks made progress slow, and it was uncertain whether she would remain afloat. The next day progress somehow continued and the ship reached Malta after a further night at sea.

The violence of the enemy could not deter the Master from his purpose. Throughout he showed skill and courage of the highest order and it was due to his determination that, in spite of the most persistent enemy opposition, the vessel, with her valuable cargo, eventually reached Malta and was safely berthed. (The award is dated 4th September, 1942)

Eagle Oil and Shipping Company Limited   Mail No

London   16 Finsbury Circus

London E.C.2

SHIPPING DEPT 13th November, 1942

We have been requested by the Director, Tanker Division, Ministry of War Transport, to advise you of the following Resolution which was passed by the Council of Government of Malta: -

'That the grateful thanks of the Council of Government be conveyed to the crews of the ships of the Royal Navy, and the Merchant Service, and to the R.A.F., who recently once again ensured the delivery of essential supplies to the people of these Islands.'

We are pleased to be able to pass on to you this appreciation of the services rendered by you whilst serving in s.s. '*OHIO*'

Yours faithfully

For Eagle Oil and Shipping Company Limited

Assistant Manager, Shipping Department

4: Typical Newspaper reporting

Associated Press March 6 1944

Famous Tanker is Slav Navy H.Q.

Malta, Monday.

The famous tanker *Ohio* has been taken over by the Yugoslav Navy as a Headquarters ship.

She was torpedoed, dive-bombed for three days, and set on fire. Captain G. W. Mason of New Malden, Surrey, sailed on and won the George Cross – A.P.

News Chronicle March 7 1944

The *Ohio* goes back to sea

The heroine of 1942 the tanker *Ohio*. Yesterday she came into the news again.

Meanwhile the tanker lay, a battered hulk, with three gaping holes in her side. No one thought she would ever put to sea again. But yesterday the *News Chronicle* correspondent in Malta cabled that dockyard workers who took her in hand have made what is virtually a new ship, and today the *Ohio* is ready for service again.

Daily Express Tuesday October 8 1945.

The ship the Germans could not sink is blown up off Malta.

A ship that has a golden page in the history of the siege of Malta goes down in waters where history was made … the tanker *Ohio* towed out to sea from Valetta, is sunk by charges placed in her holds.

Source Notes

General Sources

The Ciano Diaries (American translation), Heinemann, 1947.

Hitler's War Directives, edited by H. R. Trevor-Roper, Sidgwick & Jackson, 1964.

Memoirs, Field-Marshal Kesselring, William Kimber, 1953.

War at Sea, Vols 1 & 2, Captain S. W. Roskill, H.M.S.0. 1956–60.

Our Penelope, by Ship's Company, Guild Books, 1943.

Red Duster, White Ensign, Ian Cameron, Muller, 1959.

Action This Day, Admiral Sir Philip Vian, Muller, 1960.

Sea Warfare, Vice-Admiral Sir Frederick Ruge, Cassell, 1957.

La Marina Guerra Mondiale, Vol. V. La Guerra Nel Mediterrano Le Azione Navali Dal 1 Aprile 1941 all' 8 Settembre 1943, G. Fioravanzo, Ufficio Storico Della Marina Militare, Rome, 1960.

L'Aeronautica Italiana Nella Seconda Guerra Mondiale, Vol. 2; General Santoro; Edizioni Ease, Rome, 1957.

Sea Flight, Hugh Popham, William Kimber, 1956.

Two Small Ships, Donald Forbes, Hutchinson, 1957.

So War de U-Bootkrieg, Harald Busch, Bielefeld, 1957.

Convoy Escort Commander, Vice-Admiral Sir Peter Gretton, Cassell, 1964.

Half Time, Commander Anthony Kimmins, Heinemann, 1947.

I Sommergibili in Mediterraneo, Tomo II: Dal 1 Gennaio 1942-all' 8 Settembre 1943; M. Bertini; Ufficio Storico; Rome, 1968.

Royal Air Force, 1939–45; Dennis Richards & Hilary St. George Saunders, H.M.S.O., 1957.

The Italian Navy in World War II, Commander Marc' Antonio Bragadin, United States Naval Institute, 1957.

A Merchant Fleet at War, Captain S. W. Roskill, Collins, 1962.

The Stuka at War, Peter C. Smith, Ian Allan, 1971.

Eagle Fleet, W. Lucas, Weidenfeld & Nicholson.

The Flag of the Southern Cross, Frank C. Bowen, 1947.

In Danger's Hour, Gordon Holman, Hodder & Stoughton, 1948.

The British Destroyer, Edgar J. March, Seeley Service, 1968.

Blue Star Line, Taffrail, Gardiner Liverpool, 1948.

Union Castle Chronicle, M. Murray, Longmans, 1958.

Lest We Forget – Santa Marija' 1942 – A Tribute to Malta Convoy Heroes. *The Times of Malta*, August 13, 1967.

O.H.M.S. or All in a Day's Work – HMS *Charybdis*, David (Rocky) Royale, *Charybdis* Survivors Association, 1984. Made available to the author by David Royale.

Malta Convoy, Apprentice DAG Dickens, Personal Narrative, November, 1942, made available to the author by Captain Dickens.

Betwixt Sea and Sky – General Antonio Cumbat, SIAD, Roma, Italy. June 1972. Copy presented to the author.

Personal Speech on Operation Pedestal, Rear Admiral R. M. J. Hutton, C.B., C.B.E., D.S.O. and 3 bars, copy presented to the author.

Destroyer Captain, Roger Hill, William Kimber, London, 1975.

Unbroken, Alastair Mars, Muller, 1953.

The Second World War, Vol. IV, The Hinge of Fate, Sir Winston Churchill, Cassell, 1951.

Pelle D'Ammiraglio, Alberto da Zara, Mondadori.

Submarines Attacking, Aldo Coccia, William Kimber, 1956.

Eagles War, Peter C. Smith, Crécy Publishing 1995.

Detailed Notes

Page 25 – Air Vice-Marshal Sir Hugh Lloyd was relieved by Air Vice Marshal Sir Keith Park in July 1942.

Page 41 – Harwood on advisability of convoy in a telegram to the Prime Minister dated 18th June, 1942.

Page 42 – For main dispositions and comment see – *Report* of Vice Admiral Sir Neville Syfret submitted to Lords Commissioners of the Admiralty as a 'Despatch' on 25th August 1942 and published as a supplement in the *London Gazette* on 11th August 1948.

Page 43 – In addition to his official report Admiral Burrough subsequently set down his account of this operation in his own words and this unpublished manuscript he kindly made available to the author.

Page 44 – With regard to battleships' support through the Narrows, in an interview with Admiral Sir Harold Burrough in August 1969 he stated: 'This idea was mine but it was dropped almost at once.' Further elaboration is given in a lecture delivered to the joint Services Staff by Admiral Burrough on 27th April 1948: 'There were a large number of Ju87s available in Sicily which would have found the shorter flight the next morning to their favour. Also Vice-Admiral Malta was adverse to giving away the fact that we knew about the Sicilian Channel route as it was in constant use by our submarines.'

Indeed, during the passage of 'Pedestal' the supply submarine *Otus* did actually use this route without detection.

Page 51 – Details of Merchant Ship actions etc. in this convoy are contained in Admiralty Monograph *Reports of Interviews from British Merchant Ships Attacked, Damaged or Sunk by-Enemy Action; 1st August 1942 31st October 1942*; prepared by the Shipping Casualty Division of the Admiralty Trade Division.

Page 53 – For details of the full debate of this issue see House of Lords, *Official Report* (Vol. 4); 1941–42; Columns 647–656, 14th October 1942.

Page 54 – For Admiral Weichold's statements see *War in the Mediterranean*, a record made after his capture. Imperial War Museum copy: K.14545.

Page 55 – Captain Broome's comments in a letter to the author July 1969.

Page 74 – For German movements etc. see *War Diary of the German Naval Staff (Operations)*, Part A. August 1942, Vol. 36; US Navy translation. Declassified ART.0445; Penavinst 5510.10.

Page 74 – Luftwaffe dispositions from Air Historical Branch, Ministry of Defence.

Page 75 – For further details of the organisation of the Luftwaffe in the Mediterranean at this time see also *The Rise and Fall of the German Air Force*, 1939–45; Air Ministry (ACAS(I) 1948).

Page 93 – High-flying recce aircraft: From June until September the Luftwaffe used for reconnaissance purposes some special pressurised Junkers Ju86Ps, capable of flying at over 45,000 feet. No Allied fighter could reach them. The Germans only had six of these aircraft and there is no confirmation that they were used against 'Pedestal' although it is possible.

Page 93 – Three especially adapted Spitfire V's were modified at Aboukir, Egypt in an attempt to intercept these aircraft and Flying Officer G. W. H. Reynolds achieved the first 'kill' of a Junkers Ju86P at 40,000 feet on 24th August 1942, just too late for Pedestal. See article High Flight, page 11 in the *Spitfire Notebook* of *The Aeroplane Spotter* kindly drawn to my attention by Robert W. Gant.

Page 94 – Luftwaffe attack. Possible unit employed was *I* or *II/LG.I.LG* stood for *Lehrgeschwader* and although this implies a unit under instruction if the word *Lehr* is translated literally, these units were in fact made up of instructors and personnel from the Technical Development Flying Unit and at the start of the war they included some of the most competent and experienced crews in the Luftwaffe. By 1942 the quality had been diluted but they were still an 'above average' unit and in addition had recently undergone an intensive anti-shipping course which resulted in the easy destruction of the *Jackal*, *Kipling* and *Lively* in June. They were led by Captain Helbig.

Page 104 – The fact that 'Pedestal's' escort was so large encouraged some Italian writers in wild speculation. Signor Gayada asked in a newspaper article – 'Did the British and American Commands therefore propose to embark on the great adventure of a landing at some point on the Mediterranean shores of Europe or Africa? This question is perfectly valid and its very existence serves to confirm the exceptional scope of the Anglo-American undertaking and the superb Italian and German victory.' He cites photographic evidence that the escorting warships carried large quantities of landing materials, 'rafts, dinghies and motorboats', and also claims that the Allied battleships and carriers 'endeavoured to force a passage through the Sicilian Channel only stopping after bold attacks by the Italian submarines and E-boats'.

Page 104 – An abbreviated article dealing with the Italian side of 'Pedestal' is given in *The Italian Navy's Last Victory* [*sic*] ; Marc' Antonio Bragadin, U.S.N.I. Proceedings, Vol. 83, pp. 479–82, 1957.

Page 106 – Details of Carrier operations, not too accurate or precise, in *Fleet Air Arm*, HMSO, S070.427:1943.

Page 130 – Italian Stuka attack from an article (unsigned), in the *Popolo d'Italia*.

Page 133 – Fires on *Indomitable*: information from a letter to the author by Sir Richard Onslow, July 1969.

Page 136 – Luftwaffe aircraft. *III/ZG 26* used Bf.110c-4s during the summer of 1942 but for reconnaissance purposes some c-5s may have been used. Most of the Ju88s used were A-4s or A-4/*Trops* (Tropicalised).

Page 148— Letter to the author from Admiral Sir Harold Burrough August 1969; also letter to author from Admiral Sir Richard Onslow, July 1969.

Page 151 – Letter to the author from Mr A. H. Murphy, August 1969.

Page 152 – The following is an official description of the TSDS (Two Speed Destroyer Sweep): 'Consisting of two paravanes, each weighing half a ton, one tadpole, two 700 yard wires, tadpole wire, two floats, 100 yards wire, winches and two rotating drums, davits on stern. Speeds 15/25 knots.'

The *Fearless* class destroyers had been built with his gear plus an extra drum on which with a suitable lead to the leading davits. The *Intrepid* class destroyers had been designed for a mine*laying* role rather than minesweeping but the gear for the could be rapidly inter-changed. The difficulties in handling and operation, however, still remained.

Page 177 – Letter to the author from Admiral C. K. Roberts, July 1969.

Page 177 – On the mine menace: Admiral Sir Richard Onslow wrote to the author: 'In the glare of the searchlights I saw three or four spherical mines, newly painted, dark green in colour, passing down our port side, having been cut by the minesweeping destroyers in the van. Normally of course we should have turned towards the enemy E-boats both to engage them more closely and to comb their torpedo tracks. But if we needed any reminder that we must stick to the swept water this was it. In no account I have read have I seen the mine threat emphasised. It was very much on my mind after seeing them float by.'

Page 187 – Details of *Santa Elisa*'s actions from: *Summary of Statements by survivors of SS Santa Elisa*; prepared by Ensign W. E. Dryer, USNR, for USN Dept: Declassified, Op-16-B-5.

Page 187 – Details of *Almeria Lykes*' actions from: *Summary of Statements by survivors of SS Almeria Lykes*; prepared by Ensign E. D. Henderson, USNR, for USN Dept. Declassified OP-15-B-5. Also see note for page 41.

The following signal is of interest:

From Senior Officer, Force 'F' 1802B/15 to Vice Admiral, Malta, Cruiser Squadron 10, Captain (D) 6th Destroyer Flotilla—

'Do you know if *Almeria Lykes* and *Wairangi* were sunk? Neither CS10, *Eskimo* or *Somali* can confirm this was so.'

N.O.I.C. Malta 2253B/15 to S.O. Force 'F', CS10—'Your 1802/1. No. CS10 was instructed to sink ships on return journey as a result of *Eskimo*'s 0930/13 to FOIL, CS10. Extensive reconnaissance in the Pantelleria area has not disclosed any merchant ships.'

Page 190 – Sinking of the *Foresight* by *Tartar*: Tyrwhitt was subsequently Court Martialled for this at Gibraltar. Tyrwhitt was, in Onslow's opinion, one of the finest and most gallant destroyer officers he knew and he describes Tyrwhitt's action as an 'obviously correct decision to anyone who knew anything about destroyers'. The result of the Court Martial bore this opinion out for Tyrwhitt was honourably acquitted, which, says Sir Richard, was 'as expected'.

Page 195 – Mussolini's decision to withdraw the cruisers: commenting, on this incredible blunder, Admiral Burrough stated that he was 'always grateful to Mussolini for it'. He added: 'There is no doubt in my mind that had the Italian cruisers arrived that morning there would have been a massacre; we would have been wiped out.' Interview with Admiral Sir Harold Burrough, August 1969.

Page 206 – Information from Sir Richard Onslow, July 1969.

Page 206 – Extract from *Gazzetta del Popolo*, 15th August 1942.

Page 215 – *Manchester*'s scuttling: In Roskill's *War at Sea*, Vol. 2 it is stated that at a subsequent Court Martial Enquiry into *Manchester*'s loss the court came to the decision that her scuttling was 'premature'. The author has studied the Court Martial Proceedings contained in ADM 156/210 at the National Archives, London, and agrees with the unanimous findings of the court, that *Manchester* had been scuttled prematurely.

Page 215 – Information from Admiral C. K. Roberts, July 1969.

Page 219 – On the difficulties of destroyer towing Admiral Onslow has this to say: 'The reader should understand that a destroyer is not designed for towing and despite its great power makes a very inefficient tug. When towing from ahead there is only one towing position to which a hawser can be attached: from the towing slip right aft. In a ship designed for the job the hawser is attached to a swivelling towing position at the point of balance, usually just abaft the funnel. This arrangement allows the tug to alter course without being pulled back by the strain on the hawser. When a heavy ship is in tow by a destroyer, any tendency to yaw to port pulls the destroyer to port. The leverage of the destroyer's rudder when this occurs is virtually nil, since it is acting at a point below the point of attachment to the tow. If the ship under tow continues to carry her way the destroyer's bows are forced to starboard through the right angle until eventually the two ships are facing in opposite directions.' As can be seen, this is exactly the problem which faced the *Penn* and *Ohio*.

Page 233 – Captain Mason's citation read: 'His Majesty the King has been pleased to award the George Cross to Captain D. W. Mason in recognition of the gallantry displayed by him and his crew, as a result of which the major part of the *Ohio*'s cargo, so vital to the defence of Malta, reached its destination.'

Page 240 – On claims of aircraft destroyed: on the 8th September 1942, in a speech to the House on the general war situation, the Prime Minister described the passage of 'Pedestal' in glowing terms and was even more specific (and inaccurate) on the enemy casualties: '... fifty-six certains and fifteen probables, of which thirty-nine were destroyed by the Fleet Air Arm, seventeen by ack-ack fire and sixteen by the Malta Air Forces.' House of Commons *Official Report* (Hansard), Vol. 383, Columns 82–83.

Page 251 – For those with further interest, a film is available at the Imperial War Museum: *Malta Convoy* (One reel, 13 mins) being an eyewitness account by Commander Anthony Kimmins of the supply convoy which fought its way through to Malta in August 1942. Ministry of Information; Uk.452. Some extracts of this film were subsequently used in the British film loosely based on this operation, *The Malta Story*, which starred Jack Hawkins. There is also available an Italian film on the attacks on 'Pedestal'.

Admiralty files consulted – ADM 234/353, BS No. 32 Malta Convoys, with particular reference to M011161/42, M013525/42, M11420/42, N1086688/44, WH8267, WH8268, WH8269, WD201/749 and XP7159.

INDEX